Thinking and Rethinking the University

In the **World Library of Educationalists** series, international scholars compile career-long selections of what they judge to be among their finest pieces so the world has access to them in a single, manageable volume. Readers are able to follow the themes and strands and see how their work contributes to the development of the field.

Over more than three decades, Professor Ronald Barnett has acquired a distinctive position as a leading philosopher of the university and higher education, and this volume brings together 15 of his key writings, particularly papers from leading journals. This volume also includes, as its introductory chapter, an intellectual autobiography in which Professor Barnett recounts the history of his scholarship and writing, traces its development across five stages, and identifies the themes and sources of inspiration that lie within his academic writing.

Ronald Barnett has described his corpus of work as a social philosophy of the university that is at once conceptual, critical, practical and imaginative. His concepts of criticality, critical interdisciplinarity, supercomplexity and the ecological university have been taken up in the literature across the world. Through telling examples, and with an incisive clarity of writing, Ronald Barnett's scholarship has helped to reorient and illuminate in fresh ways practices in the university and in higher education. The chapters in this volume reveal all of these qualities, making it a compelling overview of a passionate and yet constructive critic of the university.

Ronald Barnett is Emeritus Professor of Higher Education at the Institute of Education, London.

World Library of Educationalists series

Thinking and Rethinking the University
The selected works of Ronald Barnett
Ronald Barnett

The Politics of Race, Class and Special Education
The selected works of Sally Tomlinson
Sally Tomlinson

Lessons from History of Education
The selected works of Richard Aldrich
Richard Aldrich

Knowledge, Power, and Education
The selected works of Michael W. Apple
Michael W. Apple

Education Policy and Social Class
The selected works of Stephen J. Ball
Stephen J. Ball

Race, Culture, and Education
The selected works of James A. Banks
James A. Banks

In Search of Pedagogy Volume I
The selected works of Jerome Bruner, 1957–1978
Jerome S. Bruner

In Search of Pedagogy Volume II
The selected works of Jerome Bruner, 1979–2006
Jerome S. Bruner

Reimagining Schools
The selected works of Elliot W. Eisner
Elliot W. Eisner

Reflecting Where the Action Is
The selected works of John Elliot
John Elliot

The Development and Education of the Mind
The selected works of Howard Gardner
Howard Gardner

Constructing Worlds through Science Education
The selected works of John K. Gilbert
John K. Gilbert

Making Sense of Learners Making Sense of Written Language
The selected works of Kenneth S. Goodman and Yetta M. Goodman
Kenneth S. Goodman and Yetta M. Goodman

Learning, Curriculum and Life Politics
The selected works of Ivor F. Goodson
Ivor F. Goodson

Education and the Nation State
The selected works of S. Gopinathan
S. Gopinathan

Educational Assessment, Evaluation and Research
The selected works of Mary E. James
Mary E. James

Teaching, Learning and Education in Late Modernity
The selected works of Peter Jarvis
Peter Jarvis

Education, Markets, and the Public Good
The selected works of David F. Labaree
David F. Labaree

Politics, Policies and Pedagogies in Education
The selected works of Bob Lingard
Bob Lingard

A Life in Education
The selected works of John Macbeath
John Macbeath

Overcoming Exclusion
Social justice through education
Peter Mittler

Learner-Centered English Language Education
The selected works of David Nunan
David Nunan

Educational Philosophy and Politics
The selected works of Michael A. Peters
Michael A. Peters

Encountering Education in the Global
The selected works of Fazal Rizvi
Fazal Rizvi

Landmarks in Literacy
The selected works of Frank Smith
Frank Smith

Corporatism, Social Control, and Cultural Domination in Education: From the Radical Right to Globalization
The selected works of Joel Spring
Joel Spring

The Curriculum and the Child
The selected works of John White
John White

The Art and Science of Teaching and Learning
The selected works of Ted Wragg
E.C. Wragg

China through the Lens of Comparative Education
The selected works of Ruth Hayhoe
Ruth Hayhoe

Multiculturalism in Education and Teaching
The selected works of Carl A. Grant
Carl A. Grant

Thinking and Rethinking the University

The selected works of Ronald Barnett

Ronald Barnett

LONDON AND NEW YORK

First published 2015
by Routledge
2 Park Square, Milton Park, Abingdon, Oxon OX14 4RN

and by Routledge
711 Third Avenue, New York, NY 10017

Routledge is an imprint of the Taylor & Francis Group, an informa business

© 2015 Ronald Barnett

The right of Ronald Barnett to be identified as author of this work has been asserted by him in accordance with sections 77 and 78 of the Copyright, Designs and Patents Act 1988.

All rights reserved. No part of this book may be reprinted or reproduced or utilised in any form or by any electronic, mechanical, or other means, now known or hereafter invented, including photocopying and recording, or in any information storage or retrieval system, without permission in writing from the publishers.

Trademark notice: Product or corporate names may be trademarks or registered trademarks, and are used only for identification and explanation without intent to infringe.

British Library Cataloguing in Publication Data
A catalogue record for this book is available from the British Library

Library of Congress Cataloging in Publication Data
Barnett, Ronald, 1947-
[Works. Selections]
  Thinking and rethinking the university : the selected works of Ronald Barnett / Ronald Barnett.
    pages cm
  Includes bibliographical references and index.
  1. Education, Higher—Philosophy. 2. Education, Higher—Aims and objectives. I. Title.
  LB2322.3.B37 2014
  378.001—dc23
                                                        2014020862

ISBN: 978-1-138-78507-6 (hbk)
ISBN: 978-1-138-78508-3 (pbk)
ISBN: 978-1-315-76804-5 (ebk)

Typeset in Sabon
by RefineCatch Limited, Bungay, Suffolk

For David Watson
— *who has accompanied so much of this journey*

'Thinking provokes general indifference. It is a dangerous exercise nevertheless.'

Gilles Deleuze and Felix Guattari,
What is Philosophy? (2013:41)

Contents

Acknowledgements	xi
List of sources and permissions	xii
Introduction	1

PART I
The university — 23

1 Supercomplexity and the university	25
2 Situating the learning university	35
3 Recapturing the universal in the university	48
4 The idea of the university in the 21st century: where's the imagination?	62
5 The coming of the ecological university	74

PART II
Higher education — 91

6 Higher education: legitimation crisis	93
7 Does higher education have aims?	111
8 Convergence in higher education: the strange case of 'Entrepreneurialism'	127

9 The purposes of higher education and the changing face of academia	140
10 Institutions of higher education: purposes and 'performance indicators'	156

PART III
Students and learning   175

11 Supercomplexity and the curriculum	177
12 Learning about learning: a conundrum and a possible resolution	191
13 Being and becoming: a student trajectory	203
14 Learning for an unknown future	219
15 Configuring learning spaces: noticing the invisible	235
Coda: threads of an academic life	247
Appendix: key publications	253
Bibliography	256
Name index	269
Subject index	272

Acknowledgements

A number of friends have read a draft of my Introduction to this volume and offered supportive and helpful comments on it. They are Graham Badley, Eli Bitzer, Jurgen Enders, Joelle Fanghanel, Carolina Guzmán Valenzuala, Bruce Macfarlane, Rajani Naidoo, Jon Nixon, Michael Peters, Peter Scott and Paul Temple. This volume is testimony to thirty years of writing for publication, and the support of such friends over the years – and those in the acknowledgements in my earlier books have mentioned many others – has been invaluable to me in my intellectual and professional journeying; I touch on this general matter in a more formal way within the Introduction, where I reflect on how I write and the significance of writing for me. Being aware of such support has been crucial in sustaining my own intellectual energies and, indeed, writing energies, not least in the crafting of my texts. Getting a first draft down is one thing; bringing it to a point where it might be exposed to the world is quite another.

List of sources and permissions

The author and publishers gratefully acknowledge the following for permission to reproduce material in this book. Every effort has been made to contact copyright owners. The publishers would be grateful to hear from any copyright holder who is not acknowledged here and will undertake to rectify any errors or omissions in future printings or editions of this book.

(1998) 'Supercomplexity and the University', *Social Epistemology*, 12 (1) 43–50. www.tandfonline.com

(1996) 'Situating the Learning University', *International Journal of University Adult Education*, XXX (1) 13–27.

(2005) 'Recapturing the Universal in the University', *Educational Philosophy and Theory*, 37 (6) 785–797. www.tandfonline.com

(2011) 'The Idea of the University in the Twenty-First Century: Where's the Imagination?', *Yuksekogretim Dergisi*, 1 (2) 88–94. Reproduced with kind permission of Deomed Publishing, Istanbul.

(2011) 'The Coming of the Ecological University', *Oxford Review of Education*, 37 (4) 439–455. www.tandfonline.com

(1985) 'Higher Education: Legitimation Crisis', *Studies in Higher Education*, 10 (3) 241–255. www.tandfonline.com

(1988) 'Does Higher Education have Aims?', *Journal of Philosophy of Education*, 239–250. (Permission granted by Wiley-Blackwell.)

(2005) 'Convergence in Higher Education: The Strange Case of "Entrepreneurialism"', *Higher Education and Policy*, 17 (3) 51–64. Reproduced with kind permission from OECD publishing. http://dx.doi.org/10.1787/hemp-v17-art18-en

(2004) 'The Purposes of Higher Education and the Changing Face of Academia', *London Review of Education*, 2 (1) 61–73. www.tandfonline.com

(1988) 'Institutions of Higher Education: purposes and "performance indicators"', *Oxford Review of Education*, 14 (1) 97–112. www.tandfonline.com

(2000) 'Supercomplexity and the Curriculum', *Studies in Higher Education*, 25 (3) 255–265. www.tandfonline.com

(2011) 'Learning about Learning: a conundrum and a possible resolution', *London Review of Education*, 9 (1) 5–13. www.tandfonline.com

(2006) 'Being and Becoming: a student trajectory', *International Journal of Lifelong Education*, 15 (2) 72–84. www.tandfonline.com

(2004) 'Learning for an Unknown Future', *Higher Education Research and Development*, 23 (3) 247–260. www.tandfonline.com

(2011) 'Configuring Learning Spaces: Noticing the Invisible', chapter 13 in Anne Boddington and Jos Boys (Eds.) *Re-Shaping Learning: A Critical Reader*. Reproduced with kind permission from Sense Publishers.

Introduction

Beginnings

The opportunity afforded to me by the publishers of this volume, Routledge, opens a space for some autobiographical reflections on a long personal journey (over some thirty-plus years). It is a daunting space, in which one attempts to discern patterns of one's intellectual formation, development and offerings, patterns that only in retrospect become apparent with all the dangers of wishful coherence and hubris that attend such a self-description. Still, I have been encouraged to attempt such a set of reflections and there may be value in offering an account of my scholarly intentions over these past years.

From an early age, I have been conscious of being interested in the nature of the university and intellectual life. School and university were academically quite challenging for me but even as a teenager, I began to dwell in an inner life of the mind. In the early 1960s, I became dimly aware of the debate in England (and one does have always in these matters to observe the distinctiveness of England within Great Britain) of 'the two cultures' debate sparked off by C P Snow (1959) and joined acrimoniously by the literary critic and Cambridge don, F R Leavis. (One of Leavis' books (1969) reveals some of the hostility here.) I was struck too by the inclusion in 1963, within the annual BBC radio set of Reith Lectures, of a series on *The Making of the University*, given by Albert Sloman (Sloman, 1964), the first vice-chancellor of the university of Essex. (The lectures provided an account of the formation of that university, established as part of the expansion of higher education in the UK, in the wake of the so-called Robbins Report on higher education, 1963.)

In the mid-60s, while still at school, I stumbled across – in my local library – *Thought and Change* by Ernest Gellner (1969). I could understand very little of that book at the time, with its enormous sweep across philosophy and social and political theory, but it was written with Gellner's characteristic wit and style such that I knew that I wanted, one day, to understand in some depth that work and the kind of thinking that it represented. Subsequently, I developed a fascination with Gellner's writings that has lasted to this day. (Gellner, who died in 1995, has been described as the last of the great European intellectuals (Gellner, 1998). Not only its accessible style but its huge range have been touchstones for me of the work of the intellectual, despite the considerable differences between our stances and approach.)

Following university and a year's teacher training course, I was fortunate to secure a position as a research assistant on a national project, funded by the then Department of Education and Science, into *Polytechnic Staff and Students* (Whitburn, Mealing and Cox, 1976). That work entailed, as part of the fieldwork, visiting polytechnics in England, the polytechnic sector just then establishing itself – in the early 1970s – as part of the emerging binary policy for UK higher education. Subsequently, a career in academic administration followed, firstly in a London polytechnic and then for twelve years in the Council for National Academic Awards (CNAA), the national body given authority to grant degrees and approve programmes of study in the non-university sector of UK higher education. In 1990, following a national advertisement, I applied for and was offered a post as lecturer in higher education at the Institute of Education, University of London, where I stayed through the rest of my career.

Writing as autobiography

I began my academic writing with a paper on 'Integration in Higher Education' (Barnett, 1981). That paper was written and published while I was on the staff of the CNAA and it arose out of the work of the CNAA itself. Central to the pattern of its work were interactions between panels of academics (put together by the CNAA) and course teams in polytechnics (and their equivalent institutions in Scotland, Northern Ireland and Wales), discussion focusing on the nature of the courses being proposed and offered. Often, those meetings took place on the premises of departments in the institutions concerned. A not infrequent topic of the dialogue lay in that of 'integration', a concern on the part of the CNAA being that of the extent to which a collection of course units or modules were integrated into a unified curriculum, so forming a coherent experience for students taking those programmes. This was an especially significant and even 'hot' topic in the very large modular programmes being then developed in many of the non-university institutions but it was a major topic generally across the work of the CNAA. I felt that the very concept of integration deserved some attention and so that paper came to see the light of day.

I mention this event not just because it heralded my first paper but because it illustrates a feature that has been a thread running through my intellectual work. In effect, much of my work has taken the form of autobiography in the sense that it has been much prompted by experiences and events encountered in the course of my professional life. 'Experiences and events' is, of course, a double shorthand. The phrase has broad scope for it includes here discourses, ideologies, values present in situations, institutional policies, strategies and procedures, texts (such as university 'mission statements') and identities being taken up or encouraged among both staff and students. The phrase also owes much to one's perceptions: experiences and events are not given but are constructed in part by oneself, depending on the values and insights one brings to presenting situations.

My academic writing, accordingly, has been a kind of space in which I have wrestled with many of the challenges I have found and disturbances I have encountered. Committee meetings, the classroom, interactions with students, institutional procedures that I have encountered and even endured (for example, in national audits) have not infrequently served to generate personal concerns and even angsts that have energised my writing energies. My papers and books have often in a way written themselves in the playing out of the internal dialogue sparked off within me. The act of writing, in turn, has been a painful pulling out – or extraction – of feelings, murmurings and presentiments from within me.

A will to write

My writing, accordingly, has been an acute encountering with instances but also informed by my reading in philosophy and social theory. The reading has been a continuous activity, accompanying one's professional practices and offering lenses through which one's experiences may be espied and framed.

I have long admired poets (a reflection to be expressed with caution since Heidegger could well have expressed the same sentiment, it seems (Heidegger, 1971, chIII)). But poets have an uncanny ability to see into things that are normally taken for granted, and go into things with such closeness and perspicacity that the taken-for-granted becomes re-presented to us, so that we may see it in fresh ways. The good poets, too, bring a stark authenticity to their work, never taking-off-the-shelf, as it were, words of our age but interrogating each situation freshly. However complex and interwoven their work, however subtle, however open to readings on multiple levels, their work has yet a directness about it for it is the poet speaking on her or his own terms to the reader and not relying on stock phrases. Every word is *chosen*. I hope that my own work reveals some of those qualities.

Such writing, in which every word, every phrase, is chosen and is *placed*, is hard work. This authenticity in one's writing is not, after all, lightly won. I used to have pinned close to my keyboard and computer a short quotation from John Henry Newman in which he attested to the 'bodily pain' that writing caused him. I will admit to just such a discomfiture. How could it be otherwise, when writing of this kind calls for such a juggling, such a bringing together in the one act, of reading, of words carefully chosen, of a disinclination to hide behind the texts of others, of forensic interrogation of sentiments within oneself, of the closest attention to particular experiences, of a concern for an audience and of a will to produce a text that might even delight readers as well as reaching out to them and into them?

This conern with the sheer act of writing has another aspect. As abstract and as analytical as it may be at times, I have long seen my work as that of writing fiction. I am in effect suggesting to the reader: 'Suppose we look at this familiar aspect of the university – why not look at it in *this* way? This rather *different* way.' I have been, therefore, trying to tell stories; to look into familiar matters and see them through a slightly different lens from that normally used. With this stance, a myriad – really an infinite array – of imaginative possibilities open up.

Method

My method has grown out of this will to write and to communicate through and in that writing; and its ingredients have perhaps already been intimated. They are five in number: reading, writing itself, dialogue, close attention to one's experiences and thought. These five elements interweave each other.

The thought comes through the writing (as a supervisor, I banned the use of the expression 'writing up one's research', for the writing is a crucial part of the research, in that it prompts and opens spaces for creativity and imagination and for sheer hard and new thinking). The writing is prompted by experiences and made vivid through experiences. Experiences are interpretable through the reading. Dialogue, with one's intellectual friends and in academic settings (both orally and in writing), causes reflections on one's writing efforts. And both the reading and the dialogue furnish one with internal voices with which one can interrogate one's own words in 'real time', precisely as they appear on the screen in front of one in response to the demands from the flickering cursor for yet more words.

But in all this interweaving of the elements of one's scholarship, there is a major set of patterns that can be discerned in my method. Putting it crudely, it takes the following form: from practice to concepts and back to practice. It is a kind of practical critical realism (of which more in a moment). Some nuances and elaborations are necessary at once. I have already indicated the complexity here of that term 'practice'. It has considerable scope and inheres as much in the mind of the beholder as in the observed event. Let me therefore begin here with a commentary on the term 'concepts'.

The reference to 'concepts' is here a shorthand for a number of intellectual tasks. Certainly, it includes the interrogation of already existing and often familiar concepts. In my writings, I have, for instance, dwelt upon the concepts of student, knowledge, university, higher education, learning, curriculum and competence. Such terms are part of the staple of the higher education community and lie 'ready-to-hand' (especially for an academic working in the field of higher education studies). Other terms lie not far away, to be drawn in for interrogation, such that they may then serve as resources to illuminate a topic in question. Concepts such as these on which I have dwelt have included those of ideology, complexity, imagination, space, time, being, becoming, authenticity and ecology.

What counts, though, in any conceptual exploration is its purpose. Its purpose, after all, is crucial to the direction of travel and to the outcome (and so the value) of the endeavour. My purpose has been simple. It derives from my twin beliefs both that the university is an extraordinary human institution, to which its longevity across the centuries and in so many different cultures is testimony, and/but that the university is not what it might be or, indeed, what it should be as we proceed well into the twenty-first century. I have therefore been motivated to try to identify possibilities for a new kind of university; a new kind of university becoming, indeed. My conceptual analyses have been energised by this guiding hope, that out of a close interrogation of key concepts and ideas, new possibilities might be glimpsed.

Many today, we may observe, are exercised by concerns over higher education and the university. Characteristically, their approaches are of two kinds. Some turn to philosophy and to an exploration of concepts through an exegetical exploration of key texts in the philosophical literature. The difficulty there is that those explorations then all too often become somewhat disconnected from practices and institutions. Some, alternatively, offer a sociological analysis of the contemporary nature of higher education and universities, starting from and embellishing concerns, their offerings being buttressed by recourse to a language of 'globalisation', 'neoliberalism', 'performativity' and 'New Public Management'. On the one hand, we are treated to an abstract scholarship and, on the other hand, a dismal account of unremitting bleakness. In neither case are we often provided with resources for going forward that have practical bite.

In contrast, my efforts have taken the form of a particular kind of social philosophy, namely a philosophy of hope. I use 'hope' here in the sense of work being put in hand to realise a new world – or, at least, a new kind of university, a new kind of higher education. My work springs from a sense that while there is much about which to be critical, there remain spaces for kinds of institution, and kinds of academic practices, that just might help to realise large and even universal concepts of liberty, reason, concern, authenticity, understanding and even emancipation. The task, then, of the social philosophy that I have tried to take forward is one of addressing particular problems concerning universities and higher education – problems that arise from the ways in which such universal concepts are being put at risk in the emerging formations that constitute universities and higher education – and searching for spaces in which such concepts can be realised more than ever in the past in addressing the initiating problem.

For the most part, then, my separate efforts have each originated from and so focus on a *particular* practical problem. The following are examples of such practical concerns *and* books of mine that have tackled such problems.

- What might be meant by 'quality' and the very idea of 'managing quality'? *Improving Higher Education: Total Quality Care* (1992) – in which I tackled the large set of practices concerned with 'quality' in higher education. I contended against the idea of 'total quality management' and suggested that while quality cannot ultimately be managed directly, it can at least be cared for and cared about. This thesis would surely challenge contemporary notions of what it is to manage quality.
- To what extent is 'critical thinking' a helpful leitmotif for higher education? *Higher Education: A Critical Business* – in which I focused on efforts that were going into the development of students' critical thinking. I argued that a full higher education not only involves critical thinking but also goes beyond to embrace a student's powers of 'critical action' and her very 'critical being'. This quite considerable broadening of the idea of critical thinking would have profound implications both for curricula and for teaching in higher education.
- What is the relationship between 'learning' and a student's development? *A Will to Learn: Being a Student in an Age of Uncertainty* – in which I was concerned with the very practical problem as to what it is to help a student develop. I argued that, in a world of uncertainty and challenge, knowledge and skills (the two dominant mantras) are inadequate and that instead we should understand teaching as a process of helping students to form the courage and wherewithal to keep going amid difficulty. This idea would call for a particular conception of teaching, in which affirmation and encouragement would have priority over knowledge and skills (for without self-belief and energies to keep going, a student would be unlikely to acquire knowledge and skills).
- What is it to be a university in a complex age? *Realising the University in an Age of Supercomplexity* – in which I suggested that, in addition to its having to cope with complex systems, a university has also to live amid 'supercomplexity', in which the world (and therefore universities)

- have to live with proliferating and contesting rival accounts of situations such that there can be no ultimate settlement. Accordingly, while management (as the art of the possible) is highly important, even more significant is *leadership* as the art of the *im*possible, in its enabling the university to develop, to go forward, and even to prosper while living with and helping to add to such rival and contesting accounts, even as to what it is to be a university.
- Just what is it to be a university? This is a matter being taken up politically and organisationally across the world, in all manner of governmental, inter-governmental and cross-institutional fora, but it seems to me in a wholly inadequate way. In *Being a University* (2011) and *Imagining the University* (2013) I have tried to show that 'the entrepreneurial university' need not be the only show in town and that options are open. Through our imagination, we can open the possibility of possibilities, and can identify *feasible utopias*, utopias that just might be realised (at least in part) in a challenging world and that even enable the university to live out more fully some of the universal ideas with which the university is intimately connected. In particular, I have argued in those two books for *the ecological university*, an idea that lends itself to infinite forms of university and which can go on emerging over time.

Philosophy as pot-holing

How might one depict this intellectual odyssey? I have already termed it a social philosophy but it is evidently more than that. A *social, critical, practical and imaginative philosophy* would be a more accurate term, clearly. It is a philosophy that originates from practical problems. It has a concern for the university as a social institution and higher education as a set of educational processes and is intent on trying imaginatively to develop conceptual and ideational resources that might be helpful in their development. With the work of Jurgen Habermas especially in mind (1978), I would want to term this a philosophy with a *practical intent*.

There is a further dimension of my work that might be brought out, namely that I have sought to ensure that my analyses are empirically grounded. Some of my work has actually drawn upon fieldwork that I have conducted (for instance, interviews with students, academics and institutional leaders) but for the most part I have been content to draw upon existing work in the literature. More importantly, perhaps, I have wanted my work to be empirically sensitive to and consistent with contemporary understandings of the university. This has derived from a motivation to ensure an empirical warrant for my conceptual and philosophical explorations. This motivation in turn has had two aspects, firstly a desire that my work should be empirically legitimate, according with contemporary insights into evolving patterns of higher education; and secondly, that any ideas that I open as to possibilities might be felt to be real possibilities, possibilities discerned in the spaces my explorations might have opened. And I have tried to intimate, by illustration with examples, how the ideas and the principles that I have proposed might be cashed out in the intimate practices that percolate universities.

This interest of mine in the empirical world has taken a particular form, therefore. All along, I have been concerned both to understand the contemporary world (of the university and higher education) as best as one can but in order to critique it and to help to improve it. One might venture to say that this stance has been a kind of 'transcendental empiricism' but it is not quite that of the transcendental empiricism of Deleuze (2012:25). While (as Colebrook puts it in commenting on Deleuze (2002:89)) there is 'an immanent flow of experience' (say, about the university amid globalisation and marketisation), there is more than that. We can make interventions and judgements about our experience. We can try to free ourselves from our surrounding experiences and we can endeavour to create new experiences (in academic life, and for students). We might even endeavour to create new kinds of university. Putting it rather grandly, a kind of *emancipatory empiricism* has played an important part in my philosophy.

In my recent work, I have made quite a bit of the idea of 'feasible utopias'. However, my whole oeuvre can be said to be an attempt to discern feasible utopias – for universities and higher education – in a complex and challenging world. It is a world dominated by ideologies, distorting power structures and global movements on the one hand and 'multiplicities' (Deleuze and Guattari, 2007) on the other hand. It is a world characterised by fluidity, a world in which the metaphor of the liquid has become potent (as Bauman (2000) has demonstrated). In such a world – imbued both with mighty forces *and* with forces of the mighty – it is easy to believe that constructive and imaginative work has little purchase and to offer only dismal texts, texts of unremitting melancholy and pessimism.

The only legitimate position, it sometimes appears, is that of the critic as such. For me, however, the challenge of scholarly work and writing has always been that of going beyond critique, searching for spaces for renewal, and going forward positively, even in the midst of ideology and uncertainty, and of irreconcilable contest. And hence the search for feasible utopias, those utopias that are most unlikely to be brought off, but yet where there are good grounds for believing that they could just be brought off in a world of continuing difficulty. And hence, again, the need for empirical warrant to one's philosophical journeying, to illustrate that one's probings and imaginings may just come out into the light.

This work may be understood as a kind of *philosophy as pot-holing* then. It takes place in a world of universities and higher education in which, in many ways, the walls are pressing in and the light is dimming. Reason is constrained by ideologies on campus (of marketisation, bureaucracy, managerialism), the identity of students is liable to diminish (as they take on the role of customer), the range of disciplines dwindles (the position of the humanities weakens as they are diminished or even jettisoned), the discourse of academia shrinks (as 'impact' and 'employability' render obsolete or archaic terms such as 'scholar', 'truth', 'care', 'carefulness', 'patience', 'delight', 'anxiety'), the timeframes close in (amid a freneticism of incessant pace, speed and busyness), the presentation of knowledge is sometimes distorted (as, for instance, pharmaceutical companies control the publication of drugs trials), and the liberty of academics to speak out on issues is curtailed and even students (in some of their student societies) act to limit the freedom of speech of visiting lecturers.

Within this ever-tightening environment, my work has taken the form of burrowing through close and closing walls, working with large and expansive concepts, such as reason, action, knowing, understanding, liberty, criticality, being, becoming and ecology. And then, if one is fortunate, one may just emerge from the rather dark and enclosed spaces into a much larger and even lighter space. Here, vistas may form, with potential for new beginnings. This is a philosophy as potholing, always hopeful that it is worth pressing on, even in the darkness. It is a pursuit of hope, hope that matters – so far as universities and higher education are concerned at least – may develop in a better way, even if the omens are poor. There just may be some spaces in which hopes may be realised, if only partially. Light and spaciousness may yet emerge.

Universals and the university

There is doubt over the origin of the very term 'university'. Some believe that its origin lies in the way in which the mediaeval universities of Europe were open places, and indeed attracted students and scholars from across Europe (aided by Latin as a *lingua franca*). Many of the early colleges, too, were founded by their benefactors to provide an education for poorer scholars. In that sense, the mediaeval universities were *universal* institutions. Others believe that the term 'university' reflected the ways in which those early European institutions were – to a significant degree – self-governing institutions. We are told that the term 'university' owes its origin to 'universitas', a guild, here of scholars who were on a level with each other (Cameron, 1978). Today, we might speak of them having a flat hierarchy, since they were largely without a management cadre: the rectors were appointed by the scholars themselves (a practice that still survives in continental Europe and other countries that inherited those traditions (especially in Latin America)). There was a universality, therefore, of an equal sharing in the collective governance that constituted the university.

Be this as it may, it is striking how the very term 'university' finds its equivalent in several languages ('universidad', 'université', 'universitat', 'universitet', 'universiteit' and so on). Such a commonality attaching to the term 'university' surely implies that the term has had an elastic but yet universal set of meanings. The university has universality! Over time, that universality has grown in three ways: first, to reflect a sense that the kind of reason associated with the university is a *universal reason*. The university is part of a global community – of universities – that pays homage to the idea of universal reason. A university pursues not its own local set of truths or truth of a particular dynasty or corporation or religion or even state but reason as such. To the extent that this universality is prejudiced – and to the extent that the university turns to local and even parochial concerns (as may be the case with 'the entrepreneurial university') or is managed so as to bend knowledge activities to specific ends – to that extent the university loses some of its legitimacy.

A second sense of universality that has come to be associated with the university is that of *universal knowledge*. As knowledge grew, and was both differentiated into 'disciplines' and was systematised and professionalised, so the university became a place where, in principle, all such systematic knowledge could be found. After all, in venturing seriously into an inquiry, one could never know in advance where curiosity might lead one. All manner of paths could open. The great universities of the world, accordingly, came to be 'multi-faculty' institutions. The universities, accordingly, were places of universal knowledge. Every kind of legitimate and serious knowledge could be found within its portals.

Again, the contemporary world is posing challenges here. Firstly, universities are favouring sciences and technological disciplines. The humanities and the more scholarly parts of the social sciences (such as social theory) are having a thin time of it. Increasingly, policy frameworks pump up the virtues of the so-called STEM (science, technology, engineering and mathematics) disciplines. Secondly, the emergence of the digital world, awash with data that can barely be analysed let alone be formed into and validated as 'knowledge', and where develop new ways of putting patterns of understanding into the world (and so 'multimodality' arises), is posing challenges as to what it is to come to 'know' the world. Now, knowledge claims are much more elusive, messy, complex and ephemeral. The universality of knowledge, in other words, is being put in question.

Lastly, specialisation in the academic world is reducing the universality of knowledge and, again, in more than one way. In carving out their particular missions (in a competitive academic marketplace), universities are focusing on their 'core' strengths and tending to jettison other activities. Thriving departments may find themselves being disbanded because they are surplus to such a branding strategy. Universities have few pretentions towards universality. On the other hand, knowledge itself is both spreading and separating. New journals spring up devoted to seemingly microscopic matters of study. This is a fissiparous situation, in which academic sects emerge defending and advancing their own terriorities. As such, universality will have an increasingly hard time of it here.

A third sense in which the universality attaching to universities has developed lies in the relationship between the university and life chances, with the accompanying sense of a *universality of access*. As universities have grown in size, as societies have become ever more 'knowledge societies' and as their relationships with the wider society have developed, so universities have become more significant as determinants of life chances. In turn, it has become a social and political imperative that universities enjoin themselves to a project of 'wider participation'. The arch-priest of this story, Martin Trow (2007), indeed characterised as 'universal' those higher education systems that reached out to a mere 50% of the population, in recruiting students to their programmes of study. In the UK, the so-called 'Robbins principle' of 1963 (Cmnd 2154, 1963) – in which higher education should be available to all who were qualified and willing to participate – has been at least in the shadows of national policy-making.

In short, it has become part of the social order – a social 'imaginary' indeed (Taylor, 2007) – that universities should be universal institutions in the sense that they should be open to all. And now, this should be an active openness, as universities are encouraged to venture out into society, to proclaim their openness and demonstrate it (with reduced fees or bursaries or scholarships or lightened entry qualifications or 'distance learning' opportunities or now 'MOOCs') for those who are deserving but otherwise unable to gain entry.

The universality of universities, therefore, has opened to several paths in the relatively recent history of universities (the last hundred and fifty years or so). The waxing and waning of these paths awaits a full socio-philosophical inventory. The point, though, of drawing attention here to this feature of universities – their universality – is to observe that my own work can be read in part as an exploration of the extent to which and the ways in which it can be said that universality is still part of the unfolding of universities.

The universality that I have sought to bring into view is yet a further aspect, namely that of the universal ideas that can be said to be associated with the university. A feature of this universality, not – I think – hitherto noticed is that this universality is growing, in a way. Formerly, as noted, the universals associated with the university were quite restricted, consisting of a few concepts such as knowledge, truth, reason, autonomy and freedom. Universities were institutional spaces in which such universals were pursued and safeguarded (through scholarship and then research); and a set of beliefs in their value passed on to the young (through teaching and learning).

Those universals have come under attack, the university having undergone – as I put it in my first book (*The Idea of Higher Education*) – a double undermining. On the one hand, a belief in the presence of objective knowledge (which it was the task of the university to uncover and maintain) has been dented through relativism and more recently movements such as postmodernism, post-structuralism and constructivism. The strong programme of the sociology of science declared that even the fundamental tenets of science were theory-laden and that there was no presuppositionless access to the world-in-itself. Accordingly, it can be said that the university has suffered an epistemological undermining, since all of its knowledge claims stand in the dock facing various accusations (of being partial, ideological, representative of 'discursive regimes', value-laden, social constructions and the like). On the other hand, the university has suffered a sociological undermining, as it has lost the social and institutional autonomy on which rested its claims to produce a disinterested set of knowledge claims.

Our understanding of this double undermining has deepened over the years (since the appearance of *The Idea*) and, in the process, the universals associated with the university as a space of reason (Bakhurst, 2011) have been seen to have been placed in jeopardy. Much less remarked upon, however, has been the emergence of an unfolding array of new universals that can be said to be associated with the university. Here, one thinks of liberty, justice, fairness, equity, citizenship, personal development and the public good. Still others are perhaps not far off, waiting in the wings for their entrance, including social benefit, ecology, authenticity, wellbeing, quality of life, wisdom, human transformation and virtue. Yet others, too, may be glimpsed on the horizon, such as delight, wonder, enchantment, care, respect (for persons) and mystery and even spirit.

In short, as the university and higher education have come more fully into the world, the universals with which they have been long associated have come under some strain, and even something of a battering. (No longer can we speak without pause of objectivity, neutrality, autonomy and freedom in relation to the university; and even, as intimated, knowledge, truth and understanding have been undermined.) But, at the same time, precisely on account of the university coming more firmly into the ambit of the wider society, an ever-growing penumbra of hopes come to be vested in the university. In turn, universals that may plausibly be associated with the university are widening and even proliferating. And this ever-expanding panoply of universals just may be opening spaces for values and virtues not simply to be realised by the university (even in the presence of the underminings that it has been facing) but to be realised *anew*. My work may, then, be seen as an exploration both of the universals coming into view within and close by the university, and of their problematics, *and* of the spaces for their realisation that may be opening.

University and higher education

Ever since the publication of my first book, I have wanted to keep clear water between the two concepts of *university* and *higher education*. Both are significant concepts and while they overlap, they are separate and neither is reducible to the other. The *concept of the university* is concerned with a social institution, to be found in most countries of the world. It has a social *facticity*; it has real institutional form, even if it also has a complex conceptual character. (There are many conceptions of the university, and many invest the university with hopes and ideals, and so ideas of the university often conflict with each other.)

In the past, as an institution, the university was a place of scholarship and higher learning. Subsequently, that scholarship turned into systematised and often large-scale research and the higher learning turned into formal programmes of study at bachelor, master's and doctorate levels. More recently, the university has taken on an increasing array of social functions and is taking diverse forms (to which the rise of private sector universities, distributed universities across continents, e-learning, a disinvestment from the humanities, a splitting of research and teaching, an interest in knowledge exploitability and the substitution of the term 'skills' for 'understanding' all bear witness). The question arises, in these circumstances, as to whether the *concept of the university* can be said to do work in the twenty-first century: perhaps, as some maintain, the concept has really 'hollowed out', and has become an 'empty signifier' (Laclau, 2000), simply taking on as ballast whatever various interest groups want to load into it. Perhaps, on the other hand, new possibilities are emerging for the university in the twenty-first century that can help fill it out anew.

Higher education, on the other hand, refers to particular kinds of educational process. It implies some kind of higher order level of engagement or attainment on the part of individuals. Logically, such a higher learning does not need an institutional infrastructure, although it may be aided by such an infrastructure. There is a further implication here to the effect that for an educational process to count as higher education, it should have come up to certain kinds of standard. As such, higher education is not only a value-laden concept but is also an especially *critical* concept. It always makes sense to ask as to whether programmes of study offered by a university or, say, a university sector really count as 'higher education'. Against the background of this distinction, different works of mine have been weighted more in the direction either of higher education *or* of the university.

Books of mine that have been particularly focused on *higher education* include the following. In *The Idea of Higher Education* (1990), I sought to advance a particular conception of higher education, founded on 'critical interdisciplinarity'. In *A Will to Learn: Being a Student in an Age of Uncertainty* (2007), I urged that learning at the level of higher education looks to the development of the student as a person. I argued that being a student lay not so much in knowing (in coming to know many things) or even in doing (in acquiring many skills) but coming into a certain kind of being, namely a form of human being capable of living purposefully amid uncertainty. And here, I put forward an educational theory to the effect that, at its best, higher education lay in the student taking on a certain array of foundational dispositions (six in number) and an open-ended array of qualities (dependent both on the discipline in question and on the student's own character).

Adding to that argument now, I would observe that both the dispositions and the qualities that I identified in that book are connected with what have come to be termed as 'epistemic virtues' (Brady and Pritchard (2003)). These may grow naturally out of a student's encounter with the challenges of intellectual and professional fields, but I would want to say that the dispositions and qualities stand in different ways in their relationship with such virtues. *Dispositions* constitute a dimension of the *universality* embedded in the very term 'university' – being *necessary* components of a genuine higher education – whereas *qualities* are a way in which students can express their separateness as *unique* persons. Universals *and* individuality sit together here. (I shall return to this universal-individual matter very shortly.)

In *The Limits of Competence: Knowledge, Higher Education and Society* (1994), I pointed to there being two polar concepts of competence present in higher education – an academic variant and a more instrumental and performative variant – and went on to propose a third idea of 'life-world becoming'. In *Higher Education: A Critical Business* (1997), I accepted the dominant idea that critical thinking is central to a proper higher education but argued that the contemporary conceptions of critical thinking were both shallow and narrow. In turn, I contended that the idea of critical thinking should be broadened and proposed the idea of *criticality*, precisely to widen the idea of critical thinking, and specifically to include critical *action* and critical *being*, but with each form of criticality being attainable at different levels (and I identified four levels at which such complex criticality might be achieved).

In my explorations of *the concept of the university*, I have placed my work against a sense of the university moving through a space of increasing complexity. Indeed, in *Realising the University in an Age of Supercomplexity* (2000), I coined the term 'supercomplexity' to try to do justice to the presence of competing and proliferating frameworks through which the very idea – and therefore practice and policies – of the university might be understood. And I went on to offer a set of practical principles by which universities might live purposefully in such an age of supercomplexity. In *Beyond All Reason: Living with Ideology in the University* (2003), I not only sought to identify and illustrate different forms of ideology on campus but tried to intimate ways in which the university might live with ideology in its midst (and I coined the neologism 'ide*a*logy' to suggest that the university may be a space for attending to ideals that are legitimately associated with the university). In *Being a University* (2011), I argued that the entrepreneurial university should not be thought of as the epitomé as to what it is to be a university but that there are other possibilities that may be realised. And in *Imagining the University* (2013), I urged that the imagination should be brought into play in discerning feasible utopias – which while unlikely ever to be fully realised were worth struggling for and where some measure of their feasibility could be discerned.

Journey

My intellectual work has moved through five phases, with each phase taking on a perspective or overarching theme. Initially, I was concerned with problems of knowledge – or epistemology. I was struck by a particular form of 'legitimation crisis', as I saw it (Barnett, 1985): on the one hand, the university had rested its credentials on its interest in objective knowledge. That it provided a space for the uncovering (in research and scholarship) and in passing on (in teaching and in learning) objective knowledge was being put in the dock, both philosophically and sociologically. Where, if anywhere, then, could any kind of legitimacy be found? My first phase took much from the early work of Jurgen Habermas, in particular his (1978) major work *Knowledge and Human Interests* and my book *The Idea of Higher Education* (1990) was an attempt to found a new conception of higher education on Critical Theory, especially as espoused by Habermas.

Subsequently, I came to feel that problems of knowledge could in part be addressed only through a concern with communication and dialogue and so it was perhaps not surprising that I should follow the Habermassian path into 'communicative action' (set out in his *Communication and the Evolution of Society* (1979) and his subsequent magnum opus, the two-volume *The Theory of Communicative Action* (1981)). My work at that time sought, accordingly, to explore the extent to which Habermas's ideas of an 'ideal speech situation', undistorted communication and truth as (a shared will towards) consensus were helpful in developing critical ideas of and for the university. (We should note, *en passant*, that Habermas' Critical Theory continues to inspire scholarship in educational studies, for example, Murphy and Fleming (2012).)

A third stage followed in which I came to sense that a way through problems of knowing in a complex world could be fully redeemed neither epistemologically nor communicatively but required also a conception of being. Ultimately, how are we – how are students? How is the university? – to live in a world of instability, complexity and ideology? Accordingly, my work at this point took – as I termed it – an ontological turn, leading to concerns with what it was to be a student and what it is to be a university in a world in which all bets are off. Ultimately, such matters seemed to me to be matters of being. Here, initially, I drew much on Heidegger, drawn to his view – in *Being and Time* – that being is always a matter of 'being possible' (Heidegger, 1998). However, feeling that Heidegger's sense of being was somewhat too static, I turned to the work to Deleuze and Guattari, both separately and in their joint writings. Their (2007) insistence on becoming, with their ideas of 'multiplicities', of 'smooth' and 'striated' surfaces of becoming, and of 'lines of flight', and 'reterritorialisation' opened a more open and dynamic way of looking at matters and seeing possibilities in the world.

Famously central to the work of Deleuze and Guattari has been the metaphor of the rhizome, with its unstructured nature, able to turn this way and that. We are now frequently told that we live in 'rhizomatic' times. (Papers are appearing not infrequently in the sociological and educational journals offering 'rhizomatic' analyses of social phenomena, and there is even a *Journal of Rhizomatic Studies*.) However, the metaphor of rhizome appears to me to be far too limited. A vocabulary is needed that does better justice to the unstable, fluid, liquid, fast-moving and global character of the world, which is now a digital world. I have therefore, suggested – in *Imagining the University* (2013) – that rather than the rhizome, a more apt metaphor might be that of the university as a squid, having a relatively hard shell, able to move quickly, embrace so many aspects of life, dive to depths and insert itself into small crevices (of academic identity and of communication structures).

This sense of potential depth and reach – and of the university's depth and reach – led me in a fourth phase to find resonances with Critical Realism, especially as originated and developed by Roy Bhaskar. Perhaps the central ideas there, after all, are those of the empirical, the actual and the real as ever deepening 'generative mechanisms' (Bhaskar, 2008), at deep global levels of structures, that are shaping both presences and possibilities. In drawing on that framework, I have though also pointed to the *imagination as a generative force in its own right* (and so possibly even coming to constitute a fourth and higher order level of movement beyond Bhaskar's three 'ontological' levels). Here lies the *possibility of possibilities*, namely the possibility of breaking through the given forms and understandings of the university.

My most recent move has been in the direction of Slavoj Zizek, especially in his Hegelian-inspired work. Zizek has recently developed the idea of a 'parallax gap', namely a situation (which may be the world) in which there are two perspectives between which no common ground is possible. This is not a slide back to relativism, since the two perspectives are joined together although there is no common ground between them. Zizek employs the metaphor of the Mobius strip to illuminate this idea, the two sides of the strip merging into each other, but providing 'a fundamental antimony which can never be dialectally "mediated/sublated" into a higher synthesis' (Zizek, 2009:4). Zizek observes too, that for Hegel, 'external circumstances are not an impediment to realizing inner potentials, but on the contrary the very arena in which the true nature of these inner potentials is to be tested,' (Zizek, 1993:142). 'What Hegel has in mind ... is the inherent contradiction of the notion of form which designates both the principle of universalization and the principle of individualism'. (135)

Can we not glimpse here both the nature of the contemporary university and also spaces for its realisation? The contemporary university is shot through with contractions, distortions and antagonisms – private and public spheres, personal and economic utility, inner experiential value and value as realised in performance indicators, bureaucratic systems and personal worth, knowledge for understanding and knowledge for use, criticality and obedience to rules, corporate life and pure being, dialogue and imposition, present and future – and is, thereby, an arena in which the universals that properly attach to the university (reason, liberty, dialogue, understanding and so forth) may and will be ruthlessly tested. In my book, *Higher Education: A Critical Business*, I included as a frontispiece that famous photograph of the student in Tiananmen Square, standing in front of and resisting an advancing line of tanks. That is a supreme example of the student's criticality – not just his thinking but his whole critical being – being ruthlessly tested.

A missing literature

It may have been noticed that of the authors just identified, on whose work I have especially drawn over the past decades, none has been part of the higher education literature as such. Each has worked in the mainstream of philosophy and social theory. There are two points I would make here. It may be difficult for many now working in the field of higher education studies to appreciate that when I began my studies in the 1970s, there was virtually nothing in the way of a theoretical literature on the university. There was one USA book *On the Philosophy of Higher Education* (by John S Brubacher (1977)) and a number of personal offerings, often by Vice-Chancellors and Rectors but for the most part, I was treading on new ground and had largely to step out on my own.

My other point is that right at the outset in the 1970s, and even before, I was alighting on what for me were extremely stimulating works by writers such as Gellner, Habermas, Popper and Feyerabend. Writers such as these were writing in large ways about knowledge, communication, culture, understanding and human development, all themes that spoke directly to the idea of higher education. It struck me then that in that literature lay ideas that could help to bring the idea of higher education up-to-date – it hardly having progressed much beyond John Henry Newman – and yet virtually nothing in the literature on higher education, quite apart from the wider public debate, seemed to have an understanding of that literature. I was very keen, as a result, to bring that literature into contact with issues about the university and higher education in my own writings. And indeed it is that more purely philosophical and theoretical literature that, as I have noted, has continued over the decades to provide me with continuing nourishment and inspiration.

Struggling with antagonisms

The university is an antagonistic space, in which its universals are both continually tested and fall short of being realised, but the university remains thereby a unique space in the world for upholding its universals precisely through their being tested. As suggested, the university is coming to be a space in which the universals legitimately associated with the university are even growing, as the space that is the university widens – through its public engagement and community activities, through its social action (in the media) and through the internet. The university lives and works through very particular events and actions but these concrete activities can and do embody a widening pool of universals.

Of course, the nature and form of those universals are also properly the subject of rivalrous debate (to what extent should the doors of the university be open to ever wider social participation? To what extent should the university retain a disinterestedness in its research or has it the right to take up arms for certain causes? To what extent should free speech be protected on campus?). But the very fact that such questions can be asked within universities is part of the universities keeping alive – and indeed advancing – the university as a set of universal spaces.

Indeed, the *universal-particular* polarity is yet another form of antagonism contained by and in the university (cf Butler, Laclau and Zizek, 2000). The university is in danger of succumbing to particularisms of many kinds and, for all its alleged globality, of becoming unduly parochial as a result. Local communities, particular problems in the world, individual students or groups of students, collaborations with certain businesses in the private sector or professional associations, and particular university 'brands': its busy-ness in projecting its own individuality and in engaging in a myriad of particular commitments may lead it to focus only on separate events and happenings, and locally so at that. (This 'local' nature of the university's hinterland is reflected in its epistemologies, as academic fields become more specialised and parochial.) But it is precisely in the minutiae of its particular tasks that the university can play its part in bringing its associated universals

– again, of liberty, understanding, criticality, truthfulness, carefulness, respect for persons and so forth – into play.

There cannot be, therefore, any return to the worlds either of Newman or von Humboldt. This is now a much more complex world. Now opens the much more complex task for the university of struggling not just to maintain the universals with which it has been associated – connected with reason, understanding and liberty – but the opportunity too of widening those universals; of seeing which 'lines of flight' are open to it and of which universals (perhaps equity, or ecology, or citizenship, or community, or peace, or wellbeing) with which it wishes especially to ally itself. As stated, all such universals can only be lived out in and by the university in an antagonistic space. For this task, continuing struggles lie ahead of the university and with it, continuing antagonisms. But in struggling – politically, socially, economically, culturally – in this way, the university can play its part in struggling for a better world.

Only connect

What of the selection of papers that constitute this volume? The question presses itself: is there any connecting tissue that runs across these offerings and across the several stages of my intellectual journey? Has there, indeed, been a single theme or a concern that has provided a thread through my work, and even still continues to do so? For most of my life I have been struck by the fact that much of humanity lives in an unduly enclosed world and this concern has generated an abiding theme in my work, that of emancipation in a complex world. One might say that these are two themes: emancipation *and* what it is to live in a complex world; but then there is also the rather large matter as to their intertwining, as to what emancipation might mean in a complex world.

In the hinterland of emancipation lie large concepts, more familiar in a way to the English mind, of liberty and freedom. It is the concept of emancipation to which I have been drawn with its admittedly Marxist undertones of humanity being beset with ideologies, which reflection, and action, might go some way towards dispelling. (In their different ways, my books *The Idea of Higher Education, Higher Education: A Critical Business* and *Beyond All Reason: Living with Ideology in Higher Education* could all be said to have been grappling with this problem.)

That the world is complex and that this poses particular challenges for the university is the other issue that continues to draw me back and even haunt me. For what is it to be – to be a student, to be a university – in a world in which all bets are off, in which no stability can be reached? *A Will to Learn, Realising the University in an Age of Supercomplexity* and *Being a University* are books of mine motivated by this set of issues.

But, as intimated, the really compelling matter arises when these two themes are put together: *just what might emancipation mean in a highly complex world?* If the world itself poses intractable problems – of life, of reason, of knowing, of understanding, of valuing, of acting – then how can the concept of emancipation gain a grip? This, it seems to me, is a key question of our age; perhaps, indeed, *the* key question of our age. On what foundations, if any, might resources be found in order to go on that provide some measure of security or justified edification?

The university, academic life and higher education are surely deeply implicated in all of these questions and not just abstractly. What forms of learning might be encouraged so that students are enabled to live their lives purposefully in a challenging world? What might 'the development of students' mean in such a world? What are the responsibilities that befall those engaged in research (whether of an empirical or more scholarly variety)? What kind of academic life within universities is such that the energies of their members might be enhanced rather than depleted? What relationships might develop between universities and the wider society in order that universities can fulfil their potential in helping the world to go forward (whatever that might mean in a turbulent contested age)? These questions cannot be ducked. They might not be addressed deliberately, in which case answers of some kind will be found and adopted unreflectively that characteristically will follow the flow of the sentiments (and dominant powers) of the times. That being so, to what extent might there be spaces for interventions – in thought and action – that might open the possibility of emancipatory projects, however fragile and however limited? Our views on these large matters will surely find their way into the smallest crevices of our daily practices in academic life.

Conclusion

In a sense, there cannot be a conclusion to the journey that I have tried to open up over these past thirty-five years, for I have tried to show that the university has the continuing task to try to live by and live up to the potential intimated in the big ideas – of reason, liberty, understanding, self-realisation and emancipation – that are properly associated with the university. This is not just a never-ending task but it is also an unfolding task. It is never-ending in that the world will continue to present the university with new challenges, new complexities and new instabilities. It is, too, unfolding in that the big ideas – the universals – that might be legitimately associated with the university are now all the time widening, and so part of the task lies in identifying those new concepts coming *continually* onto the university horizon (such as ecology, human rights, citizenship, global community, happiness, wellbeing and so forth) and in interrogating them and assessing the extent to which they offer resources for realising the university.

New hopes may rightly be invested in the university, as it reaches out into the wider society in a myriad of ways. In turn, the large ideas with which it is connected will grow. This widening of hopes and, indeed, values, will not stop now. The spaces that comprise the university will continue to grow.

In turn, the work to which I have devoted myself – of a philosophy of hope that is at once conceptual, critical, constructive, practical and imaginative – can go on. It calls for the examination of the large ideas that are coming to fill out ever wider the spaces of the university, for the critical interrogation of the ways in which those ideas may be facing difficulty in university life, and for the imaginative discernment of practices and policies that can help to realise those ideas, even in the midst of the antagonisms that now constitute the university. It is a never-ending quest.

Part I

The university

Chapter 1
Supercomplexity and the university

(from Social Epistemology, 1998, 12 (1) 43–50)

Outline

We are in the presence both of the knowledge society and of the end of knowledge; the university has become the home of the expert and yet, in the knowledge society, knowledge is distributed throughout society; postmodernism forbids us from claiming access to universal values but the university still has a role to play in upholding cognitive standards. In short, there are grave contradictions facing any attempt to legitimise the university. Can these contradictions be overcome or dissolved? If not, can a stance towards them be found that will offer some stability?

Introduction

Four questions arise from the apparent contradictions in this chapter's outline. First, are these apparent contradictions real? Second, should we be concerned about them or should we just live with them? Third, if concern is an appropriate response, can these contradictions be dissolved? Fourth, are these contradictions connected and, if so, is there a single general strategy or stance that we might take up so as seriously to address them *in toto*? I shall take these four questions in turn.

Real or apparent contradictions?

The contradictions identified in the outline above are real if we take them to be real. They arise from a disjunction between the ideals that have been successively invested in the Western university and the conditions in which the university finds itself today.

The ideals, have—in different eras since the medieval foundation of the university—invoked notions of service, trust, knowledge, understandings, expertise, enlightenment, personal development and citizenship. Not far from this forward value background have been other concepts such as democracy, community, enquiry, freedom and autonomy. Some concepts have tended to recede as others have become dominant; some have clearly overlapped with others; and, with the arrival of mass higher education, some concepts have been more fully taken up by some institutions than others. Nevertheless, this total value background—which we might crudely depict as one of enlightenment—has been undermined by the shifts accompanying the current positioning of the university.

The shifts are not of a piece and pull against each other. The mass university is faced both by the exigencies of modernity and postmodernity all at once. On the one hand, it is being called upon by the state to accede to the demands of technical reason both as an organization and in its internal educational and research processes. Performance indicators, managerial disciplines, skills, knowledge products, market penetration and economic regeneration: these are just a few of the characteristics that the university has acquired. What has largely been an example of the guild in operation has suddenly been required to take on the character of modernity (cf. Halsey, 1992). On the other hand, the university is not just exhibiting but may be one of the exemplars of postmodernity. Compression of time and space, globalization, detraditionalization, the switch from production to consumption, the arrival of post-Fordism and performativity: all these have their imprint on the contemporary university in different ways in all of its main activities (Scott, 1995).

The result of these structural changes—separate and even conflicting as they are—are that the value background of the Western university has been undermined (Barnett, 1990; Brecher et al., 1996). Research is judged by its use value: understanding among students gives way to performance; personal development yields to skill acquisition; the university as a community becomes the university as an organization; and truth recedes in favour of impact. The university is, rightly, felt to have been de-legitimized.

It is this de-legitimization of the Western university that gives rise to the contradictions apparent in its contemporary situation. The contradictions are only real if we wish to hang onto something of its historical value background. We are only concerned about the proliferation of sites of knowledge production if we believe that the university should be the key site of knowledge production. We are only concerned about the university becoming a site of the production of expertise if we believe that it should be a site of the development of general culture or *Bildung* or emancipation. We are only concerned about the value background of the university falling away in an age of 'postmodernism' if we believe that it should rest on an explicit value basis.

The angsts, therefore, that are arising over the Western university are an expression of a felt disjunction not just between what it has stood for and its contemporary situation. They are a symptom of a further disjunction between what it has now become and what it might yet or should yet still contain or offer. The 'is' and the 'might' or 'ought' of the contemporary Western university sit uneasily together. The difficulties arise because, despite the changes that have befallen the Western university, our hopes for it still to continue to offer something of its earlier value background of enlightenment, understanding and even of emancipation will not be extinguished easily. We continue to invest our hopes in the university even though our analyses shed a shadow over the retention of such 'metanarratives' (Lyotard, 1984).

Justifiable angst?

Gerard Delanty (2001) shows how difficult it is to free oneself of the value background of the Western university. How do we read this difficulty? Is it a logical failure, a failure scrupulously to carry through the analysis and to accept that the Western university is now delegitimized; and that's an end to it? *Or* is this retention of the value background, the wish still to make sense of the new in the traditions of the old, an indication that the analysis has to be more subtle so as to allow both for the new and for the old; paradoxically for continuing values amidst the very loss of values?

I suggest that it is the second of these situations that faces us. However, to say that in turn raises further difficulties. How is it possible to hold both the old and the new together, without self-contradiction? How can it be plausibly maintained that there is nothing special about the university in the modern era (or, rather, postmodern era) and that there remains something special about it after all? However, that is the rescue operation that faces us.

The angst present in the paper has to be justified argumentatively if we are not to succumb to the counter-argument that the angst can be dissolved simply by demonstrating its outworn and outdated retention of a value framework that is past its sell-by-date. We have to come forward with an analysis of our contemporary times in which it is plausible to hold what may seem to be incommensurable readings of our situation. However, the angst also has to be justified persuasively. In the end, hanging onto a value framework can only be justified by a persuasive argument for those values.

That, then, is the dual challenge facing those who wish—as I do—to hold the apparently contradictory position both that the traditional value background of the Western university has been undermined and that it makes sense to hang onto it. The making sense has to have two components. It has to contain a sociology; it has to offer a reading of the situation in which the contemporary university finds itself and which can contain this apparently contradictory set of analyses. Also, it has to contain a philosophical viewpoint—as we might call it—which argues cogently for the value background. In turn, that argument will have to show both that the value background is worth retaining and that it is plausible to retain it in the present circumstances.

Dissolving contradictions

Two tempting courses of action for dissolving the contradictions inherent in any legitimation of the modern university have to be repudiated. The first is that of declaring in favour of a particular large story of the university while ruling others offside. Five large stories of the modern university present themselves, each of which is built around a separate constellation of dominant concepts.[1]

First, the Western university has taken to itself a story built around the concepts of knowledge, truth and understanding. This is a relatively modern story but it is in trouble. The definitions of knowledge which the academy has developed are challenged from outside the academy: put alongside propositional knowledge are knowledge-in-use, tacit knowledge, action learning, experiential learning, process knowledge, 'transferable skills' and so forth. There are many knowledges[2] ('McCarthy, 1996), and the academy is no longer in control of them. More, knowledge is being redefined such that high marks are now being given to the multitude of forms of knowing-how (Gokulsing and DaCosta, 1997).

However, in an age of performativity (Lyotard, 1984), knowledge as giving a secure insight into our world is being downvalued in favour of relationships with the world that take us forward pragmatically. In this situation, knowledge, truth and even understanding become outworn concepts. This is a constellation of concepts that spring from a relatively disengaged relationship of knower with the world. Now, knowing is active, engaged and pragmatic in character. Concerns over relativism, and the end of truth and knowledge are symptoms of the repositioning of our social epistemologies.

A second constellation of concepts that is also in trouble as an underpinning of the university are those of freedom, autonomy, liberation and emancipation. Admittedly, postmodernity may seem to endorse such concepts. If the only universal is that there are no universals, it would seem as if constraints, boundaries, and grounds for large responsibilities must be removed. However, whatever the theoretical possibilities that postmodernity seems to open out, this cluster of concepts is in trouble pragmatically.

States across the world are seeking to divest themselves of some of the responsibilities that they have taken unto themselves in relation to higher education. Both in terms of income generation and in terms of quality assurance, self-regulation is the name of the current game (Kells, 1992).

Nevertheless, higher education remains a state apparatus (Althusser, 1971), the effects of which are felt on the autonomy of universities.

Some influences are direct. For example, while devolving responsibilities for quality assurance to institutions, such devolution takes place within ever-tighter national frameworks of quality assurance. Second, the financial envelope within which institutions operate is drawn ever-tighter, with student numbers in particular fields being determined. Third, governments—both individually and collectively (across Europe)—are seeking to develop a national or pan-national system of credit accumulation. Fourth, some governments are looking to influence teaching outcomes, encouraging work-based learning and even moves to inject competence-based teaching approaches.

Other curtailments of academic autonomy and freedom are more indirect. The most significant is the rise of the new managerialism (which comes in harder and softer forms (Trow, 1994)), which is an outcome of the complex and demanding external environment within which universities find themselves. Another indirect influence is found in the development of the student market. Intended partly as a direct curtailment of the power of the academics over the curriculum, it has also had the unintended consequence of limiting the students' own curriculum space as they work within the limited horizon of their consumers' expectations.

Quite apart, therefore, from the charge of a lurking grand narrative that can be levelled at the emancipatory conception of the university, it is in serious trouble pragmatically.

Yet other clusters of concepts have been called up in support of the modern university. One is the constellation of democracy, as we might term it, founded on such concepts as democracy, citizenship, equity, access and justice.[3] The difficulty here is that this cluster is about means, not ends. It tells us that the university should not be in the business of exclusion. It does not tell us what business it *should* be in.

A fourth cluster of concepts underpinning the modern university is the constellation of production, as we might term it, which includes work, skill, the vocational and the economy. However, this won't do either. Work cannot constitute the full ends of an educational process. In any event, work itself is changing: there is no activity that we can pin down under the heading of work.

A final cluster of concepts that is on offer to legitimate the modern university is the constellation of self, as it might be called. Personal development, personal fulfilment, and personal realization: in the Western tradition of the university (especially in England), these concepts continue to have a resonance. Indeed, we might say that a genuine higher learning calls for the injection of self into its epistemologies. Through their utterances, students are expected to give of themselves, to become themselves, to constitute themselves. However in a postmodern age, in which the self has been deconstructed, such a cluster of concepts has to be problematic.

The modern university, then, has been de-legitimized. None of its conceptual underpinnings offer it any serious support. Nor, it follows, can any of these past underpinnings be accorded priority over the others. We cannot declare ourselves in favour of any of them. Accordingly, we shall not overcome the contradictions before us by giving our allegiance to one while repudiating the others. All are in the dock together.

A second beguiling strategy for dissolving the contradictions has also been repudiated. It is that of attempting to hold all the conceptual clusters together in a coherent and coordinated formation. The difficulty here is quite simple: the conceptual constellations, both internally within themselves and collectively, contain competing if not incommensurable agendas. Within them reside agendas of technical reason and of dialogic reason, of production and of consumption, of critique and of reproduction, and of individualism and community. Such a multitude of competing agendas cannot be held coherently together with a straight face.

In short, the answer to the third question with which we started is that the contradictions before the university cannot be dissolved in any straightforward way. The university has to live with the contradictions within it and before it. Can we provide a new legitimation of the university which renders coherent such an apparently incoherent position?

The challenge of supercomplexity[4]

Recall the problem that we identified at the outset. It was that of the apparent paradox of the delegitimization of the modern university coexisting with a reluctance to disinvest of the key planks of the traditional value background. The Western university has ended but we still wish it to live on in ways that bear traces of its heritage.

To that analysis we have now added the further observations that the value background of the Western university is itself fractured. Even hanging onto the value background is itself fraught as a coherent project since the different elements within it pull against each other. The modern university turns out to be both paradoxical and incoherent at the same time.

The question we posed earlier still remains in its essentials. Should we can, can we, disinvest ourselves of the value background of the university—especially those elements oriented around the grand narratives of knowledge, emancipation and justice or should we simply accept that these grand narratives are symbols of a previous age? Instead, so the argument might run, we should surrender the university to agendas of performativity, of production and of consumption. In short, let the motto of the modern university be: seize the main chance.

Such a course of action—both as theory and as practice—should be eschewed. The incoherence and the paradoxical situation of the modern university are real. The world in which universities find themselves is a world not just of complexity and change; it is a world of supercomplexity. Supercomplexity is that state of affairs where not just individual speech acts or actions or propositions are subject to challenge. It is rather that state of affairs where our fundamental frameworks of knowing, being, and acting are challenged.

In such a world, conceptual constellations built around knowledge, work, emancipation, justice and self are manifestations of supercomplexity. They are characteristic of the manifold agendas with which the modern university has to grapple. Our frameworks for understanding the world, ourselves, our actions, our values and our relationships with each other proliferate. Those frameworks cut across each other, overlap with each other, are in tension with each other and may be incommensurable with each other. All is challengeable; there are no pools of security or stability. It is a supercomplex world.

To what cluster of concepts, then, might we turn amidst supercomplexity? It is precisely the concepts of challengeability, contestability, uncertainty, and certainty. To these key concepts, we have to add others such as ignorance, contingency, turbulence, disturbance, insecurity, risk, unpredictability and instability. This is, as we might put it, the constellation of fragility. The concepts mark out a fragile world where nothing is certain. It is a fragility that is not just presented to the university but is partly produced by the university itself for the university is implicated in the very production of the proliferating frameworks that now present it with its contemporary challenges.

Reconstructing the university

In an age of supercomplexity, the task of the university is clear. It is that of the continuing expansion of supercomplexity and of developing the capacity to live at ease amidst supercomplexity. If the university is to claim a place for itself in the modern world, it cannot simply rest on its powers of comprehending supercomplexity, of analysing the world in which it finds itself. It has itself to be a player, and preferably the key player, in helping continuously to widen and deepen supercomplexity.

The first injunction on the university is to dissolve the boundaries—both within itself and between it and the wider world—within which it has constituted itself. Those boundaries have been boundaries of organization, of ideas, and of self-identity. For example, internally, the modern university, in an era of supercomplexity, has to erode the boundaries by which academics mark out their professional territories. Not just multidisciplinarity has to be promoted if the university is to cope with supercomplexity.

Internally, too, the university has to find ways of becoming an organization capable of living with and promoting supercomplexity. Technical reason has to live with dialogic reason. Managers—the term has now to be accepted as legitimate—have to understand their limitations and responsibilities. In a supercomplex university, nothing can be managed directly (Barnett, 1992). However, the managers still have the responsibility of promoting an awareness of the uncertainties and the challenges that the university faces. The university's 'mission' has to be clarified but it has also to be continually revisited and revitalized amidst its changing environment. Ideas have to be sought; quietness cannot be assumed to indicate a state of high morale.

Externally, the boundaries between the university and the wider world will and should continue to erode. The supercomplexity facing the university is partly of its making; but, through globalization and detraditionalization (Giddens, 1994), it is also generated in and across the world. If it is to be adequate to the supercomplexity which faces it, therefore, the university has to live, to act and to be partly in that wider world. The university compounds, experiences and enhances supercomplexity by listening to and engaging with the discourses of the wider world, and, for that, it has to network itself in the 'network society' (Castells, 1996).

These considerations will be borne out in the main activities of the university. In research, for example, the role of researcher has to be recognized as problematic. Action research, consultancy and patenting knowledge products are examples of new definitions of research. These join the need for researchers to develop a repertoire of communication styles so as to reach out to manifold audiences and to accept a more public profile. This communicative competence requires not just technical competence but a self-belief and a will to engage. These, admittedly, are difficult to maintain for any self-respecting researcher sensitive to the postmodern problematic. However, these difficulties are precisely examples of the supercomplexity facing the university and, therefore, its academics as researchers.

If research is the public production of supercomplexity, teaching is the interpersonal production of supercomplexity. That is to say, the role of the academic as educator becomes the exposure of students to the angst of supercomplexity. This is not just a cognitive affair. It is experiential, emotional and overtly phenomenological in character. The task is dual, being that of producing disjunction in the mind and being of the student and of enabling the student to live at peace with that disjunction (Jarvis, 1992).

Research, construed as the production of supercomplexity, is necessarily complex. However, teaching is necessarily even more complex. Beyond being able to live with supercomplexity and being a participant in its production, *qua* educator, the academic has to impart an experiential sense of supercomplexity to the students and to enable them to live at ease with the continuing uncertainty and unpredictability of the modern world. Teaching to this end can no longer be understood as the dissemination of research or scholarly findings. Instead, it has to become a scene of pedagogical transactions of risk. Teaching approaches have to be pursued that are going to generate uncertainly, and the capacity to respond productively to it. Case studies, debates, action learning and structured dialogues are characteristic of teaching for supercomplexity. Lectures as such should be largely abandoned: they are an inadequate strategy for producing the forms of human capability appropriate to the uncertainties of supercomplexity.

Conclusion

The incoherence and paradoxes that are apparent in the modern university cannot be dissolved. They have to be lived with. No position of peace is available to the university. It will survive, it will gain a social credibility, by showing its capacities to assist in the expansion of the pools of uncertainty, unpredictability, challengeability and contestability that structure the postmodern world.

The university, accordingly, has to find ways of doing some justice to all the grand narratives that are invested in it. Technical reason, performativity, public projection and managerialism have to live with emancipation, citizenship, democracy and self-identity. To all these agendas others will be added, some by the university itself. This is not an easy set of tasks to fulfil; but easiness is not available to us. The university has both to produce and to help us to live with uncertainty.[5] That is the dual task in front of it. In a world where everything is uncertain, there is no other task.

NB: This paper was in part a response to a paper by Gerard Delanty (2001), both of which appeared in a special issue of *Social Epistemology* on 'Sites of Knowledge Production: The University'.

Notes

1 The notion of a constellation of concepts—as distinct from an 'essence'—as a means of locating meaning I take from Bernstein (1991).
2 *Contra* Gibbons *et al.* (1994), in their assertion that there are now two kinds of knowledge.

3 A recent example of this democratic constellation in operation can be found in the Report in the UK of the National Committee of Inquiry into Higher Education (the Dearing Inquiry) (NCIHE, 1997).
4 The key concepts in this paragraph are taken from my inaugural lecture. See Barnett (1997).
5 Goodlad (1976) speaks of higher education as promoting 'authoritative uncertainty' but it should be clear from the analysis offered here that there is no position available of *authoritative* uncertainty. The challenge of any pretence to authority is precisely part of the character of the global economy and postmodern world.

Chapter 2
Situating the learning university

(from International Journal of University Adult Education, *1996, XXXV (1) 13–27)*

Outline

The idea of the learning university posits three questions. In logical order, they are: (1) How might we understand the learning society? (2) How might we characterise the relationship between universities and the learning society? (3) How is the learning university to be realised? These questions are organically linked such that the learning university has to be understood as situated in the learning society. Engaging in this situating – in seeing the learning university within the learning society – is both a multidimensional and an interdisciplinary task. However, things are even more complicated than that! The learning society is barely with us. Analysing one of its key vehicles – such as the university – is therefore in part a speculative matter. If the learning society has to be constructed, imagined and worked for, so too must it be the case for the learning university.

Introduction

The idea of the learning university posits three questions. In logical order, they are: (1) How might we understand the learning society? (2) How might we characterise the relationship between universities and the learning society? (3) How is the learning university to be realised?

The questions can be posed separately but they are organically linked in two ways. Firstly, any learning characteristic is likely to be characteristic also of the university, since the university will be on most interpretations a key vehicle for inducing any learning propensities identified with the learning society. There would be something incoherent, if not to say contradictory, in looking to society to herald new conceptions of learning but against which tendencies the university stood immune. Secondly, the university is not merely an instrument for ushering in the learning society but is part of society. Again, learning characteristic of the learning society will be found in the university. Both instrumentally and intrinsically, therefore, any specification of the learning society has implications for the university within that form of society. We cannot seriously develop an account of the learning university unless and until we also develop an account of the learning society.

The learning university, accordingly, has to be situated in the learning society. Firstly, it has to be situated ontologically. The modes of being, of communication, and of self-formation of the learning society have to be carried over into the learning university. Secondly, the learning university has to be situated spatially. There may be some forms of learning characteristic of the learning society which have to be repudiated so far as the university is concerned. At least, it cannot be assumed a priori that the learning university must either draw all its definitions of learning from those characteristic of the learning society or that the learning university might not actually foster modes of learning which extend those to be found in the dominant institutions of the wider society. In short, the learning university, in its modes of learning, might be found to inhabit only some of the learning components of the learning society; even if those learning components turn out to be fundamental in certain senses.

Situating the learning university, therefore, is both a philosophical and a sociological enterprise. We need some insight into both the modes of being and the widening range of epistemologies that the learning society calls for and the potential relationships between the learning university and the wider society. Internally, within the learning university, we need to be sensitive to its various epistemologies and its widening ethical codes as well as to its changing organisational forms and its discourses.

Situating the learning university is, therefore, both a multidimensional and an interdisciplinary task. Things are even more complicated than this, however. The learning society is barely with us; indeed, is coming into being even now. Analysing the learning society or even one of its significant institutions is less a matter of conceptual or empirical description than it is speculative. The learning society has to be constructed, imagined, worked for.

To be frank, talk of the learning society is ideological. The ushering in of the learning society is a project before us. Such a project cannot be value-free but necessarily will be shot through with our values. The analysis that follows, therefore, is value-laden; it could not be otherwise. It is also argumentative: if it cannot be value-free, it can either be purely rhetorical or can attempt to offer an argument. It is the latter ploy which is adopted here.

The learning society

The learning society is, by definition, a society which takes learning seriously. Its members come to understand that learning is not fully accomplished by any age or biographical point but is a responsibility to be fulfilled more or less continually through the lifespan. Traditional societies were characterised by their enduring features. This year, this decade, this score of years are much as their predecessors. Stories and traditions could be passed on between the generations and by the generations. Indeed, there was a responsibility precisely to maintain those traditions. Durability, constancy, continuity: these were the characteristics of the life-world.

By contrast, late modernity is characterised supremely by change; or, at least, tells itself that that is so. Tomorrow will not be like today. Adaptability, flexibility, transferability of skill: these become the codewords of the modern age. As a result, responsibilities fall on individuals. We are told repeatedly that knowledge has a limited currency and that we should tolerate with equanimity several careers during our lifespan. In short, we are called upon to reproduce ourselves; to become new persons successively over time. Otherwise, we will be not just surplus to requirements but literally redundant. We have continually to create our own *habitus*. It is not just a matter of fitting ourselves to the changing labour market but of creatively reshaping the labour market through our personal changes.

This is a heavy burden to place on individuals. Individuals are enjoined to take responsibility for framing a never-ending cognitive and personal career in which their metaskills are continually reshaped. Societal reshaping becomes the responsibility of individuals. Cognitive transformation at the societal level will come about largely through personal transformation.

It is recognised, however, that the learning society will have implications at different societal levels. Discrete firm and organisations are encouraged to become learning organisations or learning universities. Questions are also posed about the learning society as such: what kind of society is it which will foster the necessary changes in individuals and organisations?

Approaches to understanding and developing the learning society, therefore, taken place on three levels:

1. **The individual.** Here, typical questions are of the kind:

    What skills will individuals require in a changing world? (Birch, 1988)

    How can those skills be replenished over time (and, in the process, the value of society's existing capital enhanced)?

2. **Institutions and organisations.** The questions here are of the kind:

    What are the responsibilities of organisations towards their employees in developing their skills and their learning potential?

    How can we bring about "learning organisations"? (Lessem, 1991)

3. **Society.** The questions typically posed here are:

    What societal and institutional barriers are there to learning which policy-making should address? (Ball, 1991)

    What learning targets should society set? (NACETT, 1994)

This schema – of individual/organisation/and society levels of analysis – yields another set of issues concerned with developing the links between the levels, for example:
Vertical and horizontal linkages, such as:

> (Individual/institutional): To what extent do the labour market and the educational system generate conflicting messages to individuals?
> (Barnett, 1992)

> (Individual/government): What tax incentives/costs attach to continuing study through the lifespan?
> (Ball, 1992)

> (Institutional/organisational lateral links): How can learning in one sector/organisation be better recognised in another, so that labour and credentials may be more mobile?
> (Robertson, 1994)

Prima facie, this set of distinctions could cover many of the issues and interpretations of the learning society. However, they are not exhaustive for they gloss over the possible meanings of the two terms "learning" and "society". Accordingly, two further sets of distinctions present themselves.

i Organisation of learning, that is, between learning of an essentially individualistic kind and learning of a collaborative kind (Jarvis, 1992);
ii Purposes of learning, that is, between learning which enhances skill and performance (Lyotard, 1984) and learning which enhances understanding and cooperation (Habermas, 1991). The first is instrumental and is wrapped up with the drive to sustain economic competitiveness in an increasingly competitive world trading environment (Gibbons, 1994); the second is dialogical and is connected with notions of civil society, of the ethical sphere, of the life-world and of human understanding (Test, 1992).

These two dimensions are independent of each other. For example, learning could be collaborative but be essentially strategic or operational (that is, instrumental) in character.

It follows that, to the analytic levels distinguished earlier, we can apply these two additional axes around the organisation and the purposes of learning. The general schema then takes on the form shown in Figure 2.1.

With the additional two dimensions now added – organisation of learning and purposes of learning – it emerges that the questions so far raised were oriented around individualistic rather than collaborative forms of learning;

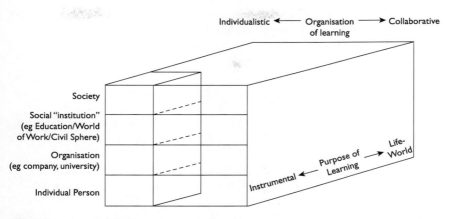

Figure 2.1 Axes of the learning society

and around learning for instrumental or strategic purposes rather than around purposes intended to promote human understanding. What might have appeared to be a fairly full range of questions turn out to be heavily weighted in one corner of the box space.

Accordingly, the rest of the box space – reflecting interests in mutual learning and the growth of human understanding and reflection – opens up a raft of new kinds of question. Some examples at the different analytic levels may be helpful:

Learning society

- What is it for society to learn about itself and be collectively more in command of itself? (Ainley, 1994)
- What possibilities are there for the development of the civil sphere in modern society? (Ranson, 1994)

Learning organisation

- In what ways might an organisation reflect upon itself and develop its understanding at the organisational level? (Duke, 1992)
- How can organisations become learning communities?

Individuals as learners

- How might individuals develop their interest in learning as such and in their own self-development?
- How can individuals become more self-reflective and self-critical? (Carr and Kemmis, 1986)

Admittedly, just as we saw there were links across the analytic levels of the learning society within its instrumental and individualistic interpretations, so there are links here within the more interactive and life-world conceptions of the learning society. For example:

- What societal and organisational processes have to be in place so as to promote self-critical learning?
- What are the conceptual links between self-learning and collective learning? Does self-learning, at any serious level, not come about through exposure to mutual learning processes?

Summarising these general remarks, we can say that the idea of the learning society is often conceived in highly restricted ways. As typically understood, the idea of the learning society is ideological, serving the strategic function of assisting in the ushering in of human capital formation and regeneration capable of withstanding global economic competition and change. In particular, it looks to producing individuals who are able to take responsibility for reproducing themselves through the lifespan in order to sustain that global competitiveness. Learning processes come to be understood in these terms: society and organisations are understood to have responsibilities to promote such learning capacities in individuals.

The corollary of these socio-conceptual orientations is that genuinely interactive learning processes which are aimed at simply enabling communities to understand themselves better and to be more effective in meeting life-world needs are marginalised, if not downright neglected altogether.

The learning university

Against the background of the above analysis of "the learning society", the idea of the learning university becomes especially problematic. The discourse of enabling students "to learn how to learn" and to acquire "transferable skills", including "communication skills" and to demonstrate a capacity "to work in teams" has to be seen as a discourse reflective of the more limited notion of the learning society. This discourse is precisely one which is oriented towards producing human capital which will reproduce itself in the interests of the learning society faced with global economic competition.

There is here not only a political economy at work but, as we might term it, an educational economy at work as well. Vocationalism, enterprise, competence, sheer performance, flexibility, and a willingness to go on learning new skills: these terms point to a certain form of pedagogical identity on the part of the student. The student role is cast as the taking on of the requisite signs of reproducing capacities required by the ever-changing labour market. "The learning society" sounds as if it is opening up new possibilities of human development, to which all right thinking persons must give their allegiance. Actually, in exchange for what is admittedly one closed set of human identity formation around disciplines, so-called objective knowledge and research expertise, this new discourse calls for the adoption of another set of closed ideas of human development. The ability successively to take on new social and economic identities without consideration for any ethical foundations they might have is the name of this game: it is a human reproducibility without inner value that is being called for and which the universities are apparently intent on supplying (as they respond with alacrity to calls to promote vocationalism, enterprise and competence).

The later set of questions potentially prompted by the learning society have, therefore, to come into the reckoning. Is it possible for the university to promote genuine interactive learning, undistorted by the press of the media of money and power? Can that learning connect with students' own existential being, their life-world, so as to make that more rational? Can the university help to set in train learning processes which are reflexive and mutually empowering so that collective learning and action are more likely? Can those learning processes be critical in character, so that the dominant institutions and processes of society are posed as problematic rather than held to be paths to be followed? Can the university help to promote a society which is intent on learning about itself and enhancing its own rationality?

To set these questions down is to do a number of things. Firstly, it is to point to the multi-dimensionality of the nature of learning: learning at both the individual and societal levels has reflexive and life-world potential, as well as instrumental and strategic utility. Secondly, it is to remind ourselves that we lack a vocabulary, a discourse, in which these questions can seriously be raised and made intelligible. That discourse has to be multi-disciplinary, involving minimally sociology, social theory, philosophy, ethics, psychology and education itself. Thirdly, it is to indicate that a programme for developing the function of the university in promoting the learning society has to proceed simultaneously on several levels: the relationships between the university and the learning society have to be built up at the individual, organisational, institutional and societal levels.

The task ahead, therefore, is analytical, political (in the sense of working out feasible strategies), discursive (developing a discourse which is one of inclusion rather than of exclusion), and ethical (since defining the learning society is necessarily a value-laden enterprise). It is also interdisciplinary, since all of these dimensions have to be integrated.

For example, the university has a history of understanding its function in relation to individuals, to individual organisations (such as in the provision of sandwich placements), whole sectors and institutions (such as particular professions) and, perhaps increasingly, even in relation to the labour market. So the university has, for long, operated at the four analytic levels to which the idea of learning might be applied (individual, organisation, sector, society). Yet, if only because the idea of societal learning is a weakly formulated notion – and, in some senses, is new – the way in which the university might assist in promoting societal learning is itself ill-formed, if formed at all.

Let us take stock. At one extreme, "the learning society" can stand for a society in which its individuals took learning seriously, understood that they had responsibilities for their own continuing learning through their life-span so that they might be able to contribute continually and effectively to the productivity of society and its capacity to maintain or enhance its place in the global competitive environment. This sense of the learning society is not to be downvalued; but it is a limited notion. At the other extreme, "the learning society" can stand for a society which is intent on developing its understanding at the societal level. This might mean:

a That the interactive components of learning are valued;
b That decision-making on major policy issues commands, if not a consensus, wide support across society;
c That understanding in support of such decision-making is widespread through society;
d That there is no a priori limit on the range of values that inform decision-making since the value base itself can be a subject for learning;
e That interaction can become progressively more rational, as truth claims, norms and aesthetic considerations all become subjects of interrogation;
f That society can, in a meaningful sense, come to understand itself and even critique itself. Reflexivity can operate at the societal level.

If this more communicative and life-world interpretation of "the learning society" is taken on board, we then have to inquire into its implications for the modern university.

One response may be that there are major limitations in the degree to which the university can help in bringing about *this* form of the learning society. It should not be thought that the university either can exhibit within itself all forms of human learning, or can be a microcosm of the learning society or can assist in promoting all those forms of learning characteristic of the learning society. There are a number of arguments that might be offered here.

It could be argued that, a priori, given a feature x in society with n forms, no one institution can feature all n forms precisely because all n forms are society-wide. Hospitals might be institutions which promote health but we do expect them to feature all examples of health promotion.

Alternatively, it could be argued that the learning characteristic of the university is not wholly identical with the forms of learning characteristic of the learning society. The latter do not exhaust the former and may even be antipathetic to it. Logically, the university may hold onto forms of learning which are not those of the learning society, as it is ordinarily conceived.

A third argument is more radical and more normative in character. It is that the university has a responsibility to sustain forms of learning which run counter to those characteristic of the learning society.

A yet further argument is again logical in character and is perhaps fundamental. It is that, by definition, the learning characteristic of the learning society is societal in its scope and nature. It captures ways in which modern society might engage with itself. Ipso facto, no one institution can exhibit such learning for it is society-wide by definition.

There is something in all of these lines of argument; and they all have a point. They remind us that the challenge of working out what learning at the level of society might mean lies before us; and they also remind us that not all institutions which are concerned with learning necessarily are fully understood if we conceive of them as institutions of and for the learning society. In particular, the university may have a responsibility to stand apart from the learning society.

But such arguments are disingenuous if they are taken to imply that the university can and should entirely stand apart from the learning society. The university does not have to fall in with the forms of learning ushered in by the learning society; but we are still left with the task of explicating the relationships between the university and the learning society. If not merely submissive, is the stance of the university towards the learning society to be simply oppositional? Neither stance can be taken to be a serious characterisation of the relationship. On the contrary, positive responsibilities can be identified which are neither compliant nor simply critical.

There is, then, in bringing about the learning university, a key distinction between the learning university as an institution for promoting learning for the learning society and as an institution which is characteristic *of* the learning society.

A university for the learning society

We have distinguished two axes along which learning in the learning society can be understood:

- instrumental – life-world;
- individualistic – collaborative.

These axes at once give us four kinds of learning; and they also offer the chance of bringing them into a relationship with each other (for example, in promoting learning which is collaborative and is oriented to the life-world).

The question which arises immediately is how does this classification map onto conventional ways in which knowledge has been packaged in the university? An immediate response is that conventional knowledge has been mostly individualistic in character and had either an instrumental (sciences and technologies) or a life-world (humanities and social sciences) focus, and that the academic world is faced with the challenge of developing more collaborative forms of learning. But this is too simple: the response neglects the extent to which life-world forms of knowing and understanding have been neglected by the academic community. Personal knowledge, tacit knowledge, experiential understanding, ethical awareness and sheer existential commitment as part of the act of understanding have all been downvalued if not entirely ruled out of court as sites of serious possibilities of learning. Learning which speaks immediately to the life-world, to students' own ontological being, to their developing sense of self has been excluded by an excessively formal and neutered approach to knowing. An education for the learning society, fully understood, would seek to articulate and incorporate these forms of learning into the curriculum *and* into new definitions of academic professionalism in relation to teaching in the university.

The four-fold set of definitions of learning opens, then, a broad territory on which new curricula, forms of learning and kinds of student experience can be mapped. That is a challenge in itself. But even this task is too simple; and in two directions.

Firstly, it is oversimple sociologically. Empirically, we have no adequate means of understanding the transformations affecting the definitions and uses of knowledge in modern society. Learning becomes problematic for a number of reasons and within a context which includes:

a   A sense that the future cannot be predicted. Not only is it one of change but it is one of risk (Beck).
b   What counts as valid knowledge is at least extending if not changing. Just as oral and craft traditions gave way to empirical techniques, now in turn they are giving way to policy studies and to operational standards. The epistemological clock is perhaps even going backwards!
c   Chaos theory and an awareness of risk imply that, at any one time, decision making is inherently unstable and must take place on the basis of ignorance. The consequences and the intervening variables cannot be predicted.
d   Lastly, postmodernism draws our attention to fundamental forms of incommensurability in our value systems and ways of appropriating the world around us. *Vive là différence*. Behind what may appear to be common concepts in our language lie, at a deep level, fundamental differences.

Sociologically, then, learning becomes a problematic concept in late modernity since knowledge itself is problematic.

Yet the learning university, wishing to promote the learning society, also has a hard task of it philosophically. The first point builds on the last about postmodernism.

On what basis can we build our epistemologies in the learning society? Postmodernism denies absolute foundations of right reason. Any attempt to lay down general rules – à la Habermas – is dismissed as totalitarianism, as the return of "terror". Those who imply that "anything goes" quickly end up by recanting their lines; but where then do we turn for some foundation to our knowing efforts? Yet unless we have that, learning has no anchorage. The concept of learning is parasitic, after all, on knowledge. There would appear to be an obligation on the university, in particular, to offer a solution here; for otherwise, it loses its point.

The second philosophical problem is that of the ethical base of our knowing efforts. What values are they intended to serve? If utilitarianism is insufficient or is no answer at all, what serves in its place? Key alternatives currently on offer are those of authenticity, of community and of universalism. Yet, especially when placed against the earlier background, each seems problematic.

Both epistemologically and sociologically, therefore, the concepts of learning, knowing and society – and, ipso facto, "the learning society" – are problematic in late modernity. The learning society, its complexion and the possibilities it opens up, should not be assumed to be given *in any sense. Accordingly, becoming clear about the character of the university for a learning society* is not to be read off automatically from a given sense of the learning society but has to be itself a matter of creative and deliberate determination. That act of clarification, insofar as it is possible, cannot be achieved as a technical act but is necessarily a value-laden enterprise. Determining what we take the learning society to be and working through its implications for a key institution such as the university is ultimately a matter of value choice around what we take society to be and the potential it might offer for human and social development.

Such a formulation of our task might seem to be entirely open-ended. The learning society and the place of the university within it are whatever we take them to be. Such a judgement should be resisted. And to bring some set of boundaries to our task, we can usefully start by delving again into the nature of the university.

Some will say, whether from a policy perspective (reminding us about diversity in a mass higher education system) or, again, from a philosophical perspective, that there is no such entity as the university. There is no single description of the university. Rather, there are at least many different kinds of university; and perhaps as many instantiations of the university as there are universities. This assumption, charitable and egalitarian as it is, should also be resisted.

The idea of the university makes no sense apart from its association with a number of ideas. These would include providing a forum for inquiry into truth, the assembly of knowledge, the development of minds through the acquisition of understanding built on truth, an interactive situation for the critical examination of truth-oriented proposals and so on. That this list could be extended fairly easily is beside the point. There is something which might be termed the western university tradition. It is a tradition which allows a multitude of diverse epistemological and value positions to exist alongside each other, certainly. But that very openendedness is testimony to the university as a site of critical discourse in which, at least as a counterfactual ideal, the central test of validity is that of the better argument.

As an institution for the learning society, rather than being simply an institution in the learning society, it may be that the first requirement on the university is to remind itself of these epistemological and value presuppositions buried in its constitution. Not merely truth-telling but an orientation towards the truth: such an orientation itself generates critical and open inquiry. Habermas' ideal speech situation may be ideal, but at least the university should approximate to it; for, otherwise, its epistemological base is irredeemably undermined.

But a critical inquiry betokens other aspects of communal life including a respect for persons, a propensity towards authenticity within the bounds of critical and collaborative reasoning, and cognitive and, indeed, experiential space in which to develop one's own thinking and being. The epistemology of academic life calls forth an ethics of academic life.

We have here a perhaps surprising, albeit tentative, first proposition: that the university becomes most fully an institution for the learning society simply by reminding itself and by realising its own presuppositions. Those epistemological, communicative, and existential presuppositions of continuing interactive inquiry and self-scrutiny through others' commentaries: these have to be, on any full assessment, key ingredients of the learning society. If continuing mutual, critical yet supportive, progressive understanding lies at the heart of the learning society, the university can become after all a microcosm of the learning society. Furthermore, by being fully itself, it can promote propensities for lifelong and mutual learning within and through the wider society.

The qualifiers "can become" and "being fully itself" are, of course, necessary because the idea of a learning university in this sense is counterfactual. The idea is an ideal. The university lays claim to a self-description of open, mutually supportive, inquiry that it cannot seriously sustain. There is a sociology, a politics and an economy at work, and that complex of stories cannot be unravelled here. But there is also an epistemology at work: the presupposition that there is a given framework of critical reasoning is under attack. The Habermasian attempt to shore it up is not being met with universal acclaim.

Conclusion: the limits of the learning society

There are, then, difficulties in front of our universities becoming learning institutions in their own right and in fulfilling their promise in promoting the learning society. The media of money, power, interests and organisational hierarchies curb the learning potential carried deep in the idea of the university.

But to say this is to remind ourselves of two things. Firstly, the modern university has become part of modem society. The university is fully an institution of society as well as being an institution in society. The price of the university's fairly willing incorporation as an instrument of social and economic planning has been its acquiring the forms, processes and operational criteria of the wider society; or even of the state. Secondly, it is to remind ourselves that the media of money, power, interests and hierarchies are ineradicable components of society. They always were, but perhaps they are more systematic features of modernity.

Consequently, to return to our opening sallies, the idea of the learning society – if it is taken to embrace mutual unfettered learning – is that; an idea, counterfactual to the possibilities before us. But it is not just an idea: it is a critical standard against which our unfolding arrangements can be tested. And it opens up imaginary possibilities to serve as beacon points to steer by, if not to reach.

Correspondingly, the learning university is also an ideal carrying utopian hopes. But it is a peculiarly apt utopian set of aspirations for the university. Putting it simply, it is the idea of the university as such. In placing the idea of the learning university at the forefront of its self-hopes, the university is reminding itself of the dialogical, critical and life-enhancing potential locked within its own presuppositions. Becoming a university for the learning society requires the university, in the first place, to take on a collective determination to achieve even more fully its own existing self-image.

Chapter 3

Recapturing the universal in the university

(from *Educational Philosophy and Theory*, 2005, 37 (6) 785–797)

Outline

The idea of the university has stood for universal themes – of knowing, truthfulness, learning, human development and critical reason. Through its affirming and sustaining of such themes, the university came to stand for universality in two senses: the university was neither partial in its truth criteria nor local in its significance (its reason was reason tout court, not merely that of the state or the crown or a religious faith per se). Now, this universalism has been shot down: on the one hand, amid postmodernism, universal pretentions have been impugned: on the other hand, globalization has been accused of being a new process of colonization. Global universities may be seen as a vehicle for the imposition of Western modes of reason. Is a new universality open to the university? Might it lie in the idea of strangeness, in living with strangeness?

Introduction

In the twenty-first century, can we identify any interconnected set of concerns or themes by which we might characterize the university? Can we, indeed, any longer speak of 'the university'? The phrase, after all, suggests precisely what has to be in doubt, namely that there is a unity to the university; that across institutions, disciplines and academic activities, there remains a set of ideas or hopes through which the university might live as a coherent human project. In the past, that unity has looked to universal features of university practices and university life. For example, it was assumed that the university, in its concern for truth, was looking to uncover universal features of human life. It was also assumed that, in principle at least, the university was interested in truth *in toto*: the university was interested in all truths; its means of establishing truth would allow it access to any truth.

The underlying point of the presence of the universal in the constitution of the university was that it was held that the university was not representative of particular interests but occupied a kind of neutral discursive space. Although established by crown and church in the mediaeval ages, and since by particular states, the university stood above the local interests of its host community; and was granted distinct freedoms not commonly enjoyed by the wider society. The university was expected to serve universal interests of truth-seeking, of knowledge garnering, of learning and critical reason. The university was partial only to such universal concerns. It stood for important aspects of human life, aspects that were universal in character.

Of late, the idea of universal features of human life has taken something of a battering, not least through the assaults of post-structuralism and post-modernism. How, in such a context, should we understand the university? Can we, indeed, talk in such terms anymore? I want, therefore, to explore here the university through the idea of universality. In doing so, I shall also implicitly be exploring the relationship between a philosophical and a sociological perspective on the university.

The idea of the universal

In its mediaeval origins, the university was a community open to all. There were no bars on a person's admission other than his ability to meet the necessary expenses; and the early mediaeval colleges were usually endowed with scholarships to provide for the poorest to attend. Scholars flowed more or less easily across Europe, Latin serving as a common language. The mediaeval universities were universal institutions, then, both in their members and in their communicative structure.

Other forms of universality emerged as universities developed. Firstly, universities were characteristically self-governing institutions. Their members were not exactly all on the same level: there was hierarchy even in the medieval universities. But the universities came to stand for an open-textured discourse, free of dogma. Indeed, the mediaeval practice of disputations bore testimony to the spirit of criticality embedded in the universities. In other words, from the inception of the universities, their communicative processes were relatively open: new ideas were positively encouraged and—as it might be termed today—a discursive space was provided for their generation and for their circulation. Such institutions later served the purposes both of the Enlightenment and of the host State precisely because of their openness: in being impartial, they became vehicles for new ideas to flourish. The universality of universities, *both* in their communicative processes and in their openness to ideas, served the interests of their local sponsors in favouring change and development.

Later, in the late eighteenth and early nineteenth centuries, the universities became associated with Truth, with a capital 'T' as it were. Philosophers and administrators, particularly in Germany, saw the university as providing a structured truth-oriented inquiry. This truth was Hegelian in character for it was itself seen not only as universal but also as a unity-in-itself. Through their uncovering of truth, the universities were illuminating and forming Spirit. With the onset of institutionalized research, particularly in the sciences and technologies, the metaphysical framework was abandoned as a justification for the university but the sense of universality was maintained in the idea of truth. For instance, it was assumed that the laws of nature were universal in character: what held for one time and place held for another time and place. The purpose of the university was to uncover those timeless universal truths.

More recently still, with the emergence of mass higher education, universities came to be seen as having if not universal then at least society-wide missions. They are to be seen as practicable: there should be no irrelevant bars to admission and universities should perceive and structure themselves so as to act in the general interests of society. Indeed, within Martin Trow's original formulation of the concept of mass higher education, 'mass higher education' was but an intermediate phase—beyond 'elite higher education'—on the way to 'universal higher education' (although, by that term, Trow admittedly had in mind systems admitting somewhat less than 100% of the age cohort; anything over 50% in fact).

The end of universality?

The senses of universality implied by the idea of the university have, however, been subject to several assaults. Just as those senses of universality have been both philosophical and sociological in character so, too, are the assaults to which those dimensions of universality have been subjected.

Firstly, the contemporary era has more or less outlawed the idea of the universal as such. While it contains many strands, perhaps the central idea in postmodernism is that we are in the presence of the end of universals. In a postmodern world, no doctrine, no value and no principle can be upheld with absolute assurance. In this fundamental sense, therefore, the idea of the university as standing for universals of any kind is put in the dock.

More specifically, the ideas that there might be universal truths or universal methods of securing truth have become suspect in the modern age. Indeed, one of the complaints of Allan Bloom in his (1987) *magnum opus*, *The Closing of the American Mind*, was that relativism had undermined the position of epistemological and cultural privilege that the university had carved out for itself. Further, *that* relativism had an internal impact within the university. No position could be adopted with any authority on campus: relativism had infected university life itself.

It may be countered that globalization offers the obverse story: in this globabalized world, universities worldwide are having to compete within a common framework, namely that bequeathed by Western nations. It is an academic world in which publication in the refereed journals of the West secures privilege, in which science and technology are in a position of disciplinary hegemony, in which states are developing intrusive evaluation systems for 'accountability', and in which students are increasingly finding themselves in a quasi-market, in which product counts for more than process. Such a globalized process of 'neo-liberalism' (Peters and Olssen, in press), it may be countered, therefore constitutes a new kind of universalism. Far from supporting the idea of the university, this is a universalism that cuts into the idea of the university. The modern idea of the university, after all, contains a sense of a social institution that continues to interrogate itself, its values and its purposes (MacIntyre, 1982): *this* globalized sense of the university, on the contrary, speaks closure in various guises, in its epistemologies, its relationships with the wider society and even in its pedagogical relationships. If there is, today, a universality in the university, it is one that both carries closure and promotes particular interests of the global economy and of the evaluative state.

However, globalization is not the only overarching account available to us. Indeed, in a sense, globalization supports relativism. It renders visible alternative and local epistemologies and value systems of universities beyond the West, even as its effects are to suffocate those particularities. And relativism grows, if only because the university has become a vehicle for the promotion of new and rival frameworks of understanding: postmodernism may be seen as just an endorsing commentary on this state of affairs.

Secondly, relativism, we should note, is a position that has received positive attention from *within* universities. It is an *academic* position. It constitutes an attack on the university's pretensions to universalism from within. A quite separate attack on the university's universalism comes largely from without. The university prides itself on its epistemological egalitarianism, on its willingness to find a home for all claimants to knowledge. The story of the university over the past two hundred or more years can be seen as one of ever widening knowledges; indeed, of the formation of disciplines themselves which continue to split and widen into an expanding universe of knowledges.

Yet the wider world condemns the university for its epistemological narrowness. Michael Gibbons and his associates gained no little interest with their (1994) thesis of a Mode 2 of knowledge outside universities. The Mode 1 of formal propositional knowledge, built up edifice-like, around which the universities had formed themselves, was witnessing the development of a new epistemology in the wider society. This Mode 2 knowledge was ephemeral, called upon multi-disciplinary teams to address specific problems, and worked through an epistemology level of praxis (although this last was not a term employed by Gibbons *et al.*, 1994).

Mode 2 knowledge supplied solutions to problems having a practical edge. It was a knowledge that even outran Lyotard's observations (1984, pp. 46–51) about the 'mercantilization' of knowledge, and the dominant criterion of its significance laying in its 'performativity', 'that is, the best possible input/output equation'. Strictly speaking, Mode 2 knowledge is not knowledge applied to practice but is knowledge derived *in* and *through* practice. There is here no 'input/output' equation; it is all output!

That the thesis attracted substantial attention perhaps said more about its tacit message than its substance. The substance, surely, was misleading. From the work of Schon, Eraut and others on professional life, and from Lewis (1986), our attention is drawn to there being not just two Knowledges but a host of knowledges. Experiential, practical, tacit, personal, process and emotional: these are just a few of the qualifiers that may be—and are—placed before 'knowledge'. We now are appreciative, for example, of the work of the midwife incorporating several such knowledges, that those knowledges may conflict in the one professional act (as bureaucratic and performative knowledges jostle with empathic and intuitive knowledges), and that those knowledges are even growing as the demands of midwifery itself grows (through, for example, the increase of multi-professional ways of working and of quality standards acting to regulate professional work). The emergence, too, of 'multi-textuality', as implied in the work of Kress and others (cf Kress and Van Leeuwen, 2001), is testimony—in a digitized and iconic age—of a multiplication of appropriations of and interventions in the world; in a word, again, 'knowledges'. In reflections such as these lie not only qualifications but surely also an endorsement of the fundamental thesis of Gibbons *et al.*, 1994: that there are more knowledges than those that are explicitly promulgated in the university.

The idea, therefore, that the university stands for universal knowledge has now to be repudiated. The knowledges to be found in the university may be growing at a rapid rate but they will—we now have to recognize—always fall short of mirroring all of the knowledges in modern society. This is inevitable: the 'Knowledge Society', after all, is not just a society that celebrates knowledge and uses it extensively: it is a society in which knowledge production is itself spread widely, if not universally. At the same time, what counts as knowledge continues to widen: epistemological literacy will always outrun the capacities of individuals and even organizations themselves to demonstrate their competence in different knowledge fields. There will be calls for knowledge brokers and knowledge managers and these, too, will be supplied from outside the university.

The challenge of supercomplexity

There is a third sense in which universalism has its limits in the university. Universalism suggests that there are to hand frameworks of understanding under which entities can be accommodated and be seen as part of the universal whole. For the university, these have been notions such as truth, openness and fairness (everyone shall have a hearing), accessibility (everyone has a right to utter) and knowledge itself (given time and effort, it is possible to know the world). However, we now live in a world of radical contestation and challengeability, a world of uncertainty and unpredictability. In such a world, all such notions—as truth, fairness, accessibility and knowledge—come in for scrutiny. In such a process of continuing reflexivity, fundamental concepts do not dissolve but, on the contrary, become systematically elaborated. In this process of infinite elaboration, concepts are broken open and subjected to multiple interpretations; and these interpretations may, and often do, conflict. As a result, we no longer have stable ways even of describing the world that we are in; the world becomes multiple worlds.

We are entitled to call this a world of proliferating and even mutually contesting frameworks a world of *supercomplexity* (Barnett, 2000): amid supercomplexity, there can never be any complete resolution of the contestability of our frameworks. That the university has to live with this conceptual fragility is only just, for the university has in large part been responsible for the generation *of* that fragility. It has, after all, been charged by the modern state to produce and to insert into society new frameworks of understanding the world that, in turn, permit new kinds of intervention in the world. In such a world, the university has become a social institution for the production both of strangeness and of human ontologies that can flourish amid strangeness: indeed, human ontologies that revel in the production of strangeness.

To put it another way, the university has become an institution for handling risk, both at the systems level and at the individual level (Beck, 1992). The notion of strangeness, however, surely captures more adequately both the epistemological and ontological challenges bearing in on the university and the task in front of the university. 'Strangeness', too, directly provides another assault on the university's pretensions. If the university is amid and for strangeness, it can hardly cling to universals; or so it may seem.

The university is a manifestly complex institution. Managing a university and leading it calls for the management of complexity: systems, infrastructure, values, information, income streams, knowledges, structures, disciplines, discourses, and activities are only some of the dimensions of universities as organizations. It is fashionable—in the social science literature—to perceive the presence of management in universities in a wholly negative way but, if they are to prosper in *any* way at all (if, for example, liberal ideals are to be realized in any way), universities need effective management and leadership, especially at this time. Small elite institutions, that were largely inward looking, did not have such pressing needs. The complexity of universities as institutions is now a universal feature of their character.

The interweaving of the elements that constitute the contemporary university in fact can be said to constitute a chaotic situation (cf Cutright, 2001), and in three senses. Firstly, change in any one element in any one dimension can affect elements in any other dimension. The university is inevitably a multi-dimensional organization. Secondly, the dimensions, elements and entities of university life are so interwoven that their interactions cannot be completely plotted and the impact of any change in any of the systems is bound to be unpredictable. Thirdly, the relationships between universities and the wider society are now 'transgressive' (Nowotny, Scott and Gibbons, 2001). With any such interleavings, overlappings and interminglings between universities and the wider society, and with the ensuing fuzzy boundaries that result, a situation of radical instability results; it is an instability that can never be overcome.

The concepts of complexity and chaos, therefore, offer considerable help in understanding the contemporary university; and they, in themselves, add weight to the end-of-universality thesis. But, as implied, there is an additional dimension of complexity at work. Universities are organizations charged with the function of generating ideas. Characteristically, these ideas have been developed in more or less systematic bodies of knowledge. However, ideas are also proliferating about the purposes of universities themselves. Talk of mission identity only has point because what it is to be a university is now not given but is *constructed*. In an open turbulent world, and amid mass higher education, those ideas proliferate. Relationships with society, forms of engagement with 'stakeholders', institutional responsibilities, key activities and their relative weight and penetration (even across the world), and the forms that those activities take (how 'virtual' they are, for instance), and modes of internal organization (such as the relationships between faculty and 'management'): all these and more are, to a degree, open matters. They are also matters that many universities are explicitly addressing, often in the form of some kind of internal strategic review.

This empirical reflection as to the construction of what it is to be a university raises two more conceptual points. Firstly, and partly to reiterate, what it is to be a university is open: there is, in principle, an infinity of possibilities in front of a university. Especially in a marketized age, amid 'academic capitalism' (Slaughter and Leslie, 1997), the very idea of the university is no longer a universal, or set of universals, in itself. Secondly, in this contemporary multiplication of the ideas of the university, some of those ideas will be found to be incompatible with each other. These are conceptual disputes, disputes over what we take a university to be.

Here, though, comes a twist in the story. Since universities are relatively open institutions, are complex organizations, and are part of communicative networks, those conceptual disputes—to a large degree—will be part of the conceptual territory of individual universities. In short, universities are bound to be sites of dispute over their own self-constitution. There is no way out of this situation even if it were desirable. But, for many, it is part of the very meaning and purpose of a university that there should be continuing dispute as to its purposes (MacIntyre, ibid.).

We see, here, that the university is again a site of supercomplexity. It is, more obviously, in the business of generating new ways of thinking substantively within the disciplines. The clash of rival frameworks of understanding that result is a situation of supercomplexity in that the rival frameworks within and across the disciplines permit of no uncontested description of situations and phenomena. That is, we cannot ever be sure what it is that confronts us in any setting: we cannot even describe—let alone determine interventions into—situations in front of us with any assuredness.

But, now, as we have seen, supercomplexity is also evident at the meta-level of the university itself. Rival discourses as to the meaning and purpose of the university abound. 'Managerialism', 'enterprise', 'market', 'collegiality', 'access', 'standards', 'research' and, more recently, 'engagement' and 'the scholarship of teaching': all these are codewords for rival discourses and ideologies. The contemporary university is a discursive swirl of contending ideas as to the proper character of each university itself. The contemporary university is a nice example of 'liquid modernity' (Bauman, 1998). In such a situation, the idea of universality historically locked up in the idea of the university may seem to have lost any lingering mileage it might have had.

Recapturing universality

The issue before us is quite simple: can we talk of the university any more? Is there a definite set of ideas—inchoate as they may be—that could be said to have some kind of universal significance with which we can associate universities? It might be tempting to come forward with a robust negative response: both that, firstly, there is no such universality available to universities *and* that, secondly, no difficulty arises from such a situation. In the modern world, one of a multitude of values, frameworks for understanding, forms of human identity, forms of human identity and orientations to action, it is right—so it may be felt—that we abandon the notion of universality as any kind of conceptual underpinning for the university. Universities have all kinds of mission and that is right: indeed, there are concerns that those missions are often unduly overlapping and even coming together. In a complex world, and in a mass higher education system, we need greater differences and not any kind of uniformity. In this milieu, 'diversity' becomes the policy watchword.

The argument may be beguiling but it is faulty. Firstly, that there can and should be legitimate differences between universities does not in itself spell the end of universality. There may still be felt to be features or attributes that universities, *qua* 'universities', should possess. For most jurisdictions around the world, indeed, 'university' is a protected title, with institutions having to meet stringent criteria to justify the appellation. And, even if tacitly, it could be reasonably suspected that that evaluation process has at least something to do with wide normative and cultural sentiments associated with the idea of 'university'.

Secondly, the old universalisms may have had their day—deriving, in part, from metaphysical ideas as to the relationship between human beings and the world, and over the perceived nature of knowledge and truth—but new universalisms may be pressing their claims. For example, if there is anything in the idea of 'globalisation', universities as global—or would-be global—institutions, are going to be implicated in that story. Thirdly, as a matter of empirical fact, the term 'university' still appears to have some general symbolic value, even if that significance is difficult to identify. That there are several hundred corporate 'universities' in the USA (cf Jarvis, 2001) implies, at least, that the term 'university' continues to have general resonance: those 'universities', while perhaps undermining some traditional senses of the university, nevertheless tacitly endorse the term and are parasitic on it; and, in endorsing the term 'university' implicitly proclaim it still as an idea.

Why does all this matter? It matters, first, because, in its universality, in its universal interests, the Western university marked itself off as having certain significances in Western society and culture. While sponsored by particular states, universities stood partly outside of any particular interests of their sponsoring states. Their interests lay in (universal) knowledge and truth *per se*. Over the past thirty years or more, the way in which these interests have been realized in practice has suggested that they have been shot through with interests—including those of gender, disciplinary hegemony, the world of work and the economy—and so the university's universality has been breached in several places. Yet, the idea that the university stands for (to some degree, at least) and is connected with universal interests gives it a particular significance precisely against the background of the university's universality, of interests that transcend those of locality, partiality and time, and justify the university and its academics having a discursive space of their own in society. In a world shot through with particularity, difference and 'context', an institution that is associated with some forms of universality may itself come to have a wider societal, if not universal, role to perform.

Secondly, through its universality, there was inbuilt in the university a sense of it offering a critical site not just within each university's host society but for humankind. Its interests in knowledge and truth supplied a vantage point from which it could critically evaluate existing knowledges and a methodology (of public communication) that would render the new understandings transparent to and for the world. Its enquiries and its new understandings, therefore, were not just *its* enquiries and understandings: they were enquiries and understandings *for* the world. Breaches in that function, for example, as is evident in the closure exerted by pharmaceutical companies over university research that they sponsor, is a matter of general public concern for they diminish the capacity of the university to assist the promotion of the public sphere.

We may observe that the juxtaposition that has been tacit in our exploration so far has been less one of universal-relative and more one of universal-particular. If we lose the university's universality, we reduce its scope to narrow interests and impoverish it through its having mere limited, local and partial significance. It can still be trusted but only to act within confined frameworks in the service of particular interests. Its significance as an institution for and of the world would have been jeopardized. The world, in effect, would have lost a major social institution.

Where, then, might a universality for and in the twenty-first century be located? If, in a world of supercomplexity, every framework, every value, and every action is contestable—as it is—how can there be any firm ground on which any form of universalism might rest? Ideas of truth and knowledge are clearly suspect; so, too, are practices such as research and teaching (for both 'research' and 'teaching' are elusive concepts and, at a policy level, arguably a university could omit either from its portfolio of activities).

Terms such as 'enquiry' and 'learning'—recently promoted by several commentators, especially from within the 'scholarship of teaching' movement—may seem to be helpful in denoting common attributes of universities but they run into two problems. Firstly, they are insufficiently specific to universities and, secondly, they run the risk of conflating universal attributes of universities with universality as such. Universality, as a feature of universities, spoke to universal concerns and interests not only of the university but also of the wider society (such as an association with universal knowledge and truth and with universally-open processes of communication). Potentially universal features such as enquiry and learning are simply means of achieving the university's universal ends: they are not features of academic universalism itself.

In a world of intellectual, cognitive and value mayhem, there seems to be little chance of regaining a universality for the university—at a moment when it is needed most of all. But the sense of mayhem that besets and even resides within the university may supply a new kind of universality. If the world is radically unknowable, if truth is always 'situated', if the university has become an organization such that its capacity to provide an 'ideal speech situation' is farther away than ever, if the university has reducing powers over its own abilities to communicate to wider publics in non-distorted ways, and if the university is beset by conflicting and ideologically loaded agendas, perhaps these very reflections—*global as they are*—suggest a new universality is within reach.

'Strangeness': the new universality

This new universality turns on the twin notions of contestability and challengeability. While linked, they have slightly different emphases. *Contestability,* we may take it, refers to that state of affairs in which a proposition or framework might be subjected to the counter punch of a rival proposition of framework. It indicates a situation in which competing voices might wish to be heard or can be heard. *Challengeability*, in contrast, refers to that state of affairs in which our orientation to the world is subject to counterintuitive experiences. Suddenly, something takes our breath away: we have the stuffing knocked out of us. The assumptions on which we depended, but of which we were hardly aware, are—in the same moment—both revealed and found to be inadequate. While their conceptual territories overlap, contestability occupies the more epistemological position while challengeability stands in the more ontological position (Barnett, 2000).

We can conflate these terms with a third (on which we have already drawn): in an uncertain and unpredictable world of contestability and challengeability, human capacities are needed that can flourish amid 'strangeness'. A world of supercomplexity, in all its fragility, requires human subjectivities that not only tolerate strangeness but can even produce it; for, ultimately, the only way, amid strangeness, to become fully human, to achieve agency and authenticity, is to have the capacity to go on producing strangeness by and for oneself.

The postmoderns are wrong: in a postmodern world, universals are not at an end. The new universal is precisely the capacity to cope, to prosper and to delight in a world in which there are no universals; and this is the new universal. And it is a task of—and challenge to—the university to provide those capacities.

Living with strangeness

This argument may be felt to be unduly abstract and not connecting with the daily experience of what it is to live and survive in universities with all their concrete messinese. But the argument has definite and several implications for both policy and practice within universities if they are to realize such a (universal) conception of the university.

Research, for example, becomes the *public* manifestation of the university. It becomes the production of strangeness through the production of new frameworks of comprehension and points also to the public projection of any such new frameworks. The life of the conventional researcher, in short, has to become even more challenging, both cognitively and experientially. Research, in the university of strangeness, cannot be constructed as work with largely given paradigms and conducted within a conversation of peer researchers. In a world of supercomplexity, researchers now acquire—whether wittingly or not—the challenge of communicating their intellectual wares to wider publics and so advancing public understanding of a chaotic world.

Of course, such projections into the public sphere of ideas, frameworks, perspectives and theories will only serve to compound the extent to which the world is supercomplex; but that heightened supercomplexity will be won through a more reflexive and even somewhat more rational society. Such a communicative role will add to the complexities of the researchers' own responsibilities and academic identities but unless universities seriously proffer their intellectual wares to the wider society, the world is bound to be not just supercomplex but also chaotic. Any possibility of a rational society emerging will have been surrendered.

Teaching, too, is challenged. Here, it becomes the production of human capacities—qualities and dispositions—for the personal assimilation and creation of strangeness. Such a conception of 'teaching' looks to a fundamental break with conventional pedagogical relationships and look to curricula that present awkward spaces to and for students. Through such spaces, they will realize for themselves their capacities for assimilating and even for producing strangeness.

In short, the teaching has to take what might be termed an *ontological turn*. From knowledge to being: instead of knowing the world, being-in-the-world has to take primary place in the conceptualizations that inform university teaching. Again, this will be unsettling to many teachers, tutors and lecturers in higher education, many if not most of whom construct their self-identities around their knowledge competences. Taking account of students as human beings as distinct from knowing beings is probably not a priority for most (even if it is included somewhere in their pedagogical repertoire). But, in a pedagogical world of supercomplexity, ontology trumps epistemology (although it by no means displaces epistemology). We can only tackle the challenge of knowing a supercomplex world if we have some degree of security in ourselves as persons. Such a reflection calls, therefore, for a 'pedagogy of recognition' as it has been termed (Nixon, 2004); or as we may also term it, *a pedagogy of affirmation*. 'Affirmation is transcendent' (Steiner, 2003). (For such a pedagogy in action, see Phipps, 2005.)

It follows, too, that universities as organizations need to take on a spirit of strangeness. Typically, universities undergo a process of strategic review once every five-ten years, often as a new vice-chancellor takes up post. A university that lives out the spirit of strangeness will understand that such periodic efforts critically to assess the developing strangeness that it faces, where it has reached in relation to those challenges and the possibilities for its positioning that lie ahead, are bound to fall short of the mark. A climate of collective self-criticality has to be developed as a continuing feature of university life. If a university is to fulfil its responsibilities as a 'university' to the world by offering a space for strangeness, it needs also to accommodate to strangeness in its own midst, especially a continuing strangeness about itself. What it is, what it might be, and what it might become has to be matters of *continuing* and collective review, not least to avoid ideological takeover which threatens a kind of malign strangeness in the university by default.

At the same time, the communicative aspects of managing and leading a university become evermore significant. At the very time that the challenges of managing a large, multifaculty university become particularly demanding, with decisions having to be made urgently amid conflicting readings of situations and inadequate information (supercomplexity and complexity all apparent at the same time), it becomes even more urgent to find ways of engaging the university as a community, both vertically and horizontally. The communicative challenge of enabling a university to prosper in the contemporary world has perhaps received less scholarly and research attention than any other large issue in higher education.

Conclusion

From their inception, universities were universal institutions: their offerings were of universal significance. In different ways, they came to reach out universally: their teaching and their research were, in certain senses, universally available. Over the last generation or so, that the universities are universal in character has been placed in doubt. It has been placed in doubt sociologically, as universities have been identified with particular interests (money, gender, disciplinary cultures, the host state, the economy) and it has been placed in doubt philosophically (as doubt has been expressed about the substance of universal categories—such as 'truth' and 'knowledge' not to mention 'right' and 'good').

The apparent loss of universality is not just a technical matter; it is not just that we can barely any longer speak of 'the university' as a general category. This loss—of the university's universality—is a matter of profound importance to the human race. With the loss of the university's universality, this social institution loses its general and world significance as it is taken over by local, partial, narrow and short-term interests. With the loss of the university's universality, the world is diminished. However, amid supercomplexity, a new universality is to hand, if only universities would seize it. It lies in the idea of strangeness, bequeathed to the university out of the combination of contestability, challengeability, uncertainty and unpredictability which the university not only faces but which the university itself has done much to engender. Realizing strangeness as the new universality, however, poses many challenges both for the universities and for those who work and have their being within them. Are they challenges that universities, and especially those in leadership positions within them, are prepared to take on?

Chapter 4

The idea of the university in the twenty-first century

Where's the imagination?

(from Journal of Higher Education (Turkey), 2011, 1 (2) 88–94)

Outline

The idea of the university is hopelessly impoverished. It is 'impoverished' in the limited range of ideas associated with the university, which confine themselves to endorsing newly emerging forms of the university. It is also 'hopelessly' impoverished in that the idea of the university is largely now without hope. Critical thinking largely takes on a shrugging-of-the-shoulders attitude, a sense that there is no alternative. Ideas about the university have closed in, therefore. A necessary condition of an opening of ideas of the university is a recovery of the imagination so as to discern feasible utopias. However, such utopias are not in themselves a sufficient condition of the formation of credible ideas. Legitimation can be derived from subjecting creative ideas of the university to criteria of adequacy: five criteria of adequacy are identified, sorting efficacious ideas of the university from non-efficacious ideas. One idea, that of the ecological university, is tested against the five criteria and so can be seen as having intellectual and practical warrant. The five criteria of adequacy accordingly will not unduly eliminate creative ideas but rather can act to help in the generation of additional ideas of the university.

At the very moment when the idea of the university should be opening out, it seems to be closing in. The idea of the university has, of course, undergone many shifts and been subject to varying conceptions over time. For some hundreds of years, the idea of the university was – as it might be said – that of the metaphysical university, reflective of an inquiry that enhanced humanity's connections with God, or the Universe, or Truth or Spirit or even the State. That conception gave way to the research university which in turn is giving way to that of the entrepreneurial university, which is closely allied to the emergence of a tacit idea of the corporate university.

What is striking about this conceptual journey that the idea of the university has undergone over nearly one thousand years is that it has gradually shrunk. Whereas the metaphysical university was associated with the largest themes of humanity's self-understanding and relationships with the world, the idea of the university has increasingly – and now especially in its contemporary entrepreneurial and corporate incarnations – closed in. The entrepreneurial university is expected to fend for itself, and attend to its potential impact on particular segments of the economy, and become distinctive. This university has abandoned any pretence with universal themes.

The idea of the university, therefore, has closed in ideologically, spatially and ethically. Ideologically, it is now intent on pursuing narrow interests, particularly those of money (in the service of a national learning economy); spatially, it is enjoined to engage with its region, especially with industrial and business organisations in its environs; and ethically, it becomes focused on its own interests. It will, as a result, close departments in chemistry, or physics, or modern languages or philosophy because it sees such closures as serving its own (usually financial) interests rather than being placed in a wider set of public interests.

Given this closing in of the idea of the university in the early part of the twenty-first century, a key question becomes this: how might the idea of the university be expanded? One answer lies in the imagination: through the imagination, we may hope to widen our conceptions of the possibilities before us. But that answer only opens up a line of inquiry: what possibilities are there for the imagination? What might be its role? Is a widening of our conceptual possibilities – for the university – necessarily beneficial? Are there any limits to the deployment of the imagination? And are there any tests that we can bring to bear on our imaginative ideas of the university, so as to demonstrate their efficacy? It is this line of inquiry that I wish to pursue in this paper.

Imaginary possibilities

Probably Charles Taylor has done more than anyone else to recover the idea of the imagination. Taylor, however, speaks of the imaginary, by which he has in mind collective sentiments of an age; those general concepts (such as those of democracy, of rights, of justice) that develop historically in societies, and which in turn are linked to social values and aspirations, in particular:

> 'the ways people imagine their social existence, how they fit together with others, how things go on between them and their fellows, the expectations that are normally met, and the deeper normative notions and images that underlie these expectations . . . the ways in which ordinary people "imagine" their social surroundings.' (Taylor, 2007, p. 23)

Another contemporary voice here is that of Richard Kearney (for whom Taylor was his teacher and supervisor for his Master's degree thesis). Kearney more explicitly links the imaginary to the imagination. We have in Kearney – as with Taylor – a sense of the imaginary as 'deeply inform(ing) our lived everyday world' but the 'lived' here is important. The imaginary shapes, colours, and patterns life itself, the lived life. It imparts understandings to an inner life; and these self-understandings are always in motion. And they are at play significantly through the stories that are important in informing life; and such narratives are themselves playing against each other. There are, therefore, for Kearney, crucially phenomenological and hermeneutic dimensions of the imaginary at play. There is, I sense, therefore, a somewhat more dynamic character to the imaginary here in Kearney (as compared with Taylor).

This link to narratives and self-understandings leads Kearney naturally to the concept of the imagination. And whereas Taylor focuses on history, Kearney focuses on fictional literature, in exploring the role of the imagination. The imagination IS dynamic, is always active if it really is 'imagination'. Consequently, reflection on the imagination takes risks:

> *'thinking about imagination is always work in progress and knows no barriers. It extends not just across disciplinary boundaries but across cultural and geographical ones as well. In traversing the imaginary we learn – for better or for worse – how to dwell in lands without frontiers.'* (Kearney, 2007, p. xiii)

The idea of the imaginary, however, goes back at least to Jean-Paul Sartre, not least in his book called simply 'The Imaginary' (2004/1940) and, here, we see a more radical notion. Whereas in both Kearney and (especially) in Taylor, we have a sense of the imaginary as being embedded in the world, for Sartre it posits escape from the world:

> *'For consciousness to be able to imagine, it must be able to escape from the world by its very nature, it must be able to stand back from the world by its own efforts. In a word, it must be free.'* (Sartre, 2004, p. 185)

There are no less than three key elements in this short quotation, those of 'escape from the world', a position won 'by its own efforts' and 'freedom'. There is here, as Sartre comments immediately afterwards, the 'possibility of negation'. In constructing an imaginary, we raise up the possibility of negation, of contending against the 'self-images of the age' (to use a phrase from MacIntyre).

For what follows, I want to draw on certain aspects of each of these three scholars in their ideas of the imaginary and the imagination

(Sartre, 2004; Kearney, 2007; Taylor, 2007). In so doing, I want first, though, to draw a sharp distinction between the ideas of the imaginary and the imagination. I take the imagination to be a power, a potential, a capability, which may or may not be exercised. I take the imaginary, or rather 'an' imaginary to be that which emerges from the exercise of the imagination. The exercise of the imagination is a necessary condition – though not a sufficient condition – of an imaginary developing.

At this point, we may bring in the positions of our three writers. From Taylor, we may take the idea of the imaginary as a set of social understandings of a large matter; from Kearney, we may take the idea of narrative as informing those social understandings; and from Sartre, we may take the idea of the imagination as denoting a strike for freedom.

To speak therefore of the ideas of the imaginary and the imagination in relation to university is to embrace the following elements. It is to point to the power of imagination as heralding a bold leap for freedom, contending against and even possibly negating the present understandings. It is also to point to the possibility of a collective imaginary eventually emerging from those imaginative efforts, an imaginary that will be sustained at least partly in virtue of it being buttressed by socially meaningful narratives. Different imaginations, different imaginative ideas, may give rise in turn, therefore, to different imaginaries.

The imagination, accordingly, is prior to the imaginary. This is a dramatic and key point here. For the imagination not only lives in individual minds (as does the imaginary) but it is energised by individual minds; it is taken forward by individual minds. Persons have to do the imagining in order that those imaginings may be taken up and – just possibly – may be transformed and sedimented over time (perhaps decades) into collective imaginaries. And that work of the imagination is a matter of vision; perhaps even of poetic vision. It is to find a new vocabulary, a new grammar, with which to read the conventional, the present. It is to leap out, to leap beyond the familiar and redescribe it in strange terms. This, then, is the task – and it would be the achievement – of the imagination in coming to bear upon the idea of the university; nothing short of recasting it so that we come to understand that our present images and concepts of the university could be quite other than they are.

Feasible utopias

Yet the possibilities for and the responsibilities upon the imagination are even larger than we have described them so far. For once we see the imagination as a resource for negation and for striking for freedom, then the exercise of the imagination becomes not only a critical project but potentially a utopian project. The imagination will not be content in simply being critical; it will not rest simply in point to a 'university in ruins' or 'the crisis in the university'. Rather, it will seek to imagine, to create, new narratives of the fullest kind that may serve the university and take it forward.

This is utopian thinking. And it is an injunction upon the imagination; to strive to form new ideas of the university that could represent the university – now in the twenty-first century – as it might be in the best of all possible worlds. Of course, there is no blue-print available (Jacoby, 2005); there are no ready-to-hand ideals of the university. That is precisely the point; they have to be created anew to suit the circumstances of our age. And that phrasing again unites Taylor, Kearney and Sartre: can new ideas of the university be created that at once critique current dominant ideologies of the university, and reach out in a way that yet does some justice to enduring sentiments of the university and can – over time – yield substantive narratives that could have collective, indeed social, appeal?

That phrasing – 'to suit the circumstances of our age' – heralds a further challenge upon such utopian thinking. For if the exercise of the utopian imagination is to be credible, is to have substance, then it has to lend itself to the possibility of practical action. That is to say, there would need to be at least a possibility of the utopian imaginary – as it would have become – leading to a change in the world. Such thinking would be utopian in that it would herald the highest form of human flourishing and it would be most unlikely to come about; and it would also be feasible in that it could yet reasonably be glimpsed as a practical venture. It could just come about in the best of all possible worlds. Such substance would be furnished, for instance, through observing examples ('case studies') of such utopias already being visibly even if embryonically present. It would consist, therefore, in the words of Deleuze (2001), of a kind of 'transcendental empiricism', acutely sensible to the present but also aware of its possibilities; in effect, 'a superior empricism'.

There are two further points I wish to make here. Firstly, this kind of utopian imaginative thinking would embody the spirit of the philosophy of 'critical realism', especially as developed over the past thirty years by Roy Bhaskar. This particular form of critical realism both posits a real world independently of our knowing efforts (hence an objective ontology) and our efforts to come to know that world, which themselves can vary considerably (hence an epistemological relativism). Bhaskar (2002) posits both a triply layered view of the world (the real, the actual, and the perceived) and a four-planar view of our being in the world (our relationship to ourselves, to others, to social structures and to the natural world). Partly, our perceptions of the possibilities for the world can reasonably emerge out of the 'absences' we detect in the world – such as an absence of equality, of general enlightenment, of life chances and so on. So while the spaces for our imaginations are infinite – there are any number of imaginative ideas of the university that we could come up with – the locus of those ideas is quite real; even if hard work needs to go on in uncovering the character of the real world, overlain as it is by unequal power structures, ideologies and obfuscations.

Secondly, I want to contend for a particular kind of anarchism, namely a 'responsible anarchism' as we may call it. In one of its variants, anarchism denotes an absence of government or regulation (Malatesta, 2001). This is, we might say, a negative sense of anarchism; an utter freedom from constraint. This idea is surely helpful to us here: if the imagination is really to take off, to fly, it has to be unconstrained. And yet flying is subject to the laws of gravity. So conceiving of the imagination here as unconstrained still allows for some overarching rule or principle.

The principle to be invoked here is that the exercise of the imagination, in bringing forth new ideas of the university, has to be responsible. Derrida (2004) urged the idea of responsibility as a key concept in thinking about the university without perhaps being able to specify what responsibility might entail. Certainly, the idea is problematic: what is to count as responsibility? But still, the idea of an irresponsible imagination would bear no weight; so responsibility as a guiding principle is of value, even if it cannot be fully cashed out. The exercise of the imagination, in attempting to usher forth new ideas of the university, has to take the form of a responsible anarchism.

We may note that, in a way, the idea of a responsible anarchism is a corollary of the idea of a feasible utopia. In being feasible, the identification of a utopia is also being responsible; it is not just a flight of fancy. And in being anarchic, it is giving itself the best chance of identifying a utopia that will be free of undue constraint, hedged in by ideology and power.

Ideas of the university

Here are some ideas of the university:

- The metaphysical university
- The entrepreneurial university
- The open university
- The civic university
- The liquid university
- The postmodern university
- The pragmatic university
- The therapeutic university
- The ecological university

This list could easily be extended manifold but, it is already sufficiently long for two points to be made about it. Firstly, each phrase represents some exercise of the imagination. The attribution in each case – of the university being or having been metaphysical, civic, entrepreneurial, or civic and so on – requires an imaginative insight into the nature of the university. Secondly, the formal structure of each phrase is exactly the same – three terms, with the definite article ('The') and the noun ('university') preceded in each case by an adjective. However, the imaginative character of the ideas expressed in those phrases varies considerably. We can sense here the makings of an imaginative structure attendant on the idea of the university.

We can begin to uncover this imaginative structure through a sense that there are different readings of the university available to us. Here are seven readings: the historic, the ideological, the actual, the emerging, the imagined, the dystopian, and the utopian. Let us briefly illustrate the character of each reading with some imaginings of the university.

The historic university (past being)

Among imaginings of the university that attempt to illuminate its past being might, for example, be 'the metaphysical university', 'the civic university', 'the liberal university', 'the service university' and even 'the research university'. Each of these expressions attempts to identify features that characterised the university in its past; they are historical imaginings, but they are nonetheless imaginings. They conjure discrete and quite distinct images of the university. For example, 'the metaphysical university' is an expression that recalls an association of the idea of the university with the largest narratives of humanity, of humanity's connection with universal concepts – alternatively – of God, humanity itself, Truth (with a capital 'T' as it were), Spirit and even the State. (Such a conception of the university lasted for several hundreds of years.)

It will be said that some, if not most, of these depictions of the university are far from historical but are present today. This is true. For instance, 'the civic university' is currently being revived as an idea (Ehrlich, 2000; McIlrath and Labhrainn, 2007). And even the metaphysical university is still with us in various incarnations (in the symbolism of the university, in its libraries and its scholarly endeavours). Ideas of the university – and even their practical forms – live on, even if other ideas emerge and supplant those earlier ideas as the dominant ideas of the university.

The ideological (present being)

Among ideological conceptions of the university are surely those of 'the entrepreneurial university', 'the enterprise university', 'the business-facing university' and even 'the European university' and 'the open university'. In order for the charge of its being ideological to be sustained, sets of structured social interests would have to be identified for whom a particular imagining of the university – as say an 'entrepreneurial university' or a 'European university' or an 'open university' – would need to be identified. Some of these imaginings of the university are, in that sense, hybrids. Each of these conceptions might be construed neutrally, with minimal ideological presences; but each of them in turn could also be harbouring large projects for the university, connected with large political and/or commercial interests.

The actual (and the critical)

Among manifestations of the actual university might be 'the bureaucratic university', 'the corporate university', 'the marketised university', 'the commodified university', 'the capitalist university' and 'the performative university'. Each of these imaginings is, or would represent, an attempt to identify a key feature of the university in its actual present form. Again, there could be an element of hybridity about some of these expressions; or, as Bernard Williams (2008) puts it, in their readings, each of these ideas of the university could be said to be 'thick concepts', being both attempts to describe the world and also to critique the world. For instance, to remark of a university that it had taken on the form of 'a bureaucratic university' or 'a commodified university' is to identify a particular feature of its contemporary form (it is becoming a bureaucracy and subjecting in substantial academic life to bureaucratic procedures) and it is at the same time to critique such a form of the university.

The emerging university

Among depictions of the emerging university might be considered to be 'the borderless university' (Erdinc, 2002), 'the liquid university' (cf Bauman), 'the supercomplex university' (Barnett, 2000), 'the virtual university' (Robins and Webster, 2002), 'the networked university' (Standaert, 2009) and 'the therapeutic university' (Ecclestone and Hayes, 2009). In each case, an attempt is made to perceive certain features of the university embryonically already present and capable of becoming a flourishing feature of the university.

Here, the imagination is heightened (as compared with the previous imaginings of the university). Now, the imagination is beginning to be loosened from the actual and is striving to glimpse future possibilities while being rooted in the present. These imaginings are projections, deriving from a careful reading of the present but striding out, going on, and drawing out a future-possible from the present. These imaginings carry something in them of a yearning for the being of the authentic university. After all, being – for Heidegger at least – is only 'being' insofar as it has 'being-possible' within it.

The dystopian university

The dystopian university represents the pessimistic imagination at work (cf. Dienstag, 2006). It identifies the bleaker aspects of the emerging university and pumps them up, giving weight to them. Such depictions of the university might include 'the soulless university', 'the subservient university', 'the selfish university' and 'the self-important university'. These are literally hopeless visions of the university, for they lack hope, hope that there might either continue to be redeeming features of the university in significant form or that new redeeming features of the university might yet emerge.

Such images of the university are unduly limited in another sense for these dystopias have already arrived. They merely pretend to be looking into the future when they are simply offering us insight into the emerging university; and offering us, as stated, unduly limited images of the emerging university at that. These dystopias are already with us; are already present. In virtue of their pessimism, their limited scope and their lack of hope, they should not detain us.

The utopian university

Visions of the utopian university might include, for example, 'the anarchic university' (or 'the iconoclastic university'), 'the authentic university', 'the dialogical university', 'the ecological university' (Barnett, 2011), 'the chrestomathic university' (Young, 1992), 'the wise university' (after Maxwell, 2008), 'the virtuous university' (Nixon, 2008) and 'the theatrical university' (Parker, 2005). Such visions of the university represent the highest form of the imagination, being imaginative ideas of the university that precisely are not present forms of the university, although in each case there are grounds for believing that each example just could be realised.

In each case, the exercise of the imagination represents a strike for freedom; and in two senses. Each vision of the university represents a break from the present; and each vision is, in its own way, reflective of a belief in a free university of some kind; in each imagining, the university is seen as free of burdens and constraints that characteristically bind the university in the early part of the twenty-first century. Each vision breaks free of the present but also offers to return to the present, claiming implicitly that it could be realised. In Heidegger's phrase, each imagining here 'leaps ahead' but never quite severs its links with the present. It opens a gap between the real and the possible but also tacitly promises to close the gap: in the best of all possible worlds, each of these utopias might just be brought fully into the world.

Criteria of adequacy

To call an imagined vision of the university a utopia rather than a dystopia is to confirm that it has been tested against certain standards and passed those tests. In other words, it has passed muster in the company of certain criteria of adequacy. I believe that we can point to five such criteria of adequacy:

- **Range:** What is the range of the imagining? Does it have theoretical backing? Is it rich in concepts and ideas? Does it lend itself to an array of practices? Does it have large implications for policies?
- **Depth:** What is the epistemological depth of the vision? Does it reflect or identify large structures, or acknowledge forces, that are present and does it address those structures? Does it connect with actors' experiences? Does it connect with the material world in its complexity?
- **Feasibility:** Given the power structures that it has identified, to what extent might the vision be implemented? How feasible is it? Could it be instantiated by individual universities? Could it even be instantiated by the university system as a whole?
- **Ethics:** To what degree does the vision reflect large ideas as to human and social wellbeing and even flourishing? In what ways could its vision be said to be worthwhile? Does it reflect large human principles such as those of fairness and openness?
- **Emergence:** To what extent does the vision lend itself to continuing further interpretations over time? Could it open itself to yet further ideas and imaginings? Could it continue to unfold over time, and in new ways as new situations arise?

Against these five criteria of adequacy, an imaginative vision of the utopian university can be examined as to its scope; that is, as to the extent it can be realised at the unit level (the department or subject level in an institution), at the institutional level, at the national level and at the global level. And so, in principle, a kind of matrix emerges in which the five criteria of adequacy would form one axis and the scope of its implementation (from unit to global manifestations) would form the other axis.

In this way, the idea of a vision being brought to bear upon the 'real world' can be cashed out. It will probably turn out that some – and perhaps several or even many – of the utopian visions cannot withstand our five criteria of adequacy. Perhaps surprisingly, it may be that many of the imaginings that are found to be inadequate are so not in virtue of their feasibility (or lack of it) but rather in virtue of their range and the weakness of their emergent qualities. Or they might be found to be epistemologically shallow, having little depth, being unable to engage with the large social and ideological structures that are bound to be present.

There is a further point to note about our five criteria of adequacy. They may appear to be unduly onerous. It may be felt that they will act as early judgements on emerging ideas of the university. Far from encouraging creative thought in the forming of new ideas of the university, they may have the unintended consequence of curtailing it. But I believe the contrary to be the case. In being brought before the tribunal of our five criteria of adequacy, new ideas that are just taking shape will now be prompted as to ways in which they can be extended – in their range, their ethical character, their depth, their feasibility and so forth.

The five criteria of adequacy will be likely to act as prompts for yet more imagining and more creativity. After all, there is no limit to the number of times any new imagining might be tested against the criteria of adequacy. Hauling imaginings before these tribunal will not in itself condemn those imaginings to an early demise; more likely, the examining and the judgments of these courts will lead to a flowering of new ideas, even quite different ideas, as the components of the ideas are encouraged first in this direction and then in that direction.

The ecological university

In these last few paragraphs, I want very sketchily to show how this tribunal might work by submitting just one of the utopian ideas of the university to it, namely that of the ecological university (Barnett, 2011). So far as its range is concerned, the idea of the ecological university can be said to extend fully: it has theoretical backing (there being an extensive literature on the idea of the ecological), and is itself rich in concepts ('sustainability', 'ecology', 'deep ecology'). But it also has considerable implications for practices and policies. So far as its depth is concerned, it gains much of its weight precisely from a recognition of the large and deep, and ideological, structures at work; and yet is capable of being readily meaningful to members of universities in their everyday experiences. So far as its feasibility is concerned, it could lend itself to implementation in all manner of spaces and arenas, within and beyond the university. So far as its ethical base is concerned, it wears its ethical credentials on its sleeve, taking its starting point from a concern with the other. And so far as its emergent qualities are concerned, it would be capable of being continuously extended and imagined anew, as it was taken into new settings and faced new oncoming situations. The idea of the ecological university can, therefore, be judged to be both efficacious and robust.

We should note, too, given our earlier depiction of a matrix of judgements, that the idea of the ecological university can be cashed out at all the levels of the academic world and its interactions with the wider world.

The spirit of the ecological university can be cashed out at the level of the 1–1 pedagogical relationship between a tutor and a student, it can be reflected in a department's or, indeed, a university's self-understanding and its actions in the community, and it can be witnessed in the ways in which a whole university sector moves and is perceived in society. Is it a force for good, for improvement? Is it releasing or making possible new energies in society that work across the whole of society, aware of its own embeddedness in wider ecologies – of society and of persons? Or is it just a competitive system, with each university seeking only to maximise its own interests and extracting value from society instead of adding to it? The idea of the ecological university, in other words, can be seen to be potent at all the ecological registers (cf. Guattari, 2005) of persons, of institutions, of communities, of society and even of the world.

Conclusions

The contemporary debate as to the idea of the university is lacking in imagination, but more than that: it is lacking in efficacious imagination. Such ideas of the university as we have for the most part lack a utopian spirit, and so are largely limited to endorsing contemporary forms of the university. And where they are utopian in spirit, they are not tested so that their substance remains unclear. Tests of adequacy can be identified which can serve to separate the conceptual goats from the conceptual sheep, so to speak; we can detect which of our imaginative ideas may really be efficacious, and be put to work in a robust way. But more than that, however, tests of adequacy may have the additional benefit of stimulating more ideas and even serve as a prompt for imaginings of yet more feasible utopias.

Chapter 5

The coming of the ecological university

(from *Oxford Review of Education*, 2011, 37 (4) 439–457)

Outline

What is it to be a university? In what does the being of the university reside in the twenty-first century? To draw on a Heideggerian expression, what is its 'being possible'? To address such questions seriously, we are drawn to imagine the university as it might unfold and so sketch out feasible utopias for it. But such a project of the imagination requires in the first place a sense as to the past and present trajectory of the university. The dominant ideas – and forms – of the university have to be identified. A further step taken here is that of furnishing conceptual resources that may help us imagine the university into the future. Four imaginaries of the university are then sketched, with allegiance being given especially to the coming of the ecological university.

Introduction

Just what is it to *be* a university? Could a rational society be imagined without a university? Universities have been with us on this Earth for at least one thousand years and will surely be with us in the future; perhaps so long as there is life on this planet that has any well-being. There is now something in not just the name of the institution but in the idea of the university that seems to have durability. But yet, the question imposes itself again: just what is it to be a university?

The question has seldom been asked seriously. There is good reason for this state of affairs for, in the past and up to the present age, the university was largely given. This is not to say that there is a single set of ideas that constitute an 'essence' of the university over time. Quite to the contrary and crucial to the thesis for which I shall contend here. The university has unfolded in such a way as to take a successive number of characteristic forms associated with certain clusters of ideas as to what it is to be a university. That unfolding has two features that are central to our story here: first, there has been a certain inevitability to the university's unfolding hitherto; and secondly, there are now options in front of the university. That 'there is no alternative' to the form now being taken by the university is precisely *not* the case: now, there are lots of alternatives.

It follows that what it is to be a university today has optionality written into it. And this is a dual optionality—in form and in idea. To draw on a Heideggerian phrasing, the university has 'being possible' (Heidegger, 1998/1962, p. 145): its being is replete with possibilities. And with possibilities comes also responsibility. That the university today has responsibilities facing it was observed by Derrida (2004) who, indeed, pressed the question: what is the responsibility of the university today? That Derrida's answer to his own question could be felt to be somewhat lacking in substance was perhaps understandable given his 'deconstructionalist' philosophy. It just may be, however, that we can at least begin to fill out more fully an answer to that question, as to the responsibility of the university. But we can seriously address the matter of responsibility only provided we can give some specification of the possibilities in front of the university, as it unfolds in the 21st century.

It is no less than a sketch of some of those possibilities that I want to offer in this paper. I want to go further than that, however, and nail my own colours to the mast of one of those conceptions of the university. Before I go on, however, I want briefly to pause to make some brief observations on the character of this inquiry.

As I see it, the task ahead is to develop *feasible utopias*. That is to say, it is to develop ideas *not* as to how the university might be in the best of all possible worlds but rather how it might be its best in *this* world. Such ideas would be *utopian* in that they would be unlikely to be realised given the empirical character of the world, with its power structures, interests and ideologies. On the other hand, such ideas would also be feasible in that we can identify instances of those ideas being instantiated to a certain extent— at least, embryonically—in the world even now. To draw on a phrase from Deleuze, such utopias would form a kind of 'transcendental empiricism' (Colebrook, 2005), rooted in the empirical world but yet imaginatively having an independence from it. We can provide evidence of such utopias being realised today.

This is a social philosophy with a critical edge. Feasible utopias are at least implicitly, and maybe also explicitly, critical of the contemporary situation. In relation to the topic at hand, far from assuming that there is no alternative to the contemporary being of the university, this social philosophy opens a space to allow for many alternatives. Part of the task, here, therefore, is to sketch out a range of alternative conceptions of the university, each of which is implicitly critical of the present situation in which the university is characteristically placed. Here, I shall want to go further even than that for I shall want to contend for what I term 'the ecological university'. This university is, I shall argue, the best kind of university that we can hope for under contemporary conditions; and it is one that still does justice to the idea of the university itself.

The metaphysical university

In its earliest incarnation, we witnessed the metaphysical university. As with all forms of the university, the metaphysical university was associated not with a single idea but with a constellation of ideas, even if those ideas contained internal instabilities (cf. Bernstein, 1991). The dominant idea behind the metaphysical university was that this was an institution that, through the learning and inquiry that it sponsored, gave access to a transcendental realm. This overarching idea took a variety of more specific forms. Here, learning made possible insight into the world as God's creation; and so into God Himself. Through learning, one came into a new relationship with God. Here, too, learning was also felt to open the way alternatively to Spirit, to Truth and to a world of Enlightenment. A yet further manifestation of the transcendental realm was even that of the State, for higher learning was also understood to draw one into a personal relationship with the State.

We are entitled to see this set of ideas as constituting 'the metaphysical university' since this university understood itself as opening the way for human being to enter a new form of being, apart from the mundane world. (The University of Aberdeen was founded in the late middle ages to offer 'personal salvation' to its students.) This was a sacred kind of learning, and with it came a hinterland of concepts such as 'mystery', 'wonder' and 'wisdom'. There was an ineffability about the learning associated with this University. The curriculum, through the quadrivium and the trivium, certainly offered forms of knowing rooted in this world but they were fundamentally forms of knowing that opened a new and transcendent set of experiences. This conception of the university lasted for several hundred years, prompting Cardinal John Henry Newman (1976 edn) to talk of its providing 'a philosophical habit of mind' (p. 57) and requiring students to 'ascend' (p. 125): the ascent was precisely an educational voyage that enabled individuals to move into a new and a higher world, and so into a separate state of human being. The metaphysical university was a *university-for-the-beyond*. It looked beyond the immediacy of (this) mundane life for its being.

There were both epistemological and ontological dimensions of this metaphysical university. Epistemologically, there was here a sense of there being a unity to knowledge. Knowledge was not exactly indivisible but yet all of its component parts were interlinked. There was a single world of knowledge even if it could be studied in different ways. Ontologically, the very process of knowing—of coming to know—not only brought changes in being, in what it was to be in the world, but also brought *beneficial* changes in being. Knowing was personally edifying. There was here, in this conception of the university, a tight and positive connection between knowing and being.

This university was associated with a particularly stratified society, in which a small caste of clerks, often with close ties to an established church, were endowed with semi-magical powers (cf. Gellner, 1988). In societies with limited levels of literacy, the clerks had something that was rare and mysterious. Through their learning, they could offer enlightenment to those who otherwise would remain unenlightened. They stood in a different universe, cognitively and socially. They represented ways of being in the world, a being for enlightenment no less, ordinarily denied to most others. So the metaphysical idea was one that both held out the promise of universal salvation and yet was available only to a select minority.

The research university

The metaphysical university gave way to the research university. For this university, knowledge was everything. This, as the American sociologist, Robert Nisbet, put it (1971), was its 'dogma'. The contrasts with the metaphysical university were stark. From scholarship and learning to knowledge and research. Knowledge became organised into disciplines and instead of knowledge being seen as forming a unity, it was now understood to be sharply differentiated, each discipline with its own properties and perspectives. This was a form of knowledge that was shorn both of its transcendental properties *and* of its personally edifying properties. This knowledge opened up new cognitive worlds: if there was mystery here, it lay internally in the procedures and the concepts that 'research' opened up in themselves and not in any divine experience opened up in the process.

In its earliest incarnations, knowledge in the research university quickly divided science, humanities and professional studies, but it was science that attracted the highest marks. Indeed, the research university could well be termed 'the scientific university'; and often was. As a result, in this privileging of science, the humanities were marginalised, so leading periodically to angst on the part of the humanities with books appearing periodically bearing the title 'The Crisis in the Humanities' or some derivation of it.

In the research university, research is more significant than teaching. Very recently, that significance has taken a financial edge as research has attracted much greater discretionary income. But the research university, as the appellation implies, has 'research' in its being. The core of its being lies in research. It understands itself as a 'research university' or at least as a 'research intensive university' (for even the research university understands that it has to engage in activities other than research). It was this focus on research-in-itself that gave rise to such popular epithets as 'ivory tower', 'knowledge for its own sake' and (even) 'academic freedom'. This was a university that was accorded freedoms from society in order to conduct research. Decision-making powers were vested in the University Senate as the supreme representative body of the academic community; the role of the University Council was—both *de jure* and *de facto*—limited (Moodie & Eustace, 1973).

We can surely explain the freedoms that were accorded the research university through the power and control that research was assumed to bring. Power and control was, as Jurgen Habermas indicated (1978), a 'knowledge-constitutive interest'. This power and control operated, we can say, on two levels. It lay in the scientific method which hinged on the possibility of isolating and controlling conditions affecting natural phenomena so as to make possible powerful predictions of those same phenomena in their natural state. But power and control also lay in more general political and state interests in science. This powerful science just might yield the possibility of exercising control over the physical environment. That the research university was given special impetus as a state funded institution during two world wars is not happenstance.

In its later manifestation, this research university gained added significance with the emergence of the so-called 'knowledge society' (Stehr, 1994, pp. 80–82) and then 'the knowledge economy' (Peters, Marginson, & Murphy, 2009). Such a university, the fulcrum of which lay in systematic knowledge, was rapidly called into service. States understood that in order to maintain and, if possible, improve their positioning in a world dependent on formal knowledge (or so it seemed), research universities were a necessary condition of their economic flourishing. Correspondingly, universities gradually understood that, in the knowledge society, knowledge production was widely distributed and that they now had competitors in knowledge production beyond themselves; and so their knowledge production efforts had to be redoubled.

The research university was a *university-in-itself*. It was concerned with its own knowledge production activities. It was an era in which researchers could, without embarrassment, declare their disinterest in any applications of their findings (even as others were discerning the technological possibilities of that research). This university was in-itself, its academics intent on publication in the journals irrespective of the numbers of readers of those journals. It prided itself on its separateness from society. Its being lay in a space that it declared its own. Academic identities were *academic* identities, produced in and sustained by the academy. The research university proclaimed a belief—even if it did not believe in its proclamation—in the uselessness of knowledge.

The entrepreneurial university

The research university—as a dominant idea—gave way to the entrepreneurial university. If the research university is a university *in-itself*, the entrepreneurial university is a university *for-itself*. This is a university that has its being amid the marketisation of what were public services. This university is told by the state that what counts in knowledge production is 'impact' but it has no need of such guidance, since impact is precisely what the entrepreneurial university understands. The entrepreneurial university is a 'performative university'; and doubly so. It understands that it has to perform in the world to survive; or at least it considers that to be the case. It has to be active in the world; an engaged university indeed. And it understands further that its knowledge products and services have to perform in the world, preferably marked by an economic return. In this milieu, knowledge is valued in terms of its exchange value before its use value.

This university might be judged to be the outcome of 'neo-liberalism', a globalised Weltanschauung of an opening of public services in general to market disciplines. But this view of the university as having been caught by large forces acting upon it would be a tendentious reading, for the entrepreneurial university has been complicit in its own emergence. 'Academic capitalism' does not just befall universities but is, to a large degree, embraced by them. (We may note, in passing, that the phrase 'academic capitalism' has been made recently popular by Sheila Slaughter and Larry Leslie (1997) but it was in fact used by Robert Nisbet (1971) who had long since seen in the emergence of academic capitalism the 'degradation' of the academic dogma, namely knowledge as such.)

Accordingly, the entrepreneurial university understands itself as changing. In this respect, this is a new form of university *being*. Whereas previously, in the research university, it was understood that its knowledge findings and claims changed, now the entrepreneurial university understands itself as changing also. This, after all, is partly why the metaphor of the entrepreneurial university is so potent, for the entrepreneur seeks to change his business, so as to move it from point A to point B. The movement carries risk, and it is no coincidence that in the UK—one of the most marketised systems of higher education—universities now regularly conduct risk assessments of their activities.

This is a university that has turned itself inside-out. *Qua* research university, it was concerned with knowledge as such and especially its own knowledge efforts. This university looked inwards, not so much at itself but to its own knowledge interests. Now, *qua* entrepreneurial university, it is concerned with the impact of its knowledge efforts on the world. Markers of that impact are sought; preferably money (as stated) but other indicators of impact come into the reckoning (such as national and international prizes and citation indices). Social and cultural capital rivals, but does not supplant, economic capital. In marketing its knowledge services and products, new knowledge activities arise, and with it a new vocabulary (of 'third stream' activities; consultancy; patenting; and knowledge transfer). Internal offices may be set up intent on extracting as much revenue as possible from the university's knowledges. Opportunities for knowledge services are identified, much to the surprise of some academics; and this endeavour reaches widely across knowledge domains, even into the humanities. Academics themselves take on entrepreneurial identities.

In this milieu, the form of knowledge production itself begins to change. If the research university was characterised by Mode 1 knowledge —formal, prepositional, disciplinary, universal and public—now the entrepreneurial university is characterised by Mode 2 knowledge— in-situ, ephemeral, multidisciplinary (and even transdisciplinary), and problem-oriented. Certainly, it was part of the thesis of Michael Gibbons and his colleague authors (1994) that Mode 2 knowledge has grown up outside the academy. But it is part of the being of the entrepreneurial university both that it seizes the main chance and engages with its potential customers; and so it is drawn naturally into the knowledge world of Mode 2.

A further characteristic of the entrepreneurial university is that it is competitive. This is but a necessary concomitant of the market situation in which the entrepreneurial university has its being. And the entrepreneurial university thrives in this situation, loudly proclaiming how little it is now dependent on the state for support. There is much hand-wringing over the various league tables—national and international—but the entrepreneurial university lives happily with such public reckonings of its relative success. For the league tables are a rather benign form of the competitiveness with which it lives daily. In this situation, therefore, universities compete against each other for contracts, for clients and customers, and for public visibility and external confirmation. The *collective* academic community fades.

Interlude

At this point, it may be helpful to make some observations about the argument I am trying to develop.

First, the story so far has not been empirical as such but it has had empirical elements. I have been suggesting that there is a temporal unfolding to the university both in its dominant ideas and its forms. The university has both being and time; and its being is in time.

At any one time, we understand the university's being in part through a set of ideas. These ideas constitute, to draw on a recent term of Charles Taylor (2007), the 'social imaginaries' of the university. They supply the dominant background understandings by which the university understands itself and is expected to understand itself. In turn, these ideas flow from, to draw on a much earlier (1969) phrase of Taylor's, the dominant 'value background' that plays upon the university. The value background is characteristically built upon large ideas that provide horizons of significance. Such horizons of significance may be dominant themes or ideas—about God or knowledge or performance in the world.

The value background attending the university changes over time; and, with its changing, so too changes the social imaginaries of the university. The social imaginaries are *social* in that they work upon the social situation of the university, in its relationship to social institutions and the wider society and individuals as members of society. The social imaginaries are *imaginary* in that they orient the university in certain directions; they suggest directions for the university's forward travel. They provide a sense of its future possibilities. To invoke the idea of 'the entrepreneurial university' is not merely to describe the university at a point in time but it is also to indicate its possibilities, the possibilities for its unfolding. Even to invoke the idea of 'the metaphysical university' is to open speculation as to the university's possibilities, for we can ask of the university *today* 'In what way and to what degree might it make sense to understand it as a metaphysical university?'

The general task in front of us is that of imagining the university: what ideas and forms of the university are possible and desirable in the 21st century? There is no reason to believe that the emergence of the entrepreneurial university marks a kind of resting point in the unfolding of the university. Certainly, there are empirical limits to the possibilities for the university but, logically, there is an infinite space in which our imaginations might work. An infinite number of conceptions are possible even within a bounded space.

Herein lies the task of which I spoke at the outset, that of identifying *feasible utopias*, namely, ideas of the university that are unlikely to be realised but which, in the best of this world, just might be realised. For such utopias, there would be a possibility both that the general conditions of the imagined universities could be realised and that, already, there would be glimpses in some places of such institutional forms. The task is that of working out a social hope for the university through the imagination but tempering that hope with an appraisal and a perception of real possibilities (cf. Halpin, 2003).

This places responsibilities and even some limitations on the exercise of the imagination; but it remains infinite in its possibilities. It has to have an eye on the empirical conditions of the age; but it also has to have an eye on the conceptual landscape. By 'conceptual landscape', I mean the kinds of concepts that might enable us to make progress in this inquiry. A fruitful tack might lie in putting together pairs of concepts and then working through their interconnections insofar as they bear on the university. For example, 'space and time'; 'culture and anarchy'; 'authenticity and responsibility' and 'being and becoming'. Such conceptual juxtapositions open up conceptual spaces in which new forms of the university might be imagined. They also would help to pose questions of any new ideas of the university.

We may take just one of these pairs of concepts by way of example. In relation to 'space and time', we can inquire into the spaces available to the university and the horizons of time attendant on the university. And we can inquire into the interrelationships between space and time. For instance, as the university moves more into global space, are the horizons of time shortening or lengthening? Perhaps both phenomena are evident. The university lives amid multiple time frames and in multiple spaces. All at once, it lives amid fast time and durable time; and it lives amid local and global spaces. Perhaps in different institutions, and in different disciplines, some spaces and timeframes are dominant; the local gives way to the global; the long-term gives way to the short-term. That would be a matter for empirical inquiry. The point is that the conceptual inquiry opens up possibilities for empirical inquiry, which in turn would be likely to prompt new conceptual challenges. The conceptual and the empirical would interweave in the working out of new ideas for the university. Imagining the university is a liberating practice but it also comes with its responsibilities and, thereby, its constraints.

Being-possible: ideas of the university's becoming

What kinds of 'being-possible' (to draw again on Heidegger's term) are in front of the university that might warrant our attention? I offer four as exemplars. In this section, I explore three of them to indicate their own possibilities and their limitations.

The liquid university

The liquid university is fluid (cf. Bauman, 2000). It moves intentionally—or to a significant extent—but lacks direction as such. It has a centre of sorts but still its parts move of their own volition in response to the world that they encounter. It is not, however, necessarily without guiding principles. To the contrary, its different parts may have their own guiding principles; it is beset by competing value systems. Accordingly, there is no one source of momentum for this university but multiple sources. Perhaps, for each university, there is a dominant set of values and sources of momentum. Science, research, knowledge transfer, public mission, impact, income generation, widening participation: each and any of these serve as goals that draw the university—or, at least, different parts of it—forward. To draw on Schopenhauer's (1997) term, each university has its own will and may even share in a collective will to be a university; so that will is both a complex and is differentially formed.

Deleuze and Guattari (2004) see human becoming as in the form of a rhizome, with its bulbous and tubular forms going in many directions, apparently with rather little shape or teleology. Perhaps more tellingly we should understand the liquid university as a kind of squid, moving this way and that, able to transport itself with extraordinary ease, power and rapidity. The liquid university is a manoeuvrable university.

Are the waters in which it moves ethically pure or muddy or even a little polluted? A challenge for the liquid university is precisely that of its ethical base. A neat gambit attracts here: the university, to warrant its name, is a space in which dialogue and even disagreement as to values are sustained. The university reflects both the Habermassian 'ideal speech situation' and the Lyotardian disinclination to opt for large narratives; and the liquid university squares this circle explicitly. It encourages and exemplifies 'dissensus' (Readings, 1997). But this is too easy a get-out, even for the liquid university. For it leads not just to value ambiguity but value incoherence. On the one hand, it lives in the world of private finance and knowledge exploitation; on the other hand, it lives in the world of public benefit and knowledge circulation. At least, the liquid university is aware of its own tendencies towards incoherence and tries to work out a *modus vivendi* for living amid such ethical mayhem.

The therapeutic university

The liquid university, then, is without a value position (other than 'let a thousand values bloom') and shrinks from declaring its values. If not logic, at least it has contemporary social theory on its side. For the contemporary world we are told is not just a liquid world but also a 'risk society' (Beck, 1992). The two features are intertwined. The uncertainty that produces its fluidity also generates risk. Risk is the propensity of situations and phenomena to bring in their wake unwelcome events. As such, risk has always been part of the human condition; an inevitable presence of the likelihood of unwelcome events. But now those unwelcome events multiply as a result of human interventions in the world. They multiply even exponentially due to human interventions themselves co-mingling and so having combined outcomes that cannot even be computed, their interactions are so complex.

Two possibilities are available to the university in this milieu. On the one hand, it seeks if not to avoid risk to itself, then to minimise it. And so universities—across the UK at least—are developing elaborate systems to assess risk and to enable themselves to conduct a 'risk audit' of virtually every act that might have consequences of risk. This is—as we noted—particularly significant in the context of the emergence of the 'entrepreneurial university' for entrepreneurial activity is, by definition, activity to which risk is attached. It has come naturally to universities to develop such systems for risk analysis since they have also become highly regulated internally (as well as externally). It is not an exaggeration to say that we have seen the rise of *the bureaucratic university*, replete with its expanding systems of regulation, surveillance and evaluation. The developing of risk audits is a natural extension of such moves. In developing risk assessment procedures, the bureaucratic university hopes to bring under control that which precisely cannot be controlled.

On the other hand, a quite different set of responses is available to the university in a world of uncertainty. This is the stance of helping the world to live purposively with uncertainty. Here, we see the potential rise of *the therapeutic university*. The therapeutic university understands both that the world cannot be fully controlled and that the idea of 'control' is anathema to the core values of an institution claiming the title of 'university'. Instead, to draw on another Heideggerian term, it has a 'care' for, a concern, for human being in a tempestuous world. Its pedagogical function becomes less one of knowing about the world and more one of bringing forth being that is capable of living positively and effectively in a world of incessant challenge. Its pedagogical function becomes less epistemological and more ontological in character, and today books and conferences are happily positioned as contributing to an 'ontological turn' (including Barnett (2007)).

Such an orientation plays out in different ways, according to whether a strong sense of the therapeutic university was being realised or a weaker sense. The weaker sense plays itself out in a concern with the university as an environment for human flourishing. Such a concern connects with the emergence of a wider interest in 'well-being'. It is to be seen in the manifold policies that universities are developing in relation to equal participation and human rights on campus (of non-harassment and so forth). Efforts will be made in helping, for example, ethnic minorities to feel that their own well-being is of concern on campus. Counselling services develop, for both students and staff. The stronger sense plays itself out in interventions in the curriculum, such that the curriculum becomes a space for working through personal anxieties. Whereas formerly, there was a boundary between the curriculum and the personal, now the personal dimension of learning is permitted into the curriculum space. Ethical dilemmas raised by curricula issues are brought explicitly into the curriculum and worked through. Differences of view among students are exposed and engaged. The curriculum becomes a space for cooling personal anxiety.

This development, the emergence of the therapeutic university, contains both pernicious and benign possibilities. In its pernicious form, failure is barely permitted. As such, students may come to expect not just that they will gain a degree but that they will gain a 'good degree', so contributing to an 'inflation' of such classes of degree (in the UK, at least). In its more benign form, students are encouraged to develop the personal dispositions that enable them to flourish even amid the challenge of the disciplinary standards that accompany their higher education.

For some, admittedly, the idea of the therapeutic university is regrettable. In the hands of these critics, the term 'the therapeutic university' is a term of near-abuse (Ecclestone & Hayes, 2009). It is intended to indicate that this idea and form of the university is a falling short of its true destiny. This is a university that 'infantalises' students (p. 87) in which its over-concern with students' well-being neglects its primary functions connected with the critical appropriation of knowledge. For these critics, students who graduate from the therapeutic university, having had their wants met, are likely to be 'passive' citizens, unable to discern sound knowledge and to exercise their critical judgement.

The critics of the therapeutic university have some point on their side but their arguments are putting up straw men. No institution worth the name of 'university' can content itself purely with a concern for well-being—whether of its employees or its students—but who is arguing for such a position? To the contrary, the claim on behalf of the therapeutic university is that the effort to come seriously to know exerts demands on the self and those demands have increased as knowledge has become evermore global and subject to the public interest. Knowing calls forth the self. Even Popper's (1975) idea of objective knowledge, in addition to entities in the world (World I) and knowledge about those entities (World III)), allowed as World II, the mind. A concern with the knowing self, therefore, is arguably an entirely proper pedagogical concern, if only in fulfilment of the university's concern with knowledge.

The authentic university

If the therapeutic university is running the risk of betraying its true identity, *the authentic university* tackles the matter head-on. This is a university that is intent (Polonius-like) on being to its own self true, but it understands that that simple self-injunction is fraught with difficulty. What is it, what might it be, for a university to be true to itself? Every university in the world is subject to the pushes and pulls of its environment. Those pushes and pulls come in the shape of expectations, resources and regulation. Some are unwanted and some are given grudging attention; yet others may even be induced by a university itself, albeit for hoped-for advancement of some kind. This state of affairs may be summarised as the coming of *the networked university*. The habitus of the contemporary university is spaghetti-like in its complexity. So the idea of a university being true to itself under these circumstances is looking to be something of a chimera.

There are two problems for the authentic university. The first is that already implied, of trying to sort out what a disencumbered position (cf. Cooper, 2002) might look like, such that it can offer the prospects of authenticity. The second is that of working out what, in even more general terms, 'authenticity' might mean for a university. Would it mean to identify and to hold onto some kind of universal position open to all institutions that warrant the title of 'university'? (This is not, we should note, to ask about an unchanging essence of the university for it might be that a new universal idea of the university is opening up or could feasibly open up in the 21st century.) Or, to the contrary, would it mean identifying a position that is particular to each university? After all, this is presumably part of the rationale for universities producing their own so-called 'mission statements'. Perhaps authenticity is to be found not in any locale that a university might attain for itself but is rather to be found in its having a set of values that can help to give it some kind of steer. Compromises with its values there may well have to be but at least the university can content itself that it has a worked-out set of values (and many mission statements these days do contain just such a statement of a university's own values).

Perhaps, to pick up a term of Stephen Rowland (2006), the authentic university is an *enquiring university*. Unless we were in the presence of enquiry, we could not be in the presence of a 'university'. The enquiring university is true to its own self in that it takes seriously its penchant for enquiry. It holds onto its self-image as a place of enquiry, an image almost lost from view but now possibly recovered. The enquiring university looks to build an internal community of enquirers, across the disciplines that it represents; and this community would include both academics and students. Students would be encouraged to see themselves as enquirers and so dent the tendency towards their self-understandings as consumers.

But the recovery of the idea of enquiry brings a discovery too, namely an understanding of the possibilities for this university in the 21st century. The mediaeval university was a cross-national place of enquiry. Now, the responsibility falls upon the enquiring university to interpret its calling globally. And this responsibility is aided by modern technology: through the use of the internet, the university can place its knowledge wares before global publics. Its academics will understand themselves in part as public intellectuals, with a responsibility to engage with publics. Such a university would not merely be offering the world new descriptions of the world or even critiques but new understandings; even new 'imaginaries' (Taylor, 2007).

'Enquiry' stands, therefore, as a possible exemplification of the authentic university in that it goes some way to fulfilling the criteria of authenticity here. The theme of enquiry looks back to the origins and traditions of the university but it does not languish there for the theme is brought up to date, in a search for its contemporary possibilities. Criteria of past resonance and contemporary relevance are both satisfied, therefore. But the enquiring university—in realising its authenticity—also takes seriously the matter of the universalism implicit in the idea of 'university'. The enquiring university seeks to promote enquiry on a global scale and does so conscious of the challenges that such a responsibility attracts (for example, over copyright, in the light of the 'new technologies of openness' (cf. Peters, 2011)). Authenticity is not simply adopted, therefore, but is a continuing task.

The coming of the ecological university

There are two questions in front of us and they have tensions between them. On the one hand lies the question with which we have just been grappling: 'What might it mean for the idea of the authentic university really to have substance today?' On the other hand lies the question (with which, as we saw, Derrida grappled): 'Can we and if so in what way might we speak today of the responsibility of the university?' The first question has its contemporary point against a suspicion that it is no longer possible for us meaningfully to talk of the university and authenticity in the same breath. The university has, it can reasonably be claimed at least, been undermined both philosophically—the large projects and ideas (such as universality) on which the university depended are no longer available—and sociologically, as its autonomies evaporate and it is called upon to heed the expectations of its societal 'stakeholders'. The second question gains its point also from a sense that the contemporary university simply falls in with the claims of its 'stakeholders'. Having a sense of its own responsibility is mere sophistry.

These two questions, then, overlap in their underlying critiques of the modern university for they both suggest that it is no longer possible for the university to be what it should be. However, they may seem to point in different directions. The idea of authenticity implies here a sense of the university's true self; the idea of authenticity has an inward quality. The idea of responsibility, on the other hand, points outwards. It implies that there is an outer realm of which the university should take note—whether of values, of service or of engagement. So there is an apparent tension here between authenticity and responsibility, between the inner and the outer callings of the university.

Perhaps this circle can be squared; perhaps the university—as it unfolds into the 21st century—can be both authentic and responsible. These two dimensions, of authenticity and responsibility, may be seen in what we may term *the ecological university*. This is a university that takes seriously both the world's interconnectedness and the university's interconnectedness with the world.

Fragments of such university becoming may already be seen. There is increasing attention being given to the idea of students as global citizens. As global citizens, students come to have a care or concern for the world and to understand their own possibilities in the world and towards the world. A concern for the world and an awareness of its interconnectedness is also evident in the newly established Talloires network, a worldwide group of major universities signed up (literally) to a mission of service to the world and 'civic engagement'. Other universities, not formally connected with this group, are reflecting on their purposes and are wanting to develop an articulated sense of their potential contribution to the world. Some universities in the developed world are deliberately working with universities in the developing world, so extending the 'capability' to which Amartya Sen has been pointing. In higher education research and scholarship, a distinct line of inquiry has been developing around the 'public goods' that a university may represent (e.g. Nixon, 2011). The University of Galway in Ireland has a research and development Centre for Civic Engagement. A particular offshoot of this work is the interest being shown in the development of the 'creative commons' (Peters, 2009) and the part that universities might play here, for example, in making their creative output freely available on the web.

A shorthand encapsulation of these developments might seem to lie in the term *'the networked university'* for these universities are taking their networking very seriously (cf. Standaert, 2009). Indeed, universities are intent on developing new networks, between themselves and the wider society and, through those networks, are making available their knowledge resources. 'The ecological university', however, is surely a more powerful term of art here. For the notion of ecology today is fact and value intertwined. It is, in Bernard Williams' (2006) terminology, a 'thick concept'. It embodies hopes and critique towards a more sustainable future built around interconnectedness as well as a critique of the world order that has led to the contemporary world order. The ecological university does not merely take its networking seriously but engages actively with the world in order to bring about a better world.

The ecological university is perhaps just able to claim that it is providing a resolution of the tension between authenticity and responsibility. It hangs onto and, indeed, widens its traditional concern with the advancement of learning in wanting to permeate society with enhanced enlightenment and understanding; and so it is authentic to its inner calling. And in so taking forward and giving life to 'the learning society', the ecological university acknowledges and discovers, all at once, a responsibility to society. As the ecological university, it does all this by forming and widening its networks across society, a task which – unlike the entrepreneurial university – it performs not in its own interests but in the interests of the world; indeed, worlds, for it acts in the interests of both the human and physical worlds.

This is a university neither *in-itself* (the research university) nor *for-itself* (the entrepreneurial university) but *for-others*. Or, we might even say simply, *for-the-other*, for the ecological university has an abiding sense of alterity (cf. Standish, 2007), of there being external realms to which it has responsibilities, even while holding fast to its traditional interest in the emancipatory power of understanding for enlightenment.

This is a university not whose time is coming but whose time has come. The ecological university cannot be a sufficient condition of the world facing up to its challenges but it is a necessary condition. The huge catalogue of challenges facing the world—of disease, illiteracy and unduly limited education, climate change, dire poverty, lack of capability and basic resource, misunderstandings across communities, excessive use of the earth's resources, energy depletion and so on and so on—requires the coming of the ecological university. This ecological university will be an engaged university, a critical and an enquiring university *and* a university-for-development, acting to put its resources to good effect in promoting world well-being. It will be active on the local and regional stages and, very often, on the world stage. The ecological university, accordingly, will live out its (new) calling, but in ways that redeem its possibilities for enlightenment and well-being.

Conclusion

Our contemporary thinking about the university is hopelessly impoverished. The university is a creation of a metaphysical viewpoint, an attempt to provide a site of higher learning that connected with universal and transcendent ideas of the relationship between humankind and the universe. That the university has survived for a thousand years or more is testimony to its capacities for self-renewal. Ideas and their associated forms of the university have succeeded each other over time. Over the last 150 years, the research university has blossomed and is now being superceded by the entrepreneurial university. In the process, the university has become focused on the here-and-now, on impact in this immediate world; the universal and infinite have given way to the finite and the parochial. Certainly, the forms of the university do not give way so easily as the ideas: a modern university is, at any one time, a layering of forms, as the new settle, uneasily at times, over the earlier incarnations.

These simple reflections lead to some large considerations and aporias. Just what is it to be a university? What is the university's 'being possible'? For now, it is apparent that there are options in front of the university. The coming of the entrepreneurial university does not or, at least, should not represent the end-game. The university may be hedged by state policies, ideologies, limitations on resources and 'stakeholder' expectations but yet it has space available to become itself. Its own becoming lies in its own hands to some extent. This, then, is our first conclusion: that there are conceptual and practical options in front of the university. But then comes the second point: that the university now has a responsibility not simply to do this or become that but to choose its own becoming, whatever that may be felt to be. This is the key responsibility, that of choosing its own idea(s) of itself; and it may seem a fearful responsibility.

The optionality before the university does not include a ratcheting back. There can be no return to the research university in its pure form, still less to the metaphysical university. But the layerings of previous sedimentations remain, to offer conceptual and practical resources for renewal. In this postmetaphysical age, even remnants of the metaphysical stubbornly remain. Given its history, and the archaeology of its conceptual journey, and the challenges of the landscape now facing the university, its options are shaped to some extent, while also being open. Its options are open partly because its value horizons are open. The university, as it reshapes itself, has to choose its values: by which values will it be steered, as the rocks appear and the gales assail it?

The metaphysical university stood apart from society. Now, the modern university interpenetrates society, as society interpenetrates the university. The university is called upon to develop a societal mission, even a global mission. Very well; let it take that calling seriously and become a fully-fledged ecological university, aware of its interconnectedness with society and putting its resources towards the development of societal and personal well-being. This would neither be merely a therapeutic university nor a liquid university but a university that worked actively and tirelessly in helping to bring about a sustainable world; and here, sustainability would be understood generously to include personal and social well-being as much as physical and material well-being. Whether this idea of the ecological university can come to overtake the entrepreneurial university and so furnish the university's becoming in the 21st century is unclear. What is surely clear is that the university has to accept its own responsibility to think seriously about the matter: just what is it to be a university in the 21st century?

Part II
Higher education

Chapter 6

Higher education
Legitimation crisis

(from *Studies in Higher Education*, 1985, 10 (3) 241–255)

Outline

Those practices and institutions which we term 'higher education' are faced with a legitimation crisis. They lack a generally recognised, coherent and secure underpinning. This deficit is readily apparent in the lack of any worked out educational theory of higher education. It is also to be seen in the language of higher education, with its competing viewpoints and ideologies. But the crisis resides at deeper analytical levels. Historically, the idea of higher education has contained an emancipatory dimension, focused on the freeing of the student's mind through the acquisition of objective knowledge, in an institution relatively independent of the wider society, where academic freedom is assured. However, this emancipatory concept has been undermined both epistemologically (the possibility of obtaining objective knowledge is in doubt) and sociologically (with the incorporation of the system of higher education into the modern state). Any attempt therefore at legitimising higher education has to recognise and counter this double undermining of its conceptual foundations.

Introduction

In his book, *Legitimation of Belief*, Ernest Gellner (1974) points out that "a term is required which conveys the fact that such and such a personage, institution or procedure is held to be authoritative, binding or valid in a given society". For Gellner, that term is legitimacy, and his book is an attempt to describe the central epistemological features of the dominant belief system of modern society (essentially that of science), and at the same time to demonstrate its legitimacy as a key institution in that society.

This paper will try to show that a parallel exercise is overdue for higher education, for it is faced with—in the terminology of Jurgen Habermas (1976)—a 'legitimation crisis'. In using the term, Habermas is pointing to the mismatch in modern society between expectations generated by society and the capacity of society to meet those expectations. That kind of legitimation deficit is just one characteristic of the legitimation crisis of higher education. The institutions and processes we label 'higher education' generate expectations which are increasingly difficult to meet. But, as we shall see, the legitimation crisis faced by higher education takes other forms as well.

Several commentators have sensed such a crisis in relation to higher education. Brubacher (1977), for example, cites Hoffman as speaking of "a crisis of legitimacy". However, no writer, so far as I am aware, has systematically mapped out the features of this particular legitimation crisis.

This paper will therefore begin to tackle the task by identifying the different components of the crisis. In the sections that follow, those components are set out in order of increasing analytic depth. We begin with its more obvious surface manifestations, and move to deeper and even foundational aspects of the crisis. The paper will end by briefly suggesting a way of resolving the crisis.

'Higher education'—a term, but not a concept?

The term higher education is a relatively recent addition to the language, following in the wake of the proliferation of new kinds of institutions of higher education which have appeared alongside the universities. (In Great Britain the process of higher education has been available in institutions other than universities for over 50 years, but until the establishment of the binary policy in the mid-1960s (HMSO, 1966) that non-university component was largely hidden from the public view, especially with the system of external university degrees.) Qua institution, higher education is no longer comprised of a set of relatively homogeneous institutions.[1]

Two consequences follow: one positive, one negative. The positive point is that it has become easier—both psychologically and socially—to raise conceptual questions about higher education, without being confined to our ideas about the university. The expansion of higher education has been salutary in driving a wedge between the concept of higher education and any particular institutional instantiation of it. The negative point is that the absence of any clear meaning and of any justification of higher education has been revealed. Institutions of higher education perform a wide range of functions but whether they have any unifying purpose is unclear. Is 'higher education' then simply a convenient umbrella term, lacking any conceptual depth? Or, to put it another way, what if anything is 'higher' about higher education?

A contested concept

This absence of any consensus about higher education has not been due to a lack of debate about higher education as such. On the contrary, the postwar exponential growth of higher education—as Edwards (1982) describes it—has been accompanied by a welter of commentary about higher education. Journals, pamphlets, a learned society (the Society for Research into Higher Education), a newspaper, and a Minister of State with special responsibility for higher education have all appeared in Great Britain in the past 20 years, quite apart from an increasing number of books on the subject. More recently has come the SRHE Leverhulme Inquiry into higher education, followed by the 'Great Debate' (culminating in major submissions to the Secretary of State from the University Grants Committee (HMSO, 1984) and the National Advisory Body (1984)).

Inevitably, in all this talk about higher education has come a profusion of views about the purposes of higher education. What is striking though is that through this debate the same themes that have characterised the debate over the idea of the university for well over a century continue to resonate.

Three themes stand out in particular as axes along which the different views range: a view of the value of knowledge as being inherently worthwhile or, on the other hand, worthwhile in so far as it fulfils other ends—the extrinsic–intrinsic axis; a view of higher education as being oriented towards the individual or towards society—the individual–society axis: and a view of higher education as promoting a culture which is either special in some way or is integrated with the meaning systems in the wider society—the elite–common culture axis. The key point here though can be expressed in the form of a simple question: given the presence of these competing views of higher education, is there any way of rationally choosing between them, or of contributing a further view no less partial than the others?

The paradox of higher education—theory without theory

The modern debate over higher education has two general characteristics. First, most of it has been focused on particular aspects of higher education, such as resource allocation, planning mechanisms, research, student learning, the use of educational technology and the structure of the system. Where the debate has been backed up by reference to the academic literature, it has drawn upon such specialisms as the economics of higher education and upon the newer areas of research into higher education—such as those in student learning and educational technology—which have developed alongside the wider social concerns in relation to higher education.

The second point—and it is a corollary of the first—is that in all this talk about higher education there has been little serious examination of the purpose—or purposes—of higher education itself. As Roy Niblett once commented (1979):

> For every book on the philosophy of higher education, it may well be that there are six on its planning, five on its administration, four on the methodology of teaching its subjects, and three even on its Curriculum.[2]

The upshot of this is that we lack an educational theory of higher education. We even lack a theoretical framework in which such theorising can take place, a framework which not only encompasses the work conducted in the philosophy of education, but also embraces recent developments in other relevant areas of inquiry such as epistemology, moral philosophy, social theory, critical theory, phenomenology, and the sociology of knowledge.

This situation is a paradox—of higher education itself. For in any society higher education is concerned with the development and transmission of elaborated linguistic structures, or theoretical frameworks. But there is very little systematic reflection upon higher education itself. Higher education is, therefore, a set of theoretical practices without a theory of those practices.

Problems with conceptual analysis of 'higher education'

There is then a theoretical vacuum in relation to higher education, not through our lack of understanding of any technical aspect of higher education, but through a general failure to make clear the idea of higher education itself. It might seem that this particular deficit could easily be overcome, since modern philosophy of education has evolved powerful tools of linguistic analysis through which concepts can be analysed and their underlying assumptions and values revealed. In the manner of R. S. Peters' early work on the concept of education (e.g. 1966, 1972, 1973) it might be possible to explicate the necessary conditions of 'higher education' so that the concept could then be used to assess the degree to which our practices bearing the term 'higher education' could be said really to be exemplifications of it.

This is an approach which could certainly bear fruit in this situation. That there is a language of higher education is in itself a matter not without significance. Not only the term higher education, but also a host of others can be readily identified: student, lecture, tutorial, seminar, degree (bachelor, master, doctor), reading for a degree, booklist, course, interdisciplinarity, credit accumulation, universities, polytechnics, academic autonomy, academic freedom, independent study, open learning, and academic community are indicative but by no means exhaustive of the terminology of this particular language community.

It would be a valuable exercise to undertake a conceptual analysis of this terminology to see what if any are the central ideas, assumptions, and values implicit within it, and so identify the dominant features—again if any—of the idea of higher education. Prima facie, the existence of 'a language of higher education' does suggest that higher education possesses a conceptual substance of its own, and is something more than 'further' education, even if we cannot be certain what it is.[3]

However, there are reasons for doubting whether conceptual analysis can provide a full analysis of 'higher education'.

First, conceptual analysis normally focuses upon ordinary language usage of terms. But as implied earlier, a number of technical languages have been spawned offering different perspectives on higher education. So we have a history of higher education, an economics, a sociology, and a politics of higher education. In addition, psychology (through student learning), management studies, policy studies, curriculum studies, and the developing subject of course evaluation are also offering their own 'languages' of higher education. If we are really to get to grips with the concept of higher education, it would seem arbitrary and unreasonably restrictive to rule out of court higher education as it is seen in those technical (or quasi-technical) languages.

Nevertheless, it could be argued that we can best clarify our key concepts in higher education precisely through an examination of their use in 'ordinary language'. But the initial promise of even this more limited objective soon dissolves on closer inspection. For what we find is that the term higher education has been the focus of an extraordinarily wide range of polemic, much of it politically and ideologically saturated. Vice-chancellors, directors of polytechnics, politicians, academics, journalists, students, and other interested parties have developed their thoughts on higher education, much of it in writing and often possessing a relatively sophisticated character. It follows then, and this is the second point in relation to the task of embarking on conceptual analysis of higher education, that 'ordinary language' usage of 'higher education' is far from ordinary and the analytic process might well end in confusion rather than clarity.

The third point is that if that kind of exercise was to end in any clear outcome it would surely have to conclude that higher education is a contested concept (Ryan, 1974; Snelders, 1981). I suggested earlier some of the different dimensions or axes which mark out the conceptual boundaries of this contest. But even if the claim that higher education is a contested concept is thought to go too far (Wilson, 1981), at least it should be readily accepted that higher education is perceived in quite different ways by the various interest groups. It follows from this that when we are offered a 'conceptual analysis' of higher education we are entitled to ask, "whose concept are we being given?" (Woods, 1973). Otherwise, instead of a neutral conceptual analysis there is the danger of a particular view being smuggled in as "*the* concept of higher education". Analysis of a concept of this kind could all too easily come to perform a normative function not only because other views would be ruled out as not really counting as higher education, but also because it could come to be seen as a prescriptive guide to ways of organising our higher education practices and arrangements.

This leads on to the fourth point. With a complex concept like higher education, which is employed not only in ordinary usage but also in different contexts by interest groups bringing different perspectives to bear, we have to recognise that conceptual analysis cannot be expected to reveal the concept 'as it really is'. The reason is not simply that the rich assortment of ways in which 'higher education' is seen and understood provides "a complicated network of similarities overlapping and criss-crossing" (Wittgenstein, 1978). It is also that, especially since higher education has become part of the apparatus of the state and subject to increasing political and economic pressures, what counts as higher education has become negotiable. Sometimes it seems as if higher education is seen as no more than a burdensome part of the economy; sometimes it seems as if it is no more than a means of supplying more or less trained recruits to meet the needs for technically skilled labour; on other occasions it appears to be seen as a way of ensuring that the research base for the sciences and the technologies is properly if not too expensively maintained; and in yet other contexts it refers to a conglomeration of institutions offering intractable problems of planning, organisation, and resource allocation. In short, according to the perspective of the individual, 'higher education' will be viewed in a particular way.

Higher education as an area of activity in which there are a number of different interest groups is a good example of social actors holding different definitions of the 'same' situation (Winch, 1958). As a result, the boundaries of the concept of higher education are fluid. There is no entity around which one can draw a conceptual circle called 'higher education' which will be universally accepted *as* higher education, with all other candidates for the title excluded.

The point can be put another way. In explicating the concept of higher education, a decision has to be made on how much of the social context to include in the concept (Gellner, 1970). For instance, is 'higher education' to be confined just to the student and to the nature of his or her learning? Is it to include a reference to the teaching? Is it to include a sense of the institutional setting in which the learning takes place? Is it to embrace a recognition of the profession or other social institution to which it is expected that the student as graduate will proceed in employment? And is it also to incorporate an acknowledgement of the wider society which makes that higher education possible?

It may be argued that this is to confuse what is meant by 'higher education' with its institutional forms. But this is to beg the question: for it is precisely what is meant by higher education that is problematic. And the range of views sketched out above suggests that for some at least the concept of higher education does include an institutional dimension.

The idea of higher education as ideology

Flowing from these reflections on the concept of higher education, we can observe that any particular definition of higher education is not arbitrarily chosen, nor is it a neutral selection from the available options. On the contrary, it reflects and is shot through with values, values which are not held fortuitously, but are associated with the fundamental outlook of the person or group concerned. Defining higher education in terms of the 'needs' of the economy, or in terms of its cultural role (à la Leavis), or in terms of its research function: each of these expressions indicates differing perceptions as to what, in the total web of its constituent parts, is of vital importance in higher education. And those contrasting values in turn reflect correspondingly different starting value positions.

On the first view, it *is* the needs of the economy that is of paramount importance, not just in this particular case, but as the base of a general outlook or—in other terms—an ideology. On the second view, it is particular aspects of the culture of society that matters, and that ought to be defended in modern society and by extension in higher education. For the last, it is the advancement of knowledge that counts; but this view in turn can be seen as in part representing the social interests of the academic community.

In short, different conceptions of higher education are not only different views of the principles that processes and institutions of higher education *as such* ought to satisfy to warrant the appellation 'higher education'. They also reflect the fundamental orientation and more pointedly the interests and values of the person or group (or even social class) concerned. They may reasonably be suspected then of being, at least partly, ideological in character.[4]

In suggesting that the different conceptions may be seen as ideological in character, it is not being said that they are nothing but ideologies, and are therefore not worth assessing. On the contrary, precisely because they are making claims to validity they can be rationally assessed (Gouldner, 1976). The characterisation of different views of the essential nature of higher education as ideological does though alert us to the possibility that those different views cannot be completely understood simply in the terms in which they are presented. It may be that their real function is to mask, but at the same time to further, hidden interests. It is often considered, for example, that Newman's (1852) *Idea of a University* (resting on the cultivation of the intellect and so providing a Liberal education which "makes not the Christian, not the Catholic, but the gentleman") is an attempt to legitimise an education for the leisure class of his day. Whether or not a reading of that kind does justice to what Newman meant by the intellect and by gentleman is certainly arguable but the point here is that it has some plausibility. In other words, it is possible to see Newman's *Idea* not just as the personal statement of one person reflecting his own ideas, personality, experience and so forth. Rather, a worked out argument of that kind can also be seen as embodying a more or less coherent set of beliefs which carry within them a structured configuration of social interests (Althusser, 1969).

In his (1982) paper on the *Ideological Influences in Higher Education*, Collier identifies and describes four ideologies dominant in British higher education: the academic ideology; the ideology of economic renewal; the egalitarian ideology; and the ideology of consensus. As Collier himself recognises, to say there are these ideologies "is not to say there are no others". We might reflect, for example, that Leavis' (1943, 1969) conception of the university as preserving a continuity of a particular kind of 'cultural consciousness' (albeit one that the university, principally through the English school, continually renews) does not easily fall into any single one of Collier's categories. Instead, it could be argued that it resonates with at least two of them (the academic ideology and the egalitarian ideology) and probably others as well (en passant, Collier mentions a conservative ideology and there is perhaps a humanistic ideology at work here too).

The detailed mapping of these ideological influences is not our concern here, however. The key point is simply that our fundamental ideas about higher education—what counts for each of us *as* higher education—are likely to be to some degree ideological in character. If this is correct, the question is raised: can we develop a non-ideological concept of higher education?

The history of the idea of higher education—development or disappearance?

One way of beginning to answer the question posed in the preceding section would be to look at a wide range of conceptions of higher education which have been developed and see if any common features emerge. Historically, the idea of higher education would seem to have passed through several different stages, the modern phases of which are:

(1) *The Nineteenth Century.* Foundation of the modern university, in which the idea of higher education took on many of its contemporary themes. These include the ideas of liberal higher education, research, and professional education (in its widest sense). Newman's *Idea of a University* contains many of these themes, but it also offers a definite view. The university was to provide a liberal education, in which knowledge was

to be its own end. The mind was to reflect on nothing other than knowledge itself.
(2) *Post World War 1–Post World War 2*. A period of critical reflection on the idea of the university, generated by a sense that the university, with the fragmentation of knowledge and its narrowing scope, had underwritten nationalism and the new technological age.[5]
(3) *The 1960s: the expansion of the system and the formation of the multiversity*. This period witnessed a massive increase in the size of the higher education system as a matter of deliberate policy on the part of the state, an expansion which was common across the western world. It was in this climate that Robbins (1963) not just provided a programme for expansion, but was also able to legitimise it within an explicitly 'liberal' view of the purposes of higher education. During this period the university was asked to take on a range of additional functions. New kinds of students, courses, research programmes, and consultancy and society-oriented services were acquired. In that multiversity, "there is no single end to be discovered; there are several ends and many groups to be served" (Kerr, 1972).
(4) *The Counter-course Conception of Higher Education* (the late 1960s and early 1970s). The sense that the expanded system of higher education was not an isolated aspect of social policy, but was underwriting the expansion of the technological society (Cockburn, 1969; Miliband, 1970), led in turn to a strongly-voiced view that higher education could and should offer a different kind of experience, and could play a radically alternative role in society. New forms of 'counter-course' were proposed (Pateman, 1972), which were to enable students critically to evaluate their educational experiences, and to assist in developing a counter-culture within modern society.
(5) *Contraction Both of the System and of the Idea of Higher Education* (early 1970s onwards). Now no longer is higher education seen by the state as a necessary vehicle for the expansion of the economy, and so the state has turned to consider ways in which its investment can be maximised. In the process, as attention has focused on ways of making the system more 'efficient' and more 'accountable', speculation about the larger aims of higher education becomes apparently redundant. So for example, the 1981–1983 SRHE-Leverhulme Inquiry[6] was conducted largely without any such reflection on the wider meaning of higher education. In the current climate the general conception of the idea of higher education seems to have shrunk to a concern with means and not ends.

This sketch of the modern development of the concept of higher education brings us to where we are today. But like all concepts and particularly those which relate to our social institutions, the general conception of higher education will never be static and there are signs that the concept is beginning to take on a new shape or at least that certain aspects are receiving an added emphasis. I have in mind the vocabulary of continuing education, of credit transfer, of education through the lifespan, of mature students (which implies that in some sense students traditionally have not been seen as mature), of part-time education, of distance learning, and of the assessment of experiential learning. There are perhaps here the beginnings of a general if not articulated shift in the public conception of higher education.[7]

Whether or not this sketch of the development of the idea of higher education is valid in every detail is not of vital concern here. Its worth in this context lies in its heuristic value for our philosophical understanding of the concept of higher education rather than as a historical exercise. The key point is that the concept of higher education has not surprisingly not remained static but has undergone various shifts. It has been stretched in all sorts of ways. On the surface it would seem as if the different perceptions of higher education have little if anything in common. The corollary is that, on the basis of this kind of analysis, it is far from clear that there is any central core of any substance to the concept. In other words, a historical examination of this kind, far from revealing the essence of the idea of higher education seems to have the opposite effect. The upshot seems to be that the term higher education means anything that can command some kind of consensus or—to put it another way—it appears to mean nothing in particular at all. The concept of higher education instead of having been drawn out and given some substance seems as a result of this exercise to have been dissolved.

The emancipatory promise of higher education

It might well be argued and it would have to be admitted that to draw such a conclusion on the basis of such a cursory outline of the history of the idea of higher education would be premature. For it could be suggested that the different 'ideas' sketched out here are not really ideas in any serious sense at all, but for the most part are merely vague unformulated sentiments. This charge has considerable validity. Indeed, I hinted earlier that if we look closely at the writings of those who have articulated an 'idea' of higher education, we find a substantial measure of agreement on the nature of higher education as a concept. We can at least without too much difficulty identify certain overlapping themes and concerns in the seminal writings on the idea of higher education. They include: knowledge, truth, objectivity, reason, culture, wholeness, community, research, criticism, (academic) freedom, dialogue, enlightenment and emancipation (through liberal education).

Clearly, in the seminal writings on the subject, these themes have received different emphases. And they have been woven together to form quite different views on key topics. Newman, for example, saw research as no part of the idea of the university. For Jaspers on the other hand research was absolutely integral to it. Nevertheless, there remains the possibility that if we penetrate beneath the surface argument we can detect a common allegiance to an admittedly undefined but relatively coherent sense of the contours of the concept of higher education.

This is the idea that, whether seen instrumentally or in terms of its intrinsic good, higher education refers to a process of individual development, through the acquisition of objective knowledge in a process of rational and open-ended discussion. In turn, this involves (so the idea continues) a process which is characterised by a lessening of the 'taken for grantedness' of the student's hold on the world. It is not just that the student comes to see the world in a different way, but even more crucially comes to realise that other (even unrealised) possibilities always exist.[8]

In short we might say that the idea of 'higher education' embodies an emancipatory concept of education.

The foundations of the emancipatory concept of higher education

This emancipatory concept of higher education is not, however, self-standing but rests on two axioms: first, that objective knowledge can be obtained (so that 'the truth' can be known); and secondly, that the processes of higher education and the institutions in which they are provided can enjoy a measure of social independence or academic freedom (so that the knowledge acquired can be really 'objective'). There is then built into this emancipatory concept of higher education both an epistemological assumption and a sociological assumption. The logic of this reflection is that if we are seriously to ground our idea of higher education then we are led into philosophy (especially epistemology) and into sociology (especially social theory—particularly for the understanding it offers of the modern state, and the sociology of knowledge). It hardly needs to be said that a worked out concept of higher education of this kind—which would in effect amount to a grounded theory of higher education—simply does not exist.

This is not the place to offer such a worked out theory of higher education, but we do not have to look very far ahead to see that the task is likely to be far from easy. For the two axioms turn out to be far from unshakeable. On the one hand, the possibility of securing objective knowledge is itself the subject of much debate from within a range of academic disciplines, including epistemology, the philosophy of and (separately) the sociology of science, the sociology of knowledge, anthropology, critical theory and the philosophy of education itself.[9] Clearly then we cannot take it for granted that objective knowledge is readily available (even if we follow certain procedures). And much less can we assume that our institutions of higher education do actually offer an encounter *with* objective knowledge.

On the other hand, the independence of the institution in which 'higher education' is normally experienced is, in the modern state, seriously limited. This point is not simply about the increasing role of the state as the provider of the funding for higher education—which is particularly evident in the United Kingdom. Rather it is about the incorporation of higher education into the apparatus of the modern state. This is admittedly an area in which we lack much in the way of real understanding, and so little can be said authoritatively. Nevertheless, we can register the reflection that the apparatus of the modern state has several components and the higher education system has its part to play in relation to each of them.[10] So the system is bound in, in turn, to the economic apparatus, the cultural (or ideological) apparatus, the technical apparatus, and what might be called the managerial apparatus. Certainly, its relationship to each of these components varies, and higher education can be said to have a measure of freedom in each sphere. Nevertheless, the incorporation of the higher education system into the modern state is a fact that we have to acknowledge in working out our idea of higher education, especially if we are to provide some kind of effective guide to our educational practices.

The double-undermining of the emancipatory concept

The two pillars or axioms on which the idea of higher education has rested—those of objective knowledge and social independence—are both then under attack. The pillars are cracking. The 'ivory tower' that they have seemed historically to support appears to be far from safe. But in fact the position, on further analysis, turns out to be far worse. To continue the metaphor for a moment, talk of cracking implies the possibility of patching up the defect, but what we have here is an undermining of the foundations.

The situation confronting higher education can be put very simply. The epistemological objectivity and the social independence on which the idea of higher education rests are not merely problematical. They are simply not available. Their unavailability is not just a local or historical difficulty that with a certain amount of goodwill or patience we might be able to overcome. They are not simply contingent difficulties which with better understanding or social skill we can put behind us. Rather they are features of the way we understand ourselves, our social arrangements and our attempts 'to know'.

These are large claims, and they cannot be fully substantiated here. Nevertheless, we can identify some of the main strands of such an argument.

First, arising especially out of sociologically and anthropologically inspired debates over relativism, we are becoming increasingly aware of the particular characteristics of modern society. What matters here is less what they are, than a recognition that they exist. The point is that despite their differences, societies which go under the heading of 'modern society' have far more significant features in common than those which do not (Gellner, 1969).

Those common features are in part picked out by such terms as scientific, industrial, commercial, technological, and bureaucratic. Again, precisely what those terms pick out is not crucial here.

Secondly, accompanying the realisation that we live in a particular kind of society comes the awareness that we are ineluctably wedded to it (Gellner, 1974, p. 207). Certainly there is scope for quite major differences in the character of its social, economic, and political institutions. But it remains the case that we cannot opt out of being a modern industrial society in any serious sense. Our situation is, as Gellner (1969) has aptly remarked, as if we were ascending in a mountain railway, where the ratchet prevents us from slipping back down the track.

Thirdly, with this massive element of 'givenness' in our social situation, there is also a certain character to the dominant cognitive apparatus of modern society. This has been hinted at already, in the reference to the scientific and technological institutions. The growth and incorporation of science as a constitutive feature of the modern state is actually a relatively recent phenomenon and is really a characteristic of the post-industrial society (Bell, 1972). In its wake have come other developments. These include the proliferation of theory as such, and the disintegration of the resulting elaborated discourses into non-communicating academic subcultures (Becher, 1981). If there is a near universal feature these elaborated codes are coming to possess, it is that of prediction and control (Habermas, 1970, 1972). The obverse of these tendencies is that the humanities are finding it increasingly difficult to justify themselves (Plumb, 1964; Niblett, 1975), unless they undergo a self-transformation so that they become quasi-sciences in appearance. Again, these observations must not be exaggerated. One of the characteristics of modern society is precisely that it offers an extraordinary cognitive pluralism. Nevertheless, that alternative ways of knowing can be identified and pursued does not reduce the influence exerted by the dominant science-based epistemology of society (Habermas, 1972; Gellner 1974; Popper, 1975).

Nevertheless, modern society has developed the capacity to reflect upon this situation. Elaborated theory itself has reflexive properties: it can understand itself. It can understand the limits of its situation—we cannot opt for the thought patterns of primitive man, or even medieval man.[11] At the same time, it can also perceive different forms of knowing that are felt to be—by some interest groups at least—potentially available. And so we see for example the introduction of various kinds of non-conventional forms of knowing (reflected in such phrases as 'experiential learning', 'education for capability',[12] 'knowing-how' and 'education for the professions'[13]).

The general picture then of modern society that emerges from these reflections is of an epistemological and a social pluralism (and with it an ideological pluralism) located within a more or less given epistemological and social framework. Another way of putting it is that the pluralism is located in a framework which constrains the conceptual and social possibilities.[14]

Turning back now to our central theme, higher education is implicated in all this on several levels, in both cognitive and social dimensions. First, higher education is itself a key institution in modern society. As such, its social independence—or academic freedom—is necessarily constrained. Secondly, the social arrangements by which it is made available represent certain interests, and fail to give serious attention to some others.

Thirdly, higher education legitimates society's dominant cognitive structures. Fourthly, what counts as knowledge within higher education cannot be accepted as objective in any absolute sense. Lastly, what is on offer must be suspected of being an ideological carrier.

The upshot for our understanding of the idea of higher education can be simply stated. The twin pillars on which the Western idea of higher education has been founded have not only been cracked: they have been undermined. This is so because the epistemological and the social foundations on which those ideas rested have themselves been demolished. Objective knowledge and the social independence of higher education are simply unavailable in any straightforward sense.

Retrospect: legitimation crisis

The argument has been twofold. First, that we have no grounded educational theory of higher education. Or to put it another way, our educational practices that we term 'higher education' take place in the absence of any coherent overarching framework by which those practices can be seriously understood and which can give some broad educational guidance as to what form those activities should take (Moore, 1974). More specifically, we have no clear idea as to the criteria that our practices and institutions need to meet in order to justify the title 'higher education'. In short, for the most part our processes of higher education are conducted without a clear idea of the principal purposes that they are intended to attain.

The second plank of the argument has been the claim that this state of affairs is explicable. It is explicable through the recognition that the central cluster of ideas for which higher education has stood have themselves become problematic and their attainment has been put in question. Those ideas include those of truth, objective knowledge, rationality, autonomy, academic freedom and an (admittedly somewhat unclear) notion of freeing the mind. This set of concepts constitutes what might be termed the emancipatory conception of higher education. Essentially, it is founded on an even more basic though again ill-defined belief in the possibility of attaining some kind of 'pure reason'.

This deep-seated hope of obtaining pure reason has, as we saw, been undermined from two directions. First, modern developments in social theory, in debates over objective knowledge and relativism, in the sociology of knowledge, in the philosophy of science and in the widening scope of the concept of ideology have undermined the theoretical possibility of obtaining knowledge which is impartial or undistorted by interest or does not contain hidden presuppositions. This we described as the epistemological undermining of higher education since this set of reflections focuses on the underlying theory of knowledge.

In contrast, we also saw that the idea of pure reason—and with it the idea of higher education—has also been undermined as a result of the institutionalisation of higher education in modern society. This sociological undermining has two aspects. On the one hand, higher education is part of the state apparatus, supplying qualified manpower and sustaining the cultural self-understandings of society. On the other hand, the academic community has itself expanded in such a way that academic knowledge has been fragmented and colonised by quasi-autonomous groups within the academic class.[15]

The argument went on to claim that this double undermining of the idea of pure reason, especially as made available in 'higher education', is not just a contemporary or merely a local difficulty. On the contrary, this undermining is irreversible. On the one hand, the epistemological undermining is a necessary feature of our condition (since it is part of our conceptual understanding of ourselves and of our attempts to know the world). On the other hand, the sociological undermining is inescapable since there can be no real prospect of opting out of modern industrial society.

We are faced then in higher education with a massive and a possibly unbridgeable gap between higher education as idea and as it is when viewed against the epistemological and sociological background on which the idea itself focuses. The epistemological and the sociological claims on which the idea of higher education rests simply do not stand up to serious scrutiny. It is, in short, a crisis of legitimation.

The message of all of this for the development of a grounded theory of higher education is quite simple. It has to recognise, counter, and overcome the double undermining that has been sketched out here. If we are going to develop an overarching theory of higher education that is going to do justice to the emancipatory aims which lie deep within the concept, then we need to show that it can deal adequately with the epistemological and sociological undermining with which it is threatened. If we seriously want to legitimise our educational practices in higher education and our beliefs and ideas associated with them, then we have to show that the double undermining that gave rise to the legitimation crisis can be overcome.

Prospect: the legitimation of higher education

At that point, we could leave matters there. The problem has been set out and its full solution will need to be attempted on another occasion. But the way in which the problem has been set out, with the undermining portrayed as being so profound, it might seem as if no satisfactory solution is available. Indeed part of the earlier argument claimed, it will be recalled, that ideas of higher education all too frequently turn out to be ideologies, reflecting narrow sets of interests. Can a grounded theory of higher education be provided which is more than one more addition to the competing babel of voices?[16]

We can perhaps end on a more positive note by following through the logic of the argument that has been presented. Implicit throughout this paper has been the suggestion that cognitively and socially we operate within frameworks. And it is because we cannot escape the bounds of frameworks that the emancipatory or liberating promise of higher education seems to be in jeopardy. We cannot escape to a situation in which there is no such framework (Popper, 1970; Gellner, 1974, p. 182). There is, we saw, in theory at least the possibility of taking up new cognitive and social options (even if only within a limited range), but those new options will have their own frameworks associated with them. A framework of sorts there has to be.

Yet it may be considered that the act of critically reflecting on the framework itself represents a limited kind of emancipation from what goes on within the framework. It might not be possible to displace the interests, partiality, and narrowness at work within the framework but it is at least in principle possible to recognise them for what they are (Habermas, 1968).

This thought surely underlines the common belief that the student's own reflections and critical evaluations lie at the centre of any programme of study intended to offer a higher education. Providing the scope of those activities is not unduly limited, it may be possible to confront the underlying epistemological and social problematics (since critical reflection can for example focus on conceptual assumptions and social implications relevant to the subject matter).

In addition to its potentially broad-ranging character, developing the student's ability to engage in critical reflection does justice to the emancipatory promise of higher education in two ways. First, the processes of communication and dialogue in which the student engages themselves need to be free from unreasonable constraint. Secondly, the student is led to reflect critically on what he or she has learnt, and so develops the art of conducting a continuing critical dialogue with oneself.

A programme of study which in this way places the development of the student's critical competences at its centre is legitimised as *higher* education since, logically, it resides in higher order activities of the kind required by reflection, evaluation, and criticism. In short, the legitimation of higher education resides in the idea of higher education as metacriticism.

Notes

1 This should not be thought to imply that the present different sectors of higher education are entirely distinct in character. As Silver (1981) has observed, assumptions and definitions about their distinctiveness are difficult to make and sustain.
2 It needs to be said that Niblett himself has gone some way towards redressing the balance, especially in his (1974) and under his editorship the (1975) collection of papers. Other modern works of a reflective kind of note are Christopherson (1973), Minogue (1973), Goodlad (1976), Gellert (undated) and Wegener (1978).
3 Perhaps the only significant attempt at conceptual analysis specifically in this field is that of Montefiore (1975); though others are beginning to appear, especially in adult education, such as Lawson (1982).
4 Admittedly, the relationships between interests and ideologies are complex, as Plamenatz (1970) helpfully shows. Other useful modern reviews of the concept of ideology include Berger and Luckman (1971), Hamilton (1974), Larrain (1979), Mapham and Ruben (1979) and Abercrombie (1980). For the application of that concept of ideology (especially as represented by Althusser) in the field of education, see Harris (1979), and Sarup (1978).
5 Writers such as Jaspers (1946), Ortega y Gasset (1946), Leavis (1943, 1969), Moberley (1949) and (undeservedly less well known) Nash (1945), were occupied with these concerns.
6 See Berrill *et al.* (1983) and the ten preceding volumes which emerged from the Inquiry.
7 See, for example, Evans (1981, 1985), the common joint chapter in the NAB and in the UGC advice to the Secretary of State (NAB, 1984; UGC, 1984); Weidemeyer (1981).
8 And so reach a state of 'authoritative uncertainty' (Goodlad, 1976, p. 85).
9 For example, Kuhn (1970); Feyerabend (1975); Lakatos and Musgrave (1977), Barnes (1974, 1977); Bloor (1976); R. J. Bernstein (1983); Hollis and Lukes (1982); Barnes and Edge (1982); Rorty (1980); Habermas (1968); Jencks (1977); Wilson (1970) and Harris (1979). By way of example, one of the strands of thought that emerge from this literature is that 'facts' cannot be read off from the world, unproblematically, but are theory-saturated (see Habermas (1968, postscript 1978) and Harris (1979); though also Gellner (1974) and Popper (1975)).
10 Useful sources here are: Galbraith (1969); Miliband (1970); Bourdieu (1971, 1973, 1979); Young and Whitty (1977); Shaw (1977); Apple (1979); Rose and Rose (1976) and Althusser (1969).
11 This, despite the similarities in thought patterns between the 'primitive' and the 'modern' mind to which Horton (1970) draws attention; though compare his qualifications in his (1982).
12 Though see Thompson's useful critique (1984).
13 As in Goodlad (1984).
14 Another apposite image employed by Gellner to describe this situation is that of 'the Rubber Cage' (1980).

15 These 'social' aspects of the legitimation crises of higher education are examined by Birnbaum (1970).
16 Althusser (1969) who, in observing that "Marx never believed that an ideology might be dissipated by a knowledge of it" (p. 230), adds that "only an ideological world outlook could have imagined societies without ideology" (p. 232), for "(ideology) is a structure essential to the historical life of societies" (p. 232).

Chapter 7

Does higher education have aims?

(from *Journal of Philosophy of Education*, 1988, 22 (2) 239–250)

Outline

Talk of aims in relation to higher education is in several senses inappropriate and misleading. This is due not only to difficulties that attach to explicating the idea of 'aims of education' in general, but more significantly to the idea of 'higher education' itself. There has been a debate about the purposes of higher education since the mid-nineteenth century – and some of that history is sketched here – but left out of that debate is any attempt to address the question: What does it mean for such aims to be realised, in order for an educational process to count as higher education? Can aims of higher education be realised in any straightforward sense and, if not, what are we to make of such aims? I suggest that the question – Does higher education have any aims? – warrants a 'yes' response, but any aims of a higher education, properly conceived, are less fixed points we steer towards than compass bearings we steer by.

Introduction

Talk of the aims of higher education takes place on at least two levels. On the one hand, there is talk of aims by those responsible for designing courses of higher education, especially within the public sector of higher education in their attempt to satisfy validating agencies, such as the UK's Council for National Academic Awards (CNAA), that the course is likely to lead to acceptable outcomes. This is, one might say, an operational usage of 'aims': the specified aims provide a means of direction for those in positions of responsibility to guide and, later, to evaluate the achievement of those outcomes. On the other hand, there is a sense employed by philosophers of education in talking, in an overarching way, of 'the aims of education'. In so far as 'aims' in this sense are ever filled out, they purport to offer a view as to the general ends that an educational process is to serve, if what is on offer is really to count as education. In higher education, the first sense is normally course-specific in the sense that the aims offered typify a particular course, even if—jointly or separately—they could also typify other courses. The second sense is intended to hold across all processes of education; it is a quasi-conceptual perspective.

Against this background, to ask the question 'Does higher education have aims?' might seem curious, to put it no stronger than that. For surely, so it might with justification be said—especially in higher education—we are faced with a surfeit of aims, in *both* senses outlined above. Not only do the separate courses have an extremely wide range of objectives, across subjects, across levels (compare a one-year postgraduate course with a four-year sandwich undergraduate course) and across curricula (compare a single honours programme with a modular multidisciplinary programme); but views as to the general aims of higher education are also quite diverse. In this paper, however, I shall try to show that talk of aims in relation to higher education is in several senses inappropriate and misleading. And this is due not only to the difficulties that attach to explicating the idea of 'the aims of education' in general, but more significantly to the idea of 'higher education' itself.

Attempts to specify aims for higher education are not new. For example, Whitehead, in considering the 'Universities and their function', suggested that the proper function of the university lay in an "imaginative acquisition of knowledge" offered to the student (1932, p. 145). Not much later, Ortega y Gasset stated that the *Mission of the University* was to sustain a broad introduction to modern culture by imparting to its students "the vital system of ideas of a period" (1946, p. 44). At the same time, Walter Moberly (1949), writing in the aftermath of the second world war which had owed much to a science-based technology, detected in the fragmentation of academic disciplines *The Crisis in the University*, and urged the academic community to recover its collegial, corporately self-critical form of life, with the students being introduced to it through broad-ranging curricula.

These, then, are examples of attempts to offer a general set of aims, which hold across the subject areas of higher education. But, before proceeding further in sketching out ways in which aims have been attributed to higher education, it is important to be clear what the discussion here, and later the argument, is *not* about.

First, this paper is not claiming that there is a complete conceptual separation between 'higher education' and the concept of 'education' as commonly employed in the context of activities in other parts of the education system. It is simply that the focus of this paper is higher education, both as concept and as practice; and in being focused in this way, may help to redress a situation in which philosophy of education, as it has developed in the UK, has taken school education as its dominant context.

Secondly, this paper is not about the idea, or the concept, of higher education as such (although something will have to be said on this front for the purpose of making the present argument). There is an important distinction to be drawn between the aims and the concept of higher education. Briefly, it is a distinction between the general direction in which the process of higher education should be pointed, and the conceptual core of the process itself. Whereas there are bound to be different views over the aims, it is at least conceivable that there could be a single concept of higher education which would command, if not universal, then a large measure of agreement amongst those concerned with higher education in a particular society.

Historical approaches to the aims of higher education

There is, in fact, a literature stretching over the last 150 years in which writers have attempted to identify a conceptual core within the idea of higher education. However, no writer on the topic—to my knowledge—has made or adhered to the distinction just drawn between concept and aims; those who have addressed themselves to 'the idea of higher education' have conflated their views on the aims of higher education with comments on the idea (or concept) as such. As a result, we tend to end up with partial views about aims masquerading as an exposition of the idea of higher education. We can see this situation in the nineteenth century debate about higher education.

In the nineteenth century, many who concerned themselves with the idea of higher education saw the central issue as residing in the developing tension between a 'liberal' conception of higher education pursued essentially for its own value and a conception which recognised the pressing claims of the wider world, whether in the form of the new professions, or the increasingly successful technologies and sciences. As is well known, Newman (1952) stood firm against the currents of the age in working out a deliberately liberal *Idea of a University*, in which he claimed that central to the "idea" was an educational process in which knowledge was perceived as being "its own end" (pp. 96–103). This was an education intended to assist "the formation of a character", specifically that of a gentleman; here Newman had in mind those aspects of a person's mental nature (p. 105) developed by a particular kind of education. It was an education in which the student formed "a connected view or grasp of things", or as Newman repeatedly describes it, a "philosophical" acquisition of knowledge, which provided the student with "an intellectual enlargement".

This was a view in which the essence of university education lay neither in the student's acquisition of certain kinds of knowledge, nor in the attainment of professional competence, but in the development of general and higher order intellectual capacities; and these capacities had a general utility, conferring on the student benefits beyond the walls of the university. Much the same view was set out by John Stuart Mill in his inaugural address at St Andrews in 1867:

> A university is not a place of professional education . . . Men are men before they are lawyers, or physicians, or manufacturers. What professional men should carry away with them from a university is . . . that which should direct the use of their professional knowledge and bring the light of general culture to illuminate the technicalities of a special pursuit.
>
> (Mill, 1969/1987)

That liberal conception, while influential, was not the sole view of higher education in the nineteenth century; the main alternative viewpoint cannot, however, simply be characterised as utilitarian. On the contrary, their most outspoken opponents, such as Playfair at the University of Glasgow (Lyons, 1983, p. 126 et seq.), were keen to ally themselves with the notion of 'liberal education'. Their major concern lay rather in its narrow interpretation, as they saw it, with the curriculum based as it was in the classics. Perhaps the most important attempt to widen the 'liberal' conception of higher education was offered by T. H. Huxley, who for the whole of the second half of the nineteenth century strove to have science assume a significant part in the curriculum for all students. Writing in 1854, he commented that: "Leave out the physiological sciences from your curriculum, and you launch the student into the world, undisciplined in that science whose subject-matter would best develop his powers of observation; ignorant of facts of the deepest importance" (Huxley, 1906, quoted in Powell, 1974).

For our purposes, there are three points to be grasped from this nineteenth century debate. First, in the nineteenth century, the aims of higher education were contested: a range of different views were on offer. Secondly, the conceptual contest was part of the surface structure of the debate: despite their differences, the various conceptions had a common feature in that, while each had something to say about the content of the curriculum, the various aims had their cash value mainly in terms of the subsequent benefits in the wider society that the student would enjoy as a result of his higher education. Part of the nineteenth century way of construing higher education lay in the general developmental advantages it conferred on the individual student, with their potential for expression in domains quite outside the immediate academic curriculum providing the student's experience.

Thirdly, at an even deeper level of the conversation, the nineteenth century was remarkable for recognising that the aims of higher education were worth discussing in their own right. *This* was the most significant feature of the debate, rather than any point made in it. Higher education had begun to be seen as a part of educational provision, deserving of its own conceptual treatment. The idea of higher education was not to be subsumed under more general talk of education.

Modern views of the aims of higher education

In the twentieth century, with one world war past and another beckoning, a new era broke, in which the link between higher education and the professions and the internal professionalisation of academic knowledge were more evident. In this situation, doubts about the non-purity of knowledge could be more easily entertained by those interested in the idea of higher education (Scott, 1984, Ch. 3). It was in this context that Karl Jaspers (1965) attempted to reconcile a liberal *Idea of the University* with a modern sense of the contextual character of knowledge claims. What counted as knowledge involves "a framework of assumptions which we know only to be relatively valid"; but it retained a "universal" validity, through its being the present point reached in a dialogue intended to reach consensus (pp. 25–27). (We see here something in embryo of the views of a subsequent and contemporary German theorist, Jurgen Habermas.)

I do not wish to take up that debate here. Rather, all I want to do is to emphasise the separateness of that debate from the issue being pursued here: whatever the particular set of aims being espoused, what does it mean for those aims to be realised, in order for an educational process to count as higher education? Can aims of higher education be realised in any straightforward sense; and if not, what are we to make of such aims?

Here, we can pick up our earlier discussion, by noting that many views about the general purposes of higher education have been developed in opposition to an alternative contemporary view. For example, Leavis's conception of the university, through the English school, as providing a revitalisation of culture, was consciously set against the "Technologico-Benthamite age" (as he termed it). By "culture", Leavis had in mind "a collaborative and creative renewal" in which values were identified and reasserted. And it was Robbins's inability to grasp, as Leavis saw it, the urgency and seriousness of the problem, that led Leavis to remark that "There is a dreadful blank unconsciousness to be faced, as Lord Robbins unconsciously testifies" (Leavis, 1969, pp. 54–58).

The point of mentioning the Leavis/Robbins debate here is that it nicely reinforces the point that the aims of higher education are contested. The divergence between the views of Robbins and Leavis is particularly interesting because it brings into play a key theme underlying the continuing debate over the ends of higher education. Robbins's conception of higher education was self-consciously liberal, in terms of its policy on access. Robbins believed (in the early 1960s) that a substantial expansion of the higher education system could take place without any loss of academic standards (Robbins, 1966, p. 4). For Leavis, by contrast, academic standards—particularly in English—could be safeguarded by accepting only students who could benefit from teaching addressed "to the top level" (ibid.). In other words, these two conceptions lay towards opposite ends of what might be described as the mass-élite axis (of views about the aims of higher education).

But this is only one of many axes along which the debate over the aims of higher education has ranged for at least 150 years. These axes include: the benefit of the individual as against society; the intrinsic–extrinsic value of knowledge ('knowledge for its own sake' as against 'relevance'); theory–practice; research–teaching; a concern with breadth of content as against depth; a technical and instrumental orientation as against a humanistic focus on meaning and reciprocal understanding; higher education as a vehicle for sustaining an élite culture (Leavis) or for promoting a common culture (Robbins's view); and a belief in the importance of the student's self-directed learning as against teaching. These pairs of ideas should not be seen as either/or in character. Rather, as suggested earlier, they should be understood as axes along which views range. The point of setting them out here, though, is less as an attempt to chart the conceptual geography of the aims of higher education, than as a means simply of indicating the range of higher education aims that have been called into play.

Contemporary philosophical approaches to aims of higher education

In the preface to his book, *The Aims of Education Restated*, John White (1982) observes that there has been little in the way of systematic philosophical examination of the aims of education. Indeed, White considered that "there just has not been as yet any book-length investigation of priorities among educational aims" (p. ix). Since in Great Britain philosophers of education have almost entirely neglected higher education as an area of inquiry, it is, therefore, not surprising that the aims of higher education have not received any serious attention. Nevertheless, philosophers of education have had something to say about higher education—even if merely in passing—and it would seem sensible briefly to focus on those offerings.

Two views are apparent in the philosophical literature about the aims of higher education. On the one hand, higher education is seen as concerned essentially with the intellectual development of students; on the other hand, higher education is seen as focused primarily on the moral development of students.

The first view—the cognitive conception of higher education—is seen in the writings of R. S. Peters. Writing in the early 1970s, Peters (1972) distinguished three aims central to the idea of the university: the advancement of knowledge and the initiation of others into it; the development of knowledge that can be applied to the practical needs of the community; and the provision of opportunities for liberal education, in the sense of all-round understanding. Each of these aims is, surely, primarily cognitive in its orientation. Admittedly, Peters did not see any sharp break between the cognitive and the moral development of students. As he reminded the reader in his book on *Ethics and Education*, "particular stress might be placed, as at Balliol in the old days, on moral awareness and a social conscience" (Peters, 1966, p. 64). Nevertheless, the balance in Peters' approach lies in its cognitive emphasis. This comes through explicitly in his comparison of the kind of education offered by universities and technical colleges. For Peters, the full achievement of "education" was especially problematic within a technological education. There were questions to be raised both over the extent to which it could impart "the grasp of fundamental principles as distinct from technical know-how", and over its capacity to develop "the whole man" involving "the cognitive perspective conveyed by 'education'" (ibid., p. 69).

The alternative view, that the central aim of higher education derives from a concern with the moral development of each student, is argued by John White (1982) in *The Aims of Education*. In countering the view that the aim of education is "knowledge for its own sake", White adds that universities—to fall within his conception of the aims of education—"would have to help students to form an integrated life-plan worked out from a moral point of view" (ibid., p. 163).

There is, then, within the philosophical literature, a differentiation between conceptions of the aims of higher education which on the one hand focus on the "knowledge functions" of education; and on the other, focus on—as White puts it—the "person integration" tasks of education (ibid., p. 164). This is not the only set of conceptual distinctions that has been made in relation to higher education, as we saw earlier in observing some of the many issues which have characterised the debate about the purposes of higher education over the past 150 years. However, the distinction being picked out here—between the intellectual and moral aims of higher education—emerges as a significance not only in the literature produced by philosophers of education, but also in the wider literature offering a conceptual perspective on higher education.

The wider academic literature on the purposes of higher education

A predominant concern with the cognitive purposes of higher education can be found, for example, in Kenneth Minogue's (1973) *The Concept of a University*. The key to the concept of the university lies, as Minogue sees it, in its separation from society—a separation characterised not by the academic world's concern with knowledge, but with its approach to what counts as knowledge. It is an approach which focuses not on the content of any set of truth claims, but on the *process* by which those claims are generated and sustained. The characteristics of the process are picked out in the various terms Minogue employs: "inquiry" (p. 57), "critical dialogue" (p. 70), "reevaluation" (p. 58), "debate" (p. 65) and "contemplation" (p. 68).

For Minogue, this is a particular kind of discourse, which is disinterested to the extent of being oblivious to its own survival (p. 99). Its concerns are not the greater efficiency of society's institutions or even their improved effectiveness, but simply the establishment of truth. For Minogue, there is no sharp distinction between the processes of teaching and research: on the contrary, the terms picked out above apply equally to both activities.

Minogue's concept of a university, therefore, parallels Peters' general concept of education: under both conceptions, it is the student's cognitive or intellectual development that is to be given emphasis. On the other hand, W. R. Niblett provides us with a parallel to White's perspective, where it is the moral development of the student that is to be paramount. In his *Universities between Two Worlds*, Niblett (1974) outlines a view of the university where its moral mission is given priority. Niblett argues that, in the modern world, the university and the other institutions of higher education have in fact (contra Minogue) been responsive to society, meeting its manifest need for highly qualified manpower. In the process, though, deeper personal and social values, towards which institutions of higher education have a particular responsibility, are in danger of neglect. In short, the universities are responsive to one world of values, but have not fully responded to the values of another.

For Niblett, these latter values are picked out by such verbs as "to sense", "to love", "to value", "to understand (one another)". This is "the world in which we live as persons . . . [and] in which we share common experiences" (p. 66). The university which responds to this set of concerns will recognise that "[students] will need to be helped to develop further and more sensitively their powers of enjoyment, their sense of purpose, their capacity for empathy and moral action" (p. 160). "Universities must remain places of personal and civilising education for an actual and living society. They need in other words to link the world of . . . the affective with the cognitive" (pp. 167–168).

There are then, in the literature, two central but contrasting views of the aims of higher education. None of the authors mentioned would argue that higher education is solely concerned with the cognitive development of students on the one hand, or the moral development of students on the other. Indeed, from whichever perspective they are offered, they explicitly point to the inescapability of the other point of view. Nevertheless, that a particular view comes through the thoughts of each writer is, I think, undeniable.

My concern in this paper, however, is not to analyse or press the claims of either point of view. On the contrary, I want to suggest that these contrasting perspectives share a profound misunderstanding of the essential nature of higher education. As a result, the aims of higher education are given a misleading perspective.

Higher education as emancipation

Before we try to establish that position, some general points about 'aims of education' are in order. First, there is an uncontroversial sense in which White is correct in arguing that the educator must have an aim. The educator, if he is serious about the task, must conduct his activities with the intention of achieving some kind of outcome. In teaching, where the achievement is effected through another person—the pupil or student—the outcome is more or less indirect. Saying that the educator has an aim or set of aims is just a less cumbersome way of describing this state of affairs.

However, as Peters pointed out 20 years ago, the application of 'aims of education' is more problematic than this. Peters argued, surely correctly, that aims do not just manifest themselves in outcomes: if held seriously, they must in some way be built into the processes of education themselves (e.g. Peters, 1959). There is, in relation to higher education, more to be said on this matter.

Before this 'something more' can be set out, we need to consider some of the features of the idea of higher education itself. Only a brief thumb-nail sketch can be offered here, since (as I emphasised earlier) the focus of this paper is the concept of aims in relation to higher education rather than the concept of higher education. Some excursion in the direction of the concept of higher education itself is necessary, however, since the argument—over the nature of aims in relation to higher education—depends on what we understand higher education to be.

Over recent years, we have often been told that there is now no single academic community, but that it has fragmented into many intellectual sub-cultures. Clark Kerr, in his *The Uses of the University* (1972), in outlining the many and varied functions which the modern university has taken on, described the modern university "as a series of individual faculty entrepreneurs held together by a common grievance over parking". And there is empirical evidence which supports this way of thinking (Becher, 1987) in terms of the formation and fragmentation of disciplinary cultures with their own values, views on the nature of knowledge, styles of research and so forth. Indeed, at times of institutional crisis, it appears that it is the disciplinary cultures which become dominant in the intra-institutional political struggles, rather than any sense of collegial responsibility for the future of the institution (Walford, 1987). The notion of 'academic community' turns out to have little empirical substance. Those discipline-specific research interests of academics have their counterpart in curriculum settings. As a result, curricular aims—where they are spelt out—are usually specific to the student's chosen subject area (compare the kinds of competences that graduates in computing or archaeology or civil engineering are expected to acquire). There must be a doubt, therefore, as to whether 'aims' can be spelt out in any way that will serve as an overarching description of higher education. In other words, it begins to look as if efforts to capture any single 'idea' of higher education as it is today must be fruitless; in practice, there are as many 'ideas' as there are disciplinary communities.

However, the task of specifying general aims of higher education should not be abandoned precipitously. Reading the literature on higher education, including surveys of students' reasons for entering higher education, and simply listening to the way in which educators in higher education describe and account for their activities (whether at graduation ceremonies, at conferences, in the process of validating courses or in public statements), suggests some commonly-held underlying concerns.

The kinds of overarching aims that can be detected in everyday perceptions about higher education seem, if anything, to include the development of the student's intellectual skills or academic competences. Where these are specified, some of the following are typically enlisted as key aspects of the student's development: critical abilities, especially the propensity to be self-critical; the ability to analyse and evaluate an argument; the capacity to relate what is learnt to a broad context and to make relevant connections; the willingness to accept the rules of rational inquiry; and the self-motivation of the student, such as to go on learning and being self-critical independently of any extrinsic influence.

This list of attributes begins to fill out the concept of higher education. If there is an underlying idea, it is that of the development of the student's autonomy as a self-sufficient rational inquirer. Following a process of higher education, a graduate (whatever his/her field of study) should have not just an understanding of the field—its key concepts, theories and findings—and be able to carry out the relevant operations, but should be able to engage with the field with a certain degree of detachment. He/she should be able to maintain a distance from the field, and be able to evaluate and be critical of it.

This is what might be described as the 'emancipatory' concept of higher education, and it appears to underlie the history, over the last 150 years, of the western idea of higher education itself (Barnett, 1985). These notions are now so built into our understanding of higher education that they have become constitutive of the concept of higher education. They are not so much aims of higher education as essential conditions of it.

The process of higher education: Action-at-a-distance

A number of implications flow from this necessarily sketchy account of the concept of higher education. Firstly, these essential conditions are realised through and by the student. The point deserves a little elaboration, because it is important to the argument here. The fulfilment of these conditions has to be, essentially, the student's own achievement not only because it is the student's self-realisation which is at stake. The emancipatory concept of higher education looks to the student making his/her way in the world intellectually. It presupposes the ultimate possibility of the student becoming self-directed and self-critical, developing the competences to make an independent contribution as a participatory member of the academic community. This is not to say that those competences have actually to be exercised, but that they could be if the student, as graduate, chose. (The use here of the term 'competence' follows that of Chomsky, 1968, in his contrast with 'behaviour' (Chs. 1 and 3).) But if the processes of higher education are directed towards the formation of the student's own judgements, ideas and intellectual achievements then it is the student who has to realise these conditions. This is many-sided: following the work of Habermas (1979, pp. 2–3), we can observe that participation in a rational discourse places demands on its participants not only of truthfulness, intelligibility and appropriateness, but also sincerity. In other words (taking particularly the first and the last of those requirements), there has to be a significant element of personal commitment to and involvement in their own truth claims on the part of individuals. Part of the hallmark of a genuinely higher education is that the student does indeed emerge with the confidence to put forward truth claims and the ability to substantiate them.

If all this is granted, it appears to make the educator in the context of higher education redundant. There is some truth in this: members of staff in institutions of higher education do often carry an exaggerated sense of their own importance. As a result, courses—especially in the physical sciences—are often unreasonably congested. (Students, too, often suffer from a corresponding overestimate of what can be done for them—a situation which is far from new. Up to the time he went up to Oxford in 1832, Mark Pattison—later to have perhaps the single greatest influence on nineteenth century Oxford—had been largely self-taught in Classics. In his memoirs, though, Pattison recollected how disappointed he had been on the standards at Oriel at that time: "Having had next to no teaching at home, I exaggerated in imagination what a teacher could do for me"; Pattison, 1969, p. 53.)

However, the conceptual point is not that the educator is actually superfluous to requirements in higher education, rather that in so far as higher education is an achievement concept (cf. Peters, 1967, p. 2), it is the student who does the achieving. Far from being redundant, the educator can play a significant role in assisting the student on the way to that achievement. There is, therefore, an achievement on the part of the educator in being effective in this way. But the key achievement—that of the development of the student's academic competences—has, in a particular sense, to be that of the student himself or herself. For it is the student's own accomplishments that count.

The educator has, therefore, in the context of higher education, an indirect role to play. Even though a strong interaction may often be helpful to a student (and certain figures may have an effect on students which lasts for the rest of their lives), it remains the student's particular response and contribution that are important.

The close and influential interaction between teacher and taught that often occurs in higher education is conceptually misleading. For in reality, it is a case of action at a distance. The achievement by the student of his/her intellectual independence does not happen simply as a result of a cloistered equivalent of the laying-on-of-hands, since it is the student's own work that is crucial. No one can achieve that for the student: the attainment of that intellectual maturity is, ultimately, a matter of the student's own perseverance (Hallden, 1987). No matter whether the number taking the student's course is large or small; or whether there is much staff–student contact or little (as in the predominantly distance-learning mode of The Open University); or whether teaching methods rely heavily on group work (Jaques, 1984): in the end, the student's realisation of the promise of higher education is the result of his/her own endeavours. There is an essential aloneness in the role of student, as indeed there is in being a full member of the academic community.

This aloneness emerges contingently in such phenomena as problems over studying and examinations which many students experience, which not infrequently lead to psychological disturbances. It is also apparent in the language of higher education, where, although we use the term 'teacher', we perhaps just as often talk of 'lecturer' or 'tutor'. Without examining the differences in role implied by these terms, we can notice that part of their meaning lies in that they do not stand for a simple model of transmission between teacher and taught. The processes of higher education are not like that. On the contrary, they are testimony to the point that, in higher education, the staff are but one kind of resource on which students can draw. They certainly are an important resource, but it is debatable to what extent they are necessary to the student's success. The development of distance learning—again, notably in the British Open University—suggests that their importance can be overplayed.

For many students, the most important resource in higher education, so far as their own development is concerned, remains the library and particularly the book-stock, despite the considerable acquisitions of new media to be found in some academic libraries. For, especially in the person-oriented disciplines, it is the student's growing awareness of a literature and his/her personal response to it that is important. And this is so whether the relevant written words are readily available in books or whether as in some subject areas—especially in the natural and medical sciences—the important written words are to be found in the latest journals. The number of titles on the shelves of an institution of higher education, and its ability to replace them with up-to-date stock, remain important indices of its status as an academic institution, even in an age of the lecture notes and other handouts available to students today.

It is worth observing, though, that the student's success is not a straightforward function of the number of words that he/she has read or remembered. Rather, it is the degree to which the student is able to form a personal evaluation of what has been learnt, or in other words, the extent to which the student has become independent of that learning.

Taking aim in higher education

From this discussion, it emerges that talk of aims of higher education—if by that we mean the aims of the teacher—is a misleading depiction of the processes of higher education. Strictly, the teacher's aims, while not exactly beside the point, are not *to* the point, since the achievement of the aims of higher education (to use the phrase for the moment) must be to a large extent, as we have seen, the work of the student. A significant degree of responsibility for the educational process is borne by the student her/himself.

To this it might be countered that, in that case, the aims of higher education could be interpreted as referring to the student's aims. But this is doubly misleading. First, it is doubtful and certainly debatable whether the student needs to have any set of aims in front of her/him in order to be able to realise, them. The success lies simply in the student achieving the emancipatory promise of higher education. It is quite possible for the student to be successful in this sense without having had any such aims. He/she simply presses on with his/her work, aiming rather to improve the relevant skills, and understanding. Here, certainly, the educator has a role to play, not so much in imparting knowledge, but in developing the student's understanding, and abilities to appraise and comment on what has been learnt.

Secondly, talk of the student's aims is misleading in another sense because aims as held by *any* actor in an educational process counting as higher education are also not to the point. For the aims of higher education (referred to earlier as the emancipatory concept of higher education) are not one set of aims in the sense that the processes of higher education could be pointed in any other direction. They are simply a spelling out of the presuppositions of the concept of higher education.

Does all this mean that talk of aims of higher education should be avoided entirely? Not necessarily. It has already been said that an educator has to have a set of aims. We have also seen that aims of higher education (those which are actually elaborated) are contested; so it is important that educators in higher education know where they stand. At the same time, within the framework of any particular set of aims which he/she holds, the educator has the key supplementary task of arranging the conditions to give the students the most favourable opportunity of achieving the emancipatory promise of higher education. The educator should, to be effective, have both the essential conditions of higher education before him as aims, and the particular aims which he holds. We can, therefore, legitimately retain the vocabulary of aims in the context of higher education, with the proviso that we remember that the educator cannot achieve either kind of aims directly, for the achievement belongs to the student.

In the context of higher education, the idea of 'aim' is, in some senses, particularly apt since, in general, once one has taken aim and fired a shot, one is normally powerless to affect the outcome. In other words, the tasks of aiming and firing are separate from the outcome: while the former can affect the latter, the latter is not a simple function of the former. Various factors may intervene to prevent the missile reaching its intended target; and it may even reach its target in spite of rather than because of the accuracy of the initial shot. We can see these occurrences in higher education. For example, students sometimes emerge with lively critical minds at the end of their course in a way which seems quite mysterious, given the dull and undemanding experience put their way by those responsible for their programme of studies. The explanation is that the students were somehow able to gain access to a wider and more challenging experience, either through their own efforts or through their extramural encounters (for example, in a training placement or in study abroad).

An appropriate home from which the term 'aim' might be taken is therefore not the military setting, where outcomes are reasonably predictable, but rather an activity like snooker. There, one cannot aim directly at the pot. Instead, one aims the cue (white) ball at an intervening object (the coloured ball). The direction of aim is seldom in line with the pot, and even where it is, the immediate focus has to be on the contact with the cue ball, rather than achieving the pot. At the same time, though, the competent player will also have in mind the further implications of the shot in the receding background, in the course of addressing the cue ball and in making the shot. There will be, in other words, an immediate set of concerns which interact with a set of larger, though less specific, strategies.

Similarly in higher education: the tutor hopes to set the student off on the right path, and hopes to see the student being successful. Once the contact has been made, the outcome is to a considerable degree unpredictable; the tutor cannot fully control it, for it is the student that is or is not successful.

It follows that if the student is unsuccessful—if he/she fails the course—the staff cannot be held directly responsible, though questions can certainly be asked (and should be) about the support given to the student. In short, the tutor–student contact should enable the student to take off on his/her own, so that the student reaches the target him/herself. And, depending on the path that the individual student takes, the tutor should modify his/her actions with the intention of securing the student's success.

Using another metaphor, we can say that aiming in higher education is more like trying to hit the end point of a stick in moving water. One cannot successfully aim directly at the target: one has to make allowances for intervening factors and hope for the best; and the water may be a little murky. To some extent, the tutor has to aim 'blind'.

It follows that in a course of study in higher education (as distinct from courses in vocational further education), the student is obliged to construct the educational process partly by him/herself. In effect, the curriculum as it is experienced is the result of a negotiation between the student and the staff responsible. This is obviously the case in instances of open learning, where the programme of study is to some degree under the control of the student. Here, the degrees in independent study offered by the University of Lancaster and North East London Polytechnic are the most striking examples, since the principle of independent study governs the student's programme. But the general point is that all programmes of study in higher education, to be worthy of the description '*higher* education', are in some sense under the control of the student. This is so because, as we saw earlier, there is a conceptual gap between teacher and taught or, more formally, between the accomplishments of the teacher and those of the taught. In the end, the student has to give something of himself if he is to develop those competences. Ultimately, the student has to become independent of, and stand outside, the curriculum on offer, and not remain a relatively passive assimilator of it.

If this account is plausible, if the connection between the aims held by members of staff and their realisation in their students is so indirect, how do staff in higher education improve their effectiveness (that is, improve their 'aim')? Quite simply, improvement comes first through critical reflection, on the part of the staff concerned, on the total process of teaching and learning. Processes of systematic evaluation are more advanced in the public sector of British higher education (Barnett, 1987), but they are developing with more rigour in universities (CVCP, 1987). The conceptual point here is that the development of systematic processes of course-evaluation is entirely justified, because (on the argument here) staff in higher education cannot aim directly at the target—that of an autonomous, self-critical, 'competent' student—but rather can only *subsequently* appraise the effectiveness of their efforts and accordingly make adjustments that seem sensible in the light of all the available evidence.

Higher education can take place, however, and be achieved, even without a designated educator as such. Admittedly, in higher education, students embark on pre-established programmes offered by individual institutions of higher education; but the conceptual point is that the student's experience cannot be entirely pre-set. This is recognised in practice through the time which is at the student's own disposal.

Conclusions

From the argument here, certain practical conclusions stand out for the way in which processes of higher education should be conducted. The first is that the key factor—the principal educator—in the process of higher education is the student. A little modesty on the part of tutors, lecturers and other members of staff in institutions of higher education would often be in order. There should, in other words, be a self-denying ordinance amongst staff. It might encourage those responsible not to overpack the curriculum with timetabled sessions, whether in the laboratory or in the lecture theatre (Bligh, 1971). Secondly, it suggests that the student's learning should be accompanied wherever possible by an encouragement to form his/her own judgements or suggest possible procedures of his/her own (for example, within programmes of professional education): the learning, even 'at the frontiers of knowledge', should be seen simply as a vehicle through which the student comes to be critical, and to be self-critical. Lastly, the course team need to recognise the value of systematic evaluation of the course, to obtain feedback, and to be in an informed position to modify the course as seems appropriate to enable the students more effectively to pursue the aims of higher education.

So, returning to our opening question: 'Does higher education have any aims?' Yes, but its aims are less fixed points we steer towards, than compass bearings we steer by.

Chapter 8
Convergence in higher education
The strange case of 'Entrepreneurialism'

(from Higher Education Management and Policy, 2005, 17 (3) 51–64)

Outline

Prima facie, in the context of higher education, 'entrpreneurialism' offers an example of systems of higher education converging across the world. However, entrepreneurialism is not undifferentiated but is to be found in different modes. Various axes identified in the paper offer spectra of entrepreneurialism and two are picked out for close inspection; on the one hand, hard-soft forms of entrepreneurialism and, on the other hand, forms of entrepreneurialism that are set in the context of strong states or strong markets. Set against each other, these two axes depict four forms of entrepreneurialism: civic, hesitant, unbridled, and curtailed. These forms of entrepreneurialism can be understood as making possible or limiting alternative modes of knowledge travel. Far from heralding convergence, entrepreneurialism turns out to be a metaphor for differences of academic identity and even of academic being. These differences are so profound that they point to value choices as to desirable forms of academic life itself.

Introduction

I want, in this chapter, to open up a space for reflecting on the matter of "convergence" or, one should perhaps say, the alleged matter of convergence in higher education. The basic idea, I take it, is that systems of higher education are converging around the world. We have here, therefore, an example of the globalisation thesis.

The idea of convergence is, of course, non-specific: in order for the term to bear any weight, we need to specify the features of higher education systems that are supposed to be converging. The development of mass higher education, emergence of markets, the opening of multiple income streams, a lessening of state involvement in higher education and a greater specificity and diversity of institutional mission are, surely, part of the convergence thesis. But these features of contemporary higher education do not just happen; they are characteristically part of a new "neo-liberal" policy framework. Here, the dominant idea perhaps is that universities have resources and services that can be made available to a range of paying clients, or customers – and so the state can play a lesser part in the conduct of higher education. No longer are academic activities to be prized for themselves, for their own internal value; now value is to be judged through the working out of an academic marketplace.

It is against the background of this "academic capitalism" (Slaughter and Leslie, 1997) that we surely have to place the emergence of the phenomenon of "entrepreneurialism". However, the concept of entrepreneurialism is itself far from clear: a wide range of modes of practice within universities may count as "entrepreneurial". In this paper, I want to tease out some modes of entrepreneurialism and to use, as one device, the idea of "knowledge travel". This idea, we shall see, cannot hope to exhaust the idea of entrepreneurialism but it can set up some perplexing suggestions. One suggestion may be that, far from being a vehicle for convergence, entrepreneurialism may turn out to be a vehicle for increasing diversity in higher education.

Entrepreneurialism and risk

The entrepreneur is a go-between. He attempts to move or even take an entity X from point A to point B, and there is some risk involved in the venture. He is willing to stake himself, his reputation and his capital, in the venture; and he may be able to persuade a third party also to risk their capital and their reputation.

Capital, as Bourdieu (2000) reminds us, does not have to be financial. In the case of the university, it might be cultural, intellectual, or social capital that could also be at stake; that is being put at risk. The entrepreneurial university, in principle, could be engaged in risking any of these forms of capital. But (and in keeping with entrepreneurs in general), the entrepreneurial university is not so much concerned to place its capital at risk so much as to generate some kind of return on its efforts. Characteristically, it wants its capital to grow, whether that is financial, intellectual, social or cultural. The financial risk, though, has attracted the most attention (and not only within the Vice-Chancellor's senior management team) but the other forms of risk deserve at least equal consideration for they do pose considerable risks in their own right.

Ultimately, what is at stake is "mission risk", in which the university lays on the line its image, reputation, and positioning – all of which may be global. In intellectual risk, the university risks its key resource, its intellectual capital. If its professoriate is unhappy with certain aspects of the new entrepreneurialism – for example, being asked themselves to be marketers and to attract "customers" for courses or even to design new market-sensitive courses – the global academic labour market lies waiting to capture the university's dissidents (although since academic entrepreneurialism is a global phenomenon, any such dissident may find that the academic grass is not that much greener elsewhere and may quickly become a returning dissident).

We speak of entrepreneurs not just in the world of business as such but also, for example, in the world of entertainment. Insofar as the entrepreneur is to be found in higher education, is the connection that is being implied that of higher education as a business or higher education as entertainment? It could be both, of course. Even as entertainment, higher education is becoming a business.

In this paper, I cannot trace the potential workings through of all these forms of capital. Instead, I shall focus on entrepreneurship as it may be exhibited through the accumulation of financial and intellectual capital; and I want to consider these two forms of capital together.

To say of a university that it is entrepreneurial is, we have already implied, to invoke sentiments of undertaking, venture (or "enterprise" [Marginson and Considine, 2000]) and risk. There is a definite undertaking (or several undertakings), it involves some movement and change, and the change in question has elements of risk. Such a university is prepared, is willing, to become other than it is, and this at both surface and deep levels. At a surface level, its new ventures may take it into uncharted paths; after all, almost by definition, the venture has not been essayed before, certainly by this institution and possibly not by any other institution.

A university may decide, for example, to establish computer-based variants of all of its programmes of study, or even determine substantially to switch its portfolio in that way. This will incur high up-front costs, not least in the training and development of its faculty, quite apart from the installation of the more physical infrastructure. The venture, undertaken systematically, has profound implications for the university: its pedagogies change, its educational relationships with its students change, the relationships that the students have with each other change (the students may become more interactive among themselves) and the pedagogical identity of the tutors changes (less a visible authority, aided by an immediate physical presence, and more an enabler of learning tasks and opportunities).

It follows that, in addition to the surface changes that entrepreneurialism heralds, changes also occur at a deep level. Indeed, in our present example, the university changes as such. It is not just that the students are less visible on campus; now, this university is marked by new kinds of identity (of both students and tutors), relationships and communicative structures.

Through entrepreneurialism, therefore, universities add to their repertoire of undertakings and undergo fairly visible *performative change* but, in the process, they may also undergo *constitutive change*. Such constitutive change is not captured by talk of mission change. On the cards is the prospect that the university becomes not even just a different university but a different *kind* of university. A question that opens up, therefore, (but one which we cannot address here) is this: under conditions of entrepreneurialism, are there any limits to the changes that might be wrought upon the university, even as it continues to claim the title of "university"? After all, the entrepreneur, we may take it, will not be spending much time reminding himself of the "idea of the university" as it has unfolded over the centuries but instead will be keen to usher in change: the entrepreneur's time horizons are largely in the future rather than in the past. It may just be that "anything goes" in this entrepreneurial dispensation.

I cannot follow that thought here. I want, instead, to focus on the idea of risk, for this is a surely a necessary component of entrepreneurialism: the "entrepreneurial university" is a university at risk (*cf.* Beck, 1992). Risk here is multileveled. At the surface or performative level, the risk may not come off: the students may not materialise for those computer-based programmes. Human and physical resources are at risk (as we have seen) but there are opportunity costs as well. The capital – intellectual and economic – may be at risk: the university may run into a "deficit" situation; staff may leave the institution as they are called upon to take on their new pedagogical identities (and undergo "training" in the process). But there is risk, as we noted, embedded at deeper levels. In the changing of its pedagogies, its academic and student identities, and its educational relationships, unpredictable changes are let loose (Again, the unpredictability is a logical feature of "risk"). And, having been let loose, such changes may be irreversible. Yes, the university may decide to return to conventional curricula and reassert itself as a conventional university, but human identities and institutional positioning, and their associated perceptions, values and orientations – both internal and external – once dislodged, will not easily be morphed back to earlier configurations.

The entrepreneurial university, therefore, is engaged on an especially risky course. It may be risking more than it understands, for it may be risking itself. In coming to be a different kind of institution, it risks coming to live by new sets of institutional values. The risk may still be felt to be worthwhile, however; although that consideration implies that the risk to the university's value structure has actually been identified and been assessed (and this is not something that is easily accomplished in the mode of "risk analysis" now being enjoined upon UK institutions of higher education). Both, therefore, an ethics of risk and a politics of risk attach to the entrepreneurial university (*cf.* Beck, 1998; Franklin, 1998).

The entrepreneurial university is between states of being, but no new stable state of being is available. A particular form of performative change may be identified as a goal and it may even be reached (the new campus is opened, perhaps even in another country) but the entrepreneurial university is never at rest; and this is its characteristic mode of being, a restless mode of being that is part of its self-understanding. The entrepreneurial university delights in risk, but does it understand the risks that it is taking?

Entrepreneurialism and convergence

Entrepreneurialism comes in many shapes and sizes. The colloquialisms are especially justified here: entrepreneurialism takes on both shape and size. If it makes sense to ask of a university: "Is this an entrepreneurial university?" it is also a consideration as to the extent and character of the entrepreneurial *presence* on campus. It may be present only to a marginal extent – in some departments, say, or as rhetoric emerging from the Senior Management Team – or it may have come to characterise an institution to a significant extent. So shape and size may be helpful metaphors in depicting the places and extent of entrepreneurialism on campus. We can envisage the university as a set of spaces and consider the penetration into those spaces of the entrepreneurial ethos and its practical manifestations.

How might those spaces be taken up by entrepreneurialism? I want to suggest two *sets of distinctions* that may help us understand the character of spaces that may exhibit an entrepreneurial presence.

1. Hard–soft entrepreneurialism.
2. Strong state – strong markets.

By "hard" and "soft" entrepreneurialism, I distinguish between those forms of entrepreneurialism where there is a definite intention to secure an economic return (preferably "profit") as against those forms where the economic drive is much less evident or is absent altogether. After all, entrepreneurialism can be found in relation to different forms of academic capital (as we noted earlier); economic capital need not feature especially strongly. What is necessary, for entrepreneurialism to be present (so we also noted) is that there be some measure of *risk* involved. The university may risk its reputation, its intellectual capital, its position, its ethos, its educational character, its role as a cultural good and so on. Why, then, restrict the appellation "hard entrepreneurialism" to the economic form? Because the economic form may not merely modify but even corrupt other forms: under market conditions, for example, the pedagogical relationship may be damaged by the undue presence of money: the transactions between teacher and taught may be irredeemably distorted, as the student becomes a customer seeking a return on her own financial investment.

I want to set off this idea of soft–hard entrepreneurialism against a sense of the presence of markets. And here, I want to distinguish between open markets and controlled markets, between situations where institutions offer the services they wish to offer at prices they themselves determine to whomsoever customers they choose and situations where any of these three aspects of markets (services, prices and customers) are subject to some kind of control. It is surely manifestly evident that both open and controlled markets exist to a greater or larger extent and that there is no sharp boundary between the two situations: open and controlled markets present us with a second axis, therefore.

In speaking of the presence of markets, clearly, too, the state must loom into view: these days, open markets or controlled markets *both* arise characteristically as a result of state policies and actions in respect of higher education (It is because the state in the United Kingdom, despite the ideological trappings of introducing the market to higher education, remains a strong player in the evolution of higher education in the United Kingdom, that we have to resort to talk of a "quasi-market"). In picking out the presence of markets to help our understanding of entrepreneurialism in higher education, "the state", therefore, cannot be far from our analysis. However, we cannot go deeply into the state–market relationship here: simply unraveling the two scales – of soft–hard entrepreneurialism and of open–controlled markets – offers us sufficient complexities for our present purposes.

We can place these two scales against each other and so (Figure 8.1) illuminate the character of the spaces of the entrepreneurial university.

In quadrant (a), we have the case of an entrepreneurial university – or it might be, say, an entrepreneurial department – that is keen to develop and promote itself in a relatively free market. It is *proactive:* its music

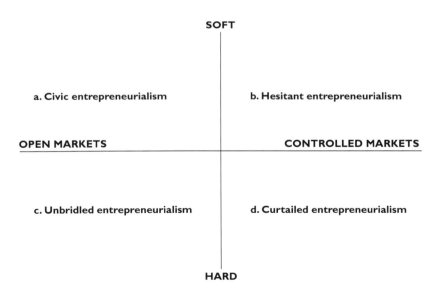

Figure 8.1 Forms of entrepreneurialism in higher education

department, say, is active in the multi-ethnic community, exploring different music traditions as a way of developing multi-ethnic relationships in the community; its archaeology department is both widening intellectually to forge links with other departments (chemistry, computing, anthropology, statistics, anatomy, biochemistry) but is also engaged with projects in the wider society, perhaps on television, taking advantage of the interests in archaeology among the general public. There may be income streams attaching to these activities but that does not provide a motivation or criterion of success. The level of *risk*, here, is relatively low but attaches to esteem (in seeming to "sell out" to academic minds of a purer persuasion), to opportunity costs in pursuing ventures that end in blind alleys and also in running against the mainstream such that traditional academic outputs (in the form of papers in learned journals) might not be so readily available and, thereby, diminish a department's potential in formal national evaluations, especially but not only in research. Let us term this form of entrepreneurialism *civic entrepreneurialism*.

In quadrant (b), we have the case, at least in principle, of a university or department that is willing to essay forth (as in (*a*)) but where institutions are steered in the direction of an understanding of higher education as a public good. It may be that institutions are encouraged to compete with each other for students but that those institutions are also, at the same time, expected to demonstrate that they are each playing their parts in offering educational opportunities to applicants from across the social class range. Or it may be that institutions are encouraged to be engaged in research – or even "third stream" activities – but that, in being so engaged, they are expected also to demonstrate ways in which society itself benefits from such activities. Or it may be that the state's marketisation agenda has to take account of other state agendas such as "quality" (where a state's quality regime plays its part alongside market disciplines) or "selectivity" (where a wish to deploy the state's resources to maximum effect limits the extent to which institutions can be active in particular activities, such as the teaching of students in "costly" subjects, the registering of research students and being involved in research itself, especially in science and technologically-based subjects). In all these ways, the market would be being limited quite deliberately by the state for reasons that were connected with relevant public goods. Public capital, in other words, may vie with economic capital.

Under such circumstances, the incentives for an institution actually to become engaged in entrepreneurial activities would be rather few, for here, after all, the risks would be greater than in (*a*) but the potential gains would be smaller. An institution might here be interested, in principle, in being entrepreneurial but it would surely hesitate in going in such a direction. Accordingly, let us call any such entrepreneurialism a *hesitant entrepreneurialism*.

In quadrant (c), we have a form of entrepreneurialism in which money as such counts. The message would go out to all members of staff that they needed to generate, say, three times their salary, both to cover the institution's overheads but also to secure a "profit" for the institution. Here, the institution would understand itself to be a major source of exploitable knowledge capital in the wider "knowledge economy" and it would seek to deploy that capital effectively and so secure the maximum financial return. It would set monetary targets for third-stream activities in its corporate plans and a culture would be developed, department by department, in which ventures were created and seen through that were intended to generate income (and, indeed, profit). Here, too, it would have every incentive to act in this way because, in this setting, the state would have opened markets to the higher education sector in the fullest way, such that our institution could charge whatever it felt it wished to charge, taking its own view of the market and the market attractiveness of its knowledge products and services. Call this an *unbridled entrepreneurialism*.

In quadrant (d), we see institutions that are playing out their entrepreneurialism in an environment in which the state in particular is managing the market, such that the most glaring excesses of unbridled entrepreneurialism were curbed. Either the amount of profit or the range of goods and services over which institutions could extend their entrepreneurial inclinations would be limited. Institutions might have their missions limited, third stream activities might be forbidden – or any monies derived from such "third stream" activities as additional income might be discounted against other core funding from the state – or institutions might not be permitted to charge the market rate either for their teaching or for their research (or both).

In circumstances such as those just sketched out, the incentives to engage in entrepreneurial activities would be limited by the state controlling the market (as in *(b)*) but (unlike *(b)*, where public or social goods were coming into play in the steering of the market) here, the market would be curtailed through the acting out of the state's own economic interests. Call this a *curtailed entrepreneurialism*.

From this analytical exercise, we may see straightaway that entrepreneurialism may appear in different forms. Of course, in practice, hardly any one institution or even any one department is going to find itself situated in any one single quadrant: it will tend to spread, to some extent, across the box spaces; but there may be a dominant point or fulcrum, even amid the fuzziness of the outline, around which such an institution or department will be positioned.

I make just one other observation here. Little, if anything, for our purposes, hangs on the two axes. Other axes could have been chosen. For example, we might have plotted the following two axes against each other:

1. *Extractive–Providing*; where the axes indicate institutions that are using their entrepreneurial activities to extract capital/profit from their environment as against institutions that are seeing their entpreneurialism as a means of gifting their resources to the wider society and so adding value (instead of extracting it) from the wider society; a distinction, we may say, between *exploitative entrepreneurialism* and *beneficent entrepreneurialism*.
2. *External mission–Internal mission*; where the institution is focused primarily on the external environment on the one hand and is seeking to engage anew with and *in* the wider society, as against an institution that is seeking to be entrepreneurial through extending its inner academic activities (where academics would continue to give external talks but would seek a fee on each occasion or where academics might give advice to governmental committees). This distinction, we may say, would help us to distinguish an *other-oriented entrepreneurialism* from an *inner-oriented entrepreneurialism*.

I shall not follow those two sets of distinctions here. I offer them to emphasise the point that we have already made that entrepreneurialism comes in many varieties but that, also, those varieties may be distinguished through different kinds of structuring dimensions. Those structuring dimensions are dimensions that we place, in our analytical endeavours, on our readings of higher education; they are not naturally there in the world to be read off it. At the same time, they serve to open up or to chart *entrepreneurial spaces* of different kinds, with different textures, in the university.

Two observations follow from that reflection, obvious as it may be. The first is that we should abandon talk of, for example, "the self-reliant university", or "the adaptive university" or "the innovative university" *unless* we can also supply the structuring conditions that lead to one kind of university or another. Without some understanding of the structures at work (that is, the dimensions or axes that prompt or hinder such forms of university life), such phrases, beguiling as they may seem to help us understand forms of entrepreneurialism, really do no serious analytical work. Without that analytical work, the "archaeology" of the concept and nature of entrepreneurialism will remain mysterious.

My other point takes us, at last, to the title of this section, *Entrepreneurialism and convergence*; and it is the main point of my paper, elementary as it may be. It is now clear that despite the possibly apparent obviousness of the idea that "entrepreneurialism" can be readily understood an example of convergence – the tendency of higher education sectors across the world to come to resemble each other – it may actually herald much more difference that it heralds convergence. Particularity rather than universality: that is the lesson of the emergence of entrepreneurialism in higher education.

Entrepreneurialism and knowledge travel

I now want to follow up these admittedly schematic observations by filling them out through an exploration of the idea and metaphor of "knowledge travel".

Whatever changes are befalling higher education worldwide – and, amid the neo-liberal revolution and the onset of "academic capitalism", they are many – universities remain knowledge institutions. Knowledge itself may be changing, but still knowledge remains important. It is not just that that Mode 1 knowledge is giving way to Mode 2 (Gibbons *et al.*, 1994); rather, the university has long been a repository of different forms of knowledge and those multiple forms are being challenged, developed, and modified as the university is beset with proliferating forms of knowledge. I cannot, however, go into that matter here.

Accordingly, we may understand entrepreneurialism to be an entreaty to academics and the academic community to engage in forms of "knowledge travel" (*cf.* Barnett and Phipps, 2005). What is entrepreneurialism if, at its core, it is none other than an enjoinder to academics to use their knowledge in new ways, to find new ways of communicating their knowledge, to seek new forms of knowledge production, to establish new knowledge partners and so on and so forth. This is to travel, epistemologically speaking, in a new way. This is knowledge travel.

It follows, too, that the different structuring principles that we have encountered will lend themselves characteristically to different forms of knowledge travel. Is one travelling with an eye on the economic return on the journey or is one engaged on the journey because it may be intrinsically interesting? Is one engaged on the journey because, through it, one may get to know others and speak their languages better, or is one engaged in it simply as a form of personal aggrandisement?

Knowledge travel occurs in various modes, each of which *may* come into play amid entrepreneurialism:

Mode (*a*): This is an *academic form of knowledge travel*, and is a mode that itself takes two forms: either the crossing of existing knowledge fields through multidisciplinary and interdisciplinary ventures or through the development of new knowledge fields (Strathern, 2004). Both these forms of knowledge travel take place across knowledge fields *within* the academy. Here, we may envisage – as academic and ethical virtues – both epistemological courage, as our knowledge travellers venture out into what are for them new knowledge lands and, particularly in multidisciplinary enquiry, academic hospitality, as they are received by academics in different academic tribes.

Mode (*b*) travel – where the knowledge traveller crosses into the practical domain. This form of knowledge travel is prompted where academic entrepreneurialism is addressed to the solving of practical problems. This knowledge traveller is going to be active in the world and, we may observe, will necessarily take on a hybrid academic identity that consists of different relationships with the world being held together: the contemplative and the practical; understanding and action-in-the-world.

Mode (c) travel – where connections are made with the public realm (as, in our grid above, in quadrant (a)): this will call for communicative dexterity within language, though "language" here can be spoken and visual/representational as well as written. Interactions with local groups in the community, professional groups, the media and consumer groups: civic entrepreneurialism will call for productive engagement with all such manner of interest groups, each with their communicative challenges. Judgements will have to be made as to how to "pitch things" for an audience: the style required for a television film may be quite different from engagement in a local community project.

Of course, in practice, many – or, indeed, all – of these forms of knowledge travel may run together. A group drawn from a university department of engineering offering specialist advice in the construction of a huge project in another country may well find themselves involved in interdisciplinary, practical and intercultural forms of knowledge travel. In turn, our engineering entrepreneurs may find themselves having to attend to their mode of self-presentation, their gestures, their dress sense and their communicative tone.

Ultimately, entrepreneurialism calls for complex academic identities. What starts as a purely epistemological matter turns out to be an ontological matter: what counts for effective entrepreneurialism is the mode of being that academic entrepreneurs are willing to embrace. If academics show a reluctance to take on an entrepreneurial spirit, it may reflect a reluctance to depart from or even to widen their state of academic being. Resistant academics may be exhibiting not just an epistemological conservatism but also an ontological self-limitation; and the latter may have some right on its side. The idea of "academic integrity" may just come into view here.

But for those brave souls who are willing to become academic entrepreneurs, to venture into new epistemological lands, academic identities may be lost but they may also be reshaped in a richer, more complex form. The logic here, of course, is that these epistemological entrepreneurs live happily with fluidity, a state of perpetual ontological voyaging. One just never knows which group or community one will be engaging with, from one day to another; one never knows the adjustments and negotiations one will have to make, in order to affect some kind of rapprochement. Our knowledge entrepreneurs have to think, and translate, and represent themselves in new and subtle ways "on their feet"; and, very often, literally so at times.

Academic entrepreneurs have to be able to empathise with new audiences. They are perpetual translators, effecting translations of their ideas, in new modes, for others to take them on board in settings that are new for all concerned; and they effect translations of others' work and language in assimilating them into their own language and frameworks. This is ontologically taxing; knowledge entrepreneurs will always be willing to go on remaking themselves in a continuing process of accommodation and assimilation. In turn, the individual changes.

Does the individual merely change or does the individual grow? Or is the academic entrepreneur a carrier of system-wide change that is enhancing of the system or corrupting of the system? Fortunately, although our earlier grid may be suggestive of some answers to these questions, we do not have to tackle those matters here.

What we can conclude here, however, is the more prosaic observation that knowledge travel is endemic to academic entrepreneurialism but that it can move in directions that are so different from each other that they are, in effect, quite different forms of epistemic travel. The mode of academic identity being called forth may be hugely varying. The journeys go in different directions, encounter quite different communities and call for different languages and forms of intertextuality.

The forms of knowledge travel and inter-communication in which the engineers engage, with their eye on definite time-schedules, and a precise design problem, is a long way from ecologists engaging in a long-term project with Amazonian Indians which again is a long distance from archaeologists engaging with local councillors and planners on the occasion of a major "find" on an industrial site and turning the find into a museum of national importance. These forms of knowledge travel, we may observe too, overlap in intricate ways with our earlier classifications of entrepreneuriliasm (hard/soft; open/controlled markets; exploitative–beneficent entrepreneurialism; other-inner oriented entrepreneurialism).

Conclusions

Our theme, even if it has barely surfaced, has been that of entrepreneurialism as a possible example of convergence. Is entrepreneurialism an example of the apparent tendency of higher education systems, worldwide, to ape each other? If we can see signs of entrepreneurialism taking off, however sketchily, in systems of higher education all across the world, does that help to confirm the convergence thesis?

Our analysis has shown that, short of a large number of qualifying statements, no such judgement can be made. Behind "entrepreneurialism" stands all manner of academic identity, of academic movement, of interplays between knowledge fields, of political and social values, and ultimately of human being itself. A term such as entrepreneurialism that just may seem to offer some confirmation of the "convergence" thesis in higher education serves, on analysis, to offer no such support. Indeed, the differences that we have unearthed perhaps to the contrary may even begin to raise fundamental doubts about the phenomenon of convergence itself. It has at least to be doubted whether there exists such a phenomenon.

More significantly, still, such talk – of "entrepreneurialism", of "convergence" – may, if taken on uncritically, serve as a pernicious discourse that closes off awkward value judgements and ethical choices about the forms of academic life – of "entrepreneurialism", of "convergence" – that are desirable or even undesirable.

Chapter 9

The purposes of higher education and the changing face of academia

(from London Review of Education, 2004, 2 (1) 61–73)

Outline

While there is no recognised sub-discipline of 'the philosophy of higher education', there has been a steady flow of writings that have just such an orientation. That flow has mainly takes two courses. On the one hand, those of a conservative persuasion hold to an ideal of higher education largely separate from society and find themselves trying to identify any possible intellectual spaces in which universities may enjoy a position of being their own end. On the other hand, those of a postmodern persuasion convince themselves that no large purposes of their own can seriously be entertained by universities and that only instrumental ends are available or that universities are simply to content themselves with their own form rather than their substance. Such a limited set of responses to the contemporary situation of universities is unnecessary. The very complexity of that situation, intermeshed as it is with the wider society, opens up new spaces and new universal challenges. It is possible for there to be a philosophical enterprise in relation to the university that also embraces large concerns and large future-oriented possibilities.

Introduction

In this chapter, I shall attempt to lay out the current state of play in regard to what might be termed 'the philosophy of higher education'. Such a task, however, presents some rather large difficulties.

Firstly, there is no branch of the philosophy of education that has been systematically developed so as to form such a philosophy. Partly, this is a consequence of there being no infrastructure: to my knowledge, there are no departments, units or research centres in the world that even have a primary interest in the philosophy of higher education. As a result, there is, for example, no journal that is devoted to the matter.

Secondly, unlike 'education', 'higher education' is more or less entirely coincident with institutions of higher education. While we can speak of educational activities and talk, for instance, of a person educating themselves outside of a formal institutional setting, this is much more difficult if not impossible in relation to higher education. That someone could be engaged in 'higher education' informally or could give themselves a 'higher education' makes little sense.

The concept of higher education refers to particular institutions in the world in a way that the concept of education does not. Accordingly, there can be no pure 'philosophy of higher education': any such activity, if it is to have any legitimacy, would have to have its feet fairly firmly on the ground and take account of empirical dimensions of the institutional and organisational features of higher education as it exists at any one time.

Thirdly, institutions of higher education are significantly different between themselves: it is not obvious that a research-led internationally respected university, with an annual budget of well over a billion dollars per year, has much in common with a community college that conducts no research. This diversity within higher education is being compounded by new developments across the world. The emergence of corporate universities, the use of digital technologies so creating virtual universities, the development of markets in higher education, and the formation of global alliances: developments such as these are changing rapidly the character of universities and increasing the diversity between them. We can no longer talk with confidence about 'the university'. Under those circumstances, the task of a philosophy of higher education cannot sensibly be seen as a project that defines the conceptual conditions of what it is to be a 'university', for universities, self-evidently, no longer possess an obvious unity among themselves.

Lastly, the concepts of 'higher education' and 'university' are different. Not all institutions of higher education are universities although, in some countries, institutions that do not enjoy the title often aspire to it while elsewhere (notably, the USA) any organisation can call itself a university. More importantly, however, we may want to question whether it is the case that all universities are providing a genuine 'higher education'. There are two points here. On the one hand, there is at work here an internal politics of the language: in particular, the term 'university,' characteristically has certain resonances—such that it becomes a prized label to an enterprise. On the other hand, in most countries, the term 'university' is a protected title and is conferred by the state only under certain conditions.

We have to start, therefore, with what may appear to be two negative and even dismal observations. Firstly, there is no sub-discipline of the philosophy of education that we can seriously suggest amounts to a 'philosophy of higher education'; and secondly, it is by no means clear in the twenty-first century as to what a philosophy of higher education could look like. As a consequence, debate over the ends that higher education might serve is impoverished and a possible opportunity to identify imaginative purposes is being lost.

Purposes, changes and context

Before trying to bring some more positive perspective to bear, our initial observations as to the complexity of the context of any would-be philosophy of higher education have first to be compounded.

Perhaps even more than school education, higher education is changing with remarkable rapidity. Many advanced societies have witnessed or are witnessing at this time the transformation of an elite system of higher education into a mass system, a situation that the USA has enjoyed—if that is the term—for perhaps fifty or more years. There are certain other large changes that are also near universal across the world. We have just touched on some, but a more precise specification may be helpful:

- globalisation;
- the revolution brought by the arrival of digital technologies;
- the interpenetration of higher education with the wider host society;
- agendas of participation, access and equal opportunities;
- marketisation of higher education, with institutions identifying their knowledge services for potential customers;
- competition;
- the development of systematic and nationwide state-sponsored quality evaluation mechanisms.

This list amounts to a formidable set of challenges to institutions of higher education and it brings other changes in their wake, which have even more direct philosophical implications. I shall pick out just two. Firstly, the interpenetration of higher education and the wider society has an immediate impact on the knowledge base of universities. That wider society is taken to be a 'knowledge society' of which two features stand out. On the one hand, the knowledge society is a society in which the production of knowledge is distributed widely across society. Not yet everyone is involved in knowledge creation, but it is a widespread business. Transnational corporations, indeed, have their own 'knowledge officers'. On the other hand, and following on, what counts as knowledge becomes open: the wider society spawns its own definitions of legitimate knowledge, characteristically more performative, more transactional and more founded on multi forms of representation. The interpenetration of higher education and the wider society, therefore, raises sharp epistemological questions: what are to be the criteria of valid knowledge by which the university orients itself? Are these criteria to be furnished to any degree by the wider society? Under these circumstances, can there be firm criteria of knowledge?

As a second example of the philosophical implications of the interpenetration of higher education and the wider society, the concepts of 'academic freedom' and even 'academic community' are placed in some difficulty. The reasons are mixed and only a brief resumé is possible here. As the university seeks to identify and market its knowledge services, academics are placed differentially in that endeavour. Most academics, in almost any discipline, are able to find market opportunities, but the opportunities for those in biotechnology, computer sciences and electronic engineering characteristically exceed those opportunities available to their colleagues in classical civilisation, philosophy, English literature and anthropology. There develops, as a result, even sharper divisions across the 'academic community'; it is not clear that there is much that binds together academics into a community, even in the same institution. The idea of academic community is, therefore, in jeopardy, but so is the idea of academic freedom.

If academics are freely marketing their services, often for considerable economic return, to the wider society, it is not clear that the concept of academic freedom has much purchase; or at least, it seems to be undergoing a radical shift. It stood for the right freely to research, to teach and to speak out in academic settings (the university being regarded as a haven for critical thought). Now, academic freedom appears to be becoming the right to exploit the exchange value inherent in academics' knowledge. 'Academic freedom' marked a calling from within: now, it seems to herald simply a personal interest indicative of a calling from without and, with it, a dissipation of former responsibilities to an academic ethic (Shils, 1983).

I cite these two examples—of the epistemological base of the university and the problematic nature of the two concepts of academic freedom and academic community—simply as that: examples of the philosophical implications of the societal and global transformations to the university's environment. This reflection suggests that the title of this paper could equally be reversed. It is the changing face of academia that gives rise to questions about the purposes of higher education at least as much as it is that considerations of the purposes of higher education raise questions about the changes that are occurring to academia.

In summary, then, we can say that a philosophy of higher education is in for a challenging time. Any philosophising in the context of higher education has to be impure: it cannot just content itself with an examination and a proffering of concepts. Such an exercise will be bound to be jejune, becoming a wordplay that fails to engage with the large transformations that are happening in higher education. Further, a failure to be empirical in part will be likely to result in analyses and ideas that are non-feasible. There will be a likelihood that the analysis implicitly relies on a conception of higher education as it was at some 'golden point' in the past and that the ensuing ideas lack any legitimacy as a realistic project. An attempt to produce a pure philosophy of higher education—constructed by the philosophers and through their frameworks—would run the risk of being an ideology, a wish fulfilment on the part of the philosophers hankering after—as they would see it—better times, being a tacit parading of hopes of and a longing for an age that is gone in which academic life was simpler, clearer and purer. To put the point more positively, a philosophy of higher education, if it is to command any respect outside of that very small group of academics who are interested in such matters, has to be a *social* philosophy of higher education (cf., Williams, 2002). It has not only to start from the empirical conditions in which higher education finds itself, but also emerge with ideas that have some practical as well as conceptual feasibility. Any philosophy of higher education that fell short of that dual aim would enjoy neither legitimacy nor effectiveness.

The end of the idea of higher education?

Over the past twenty years, a philosophical literature on the university has emerged, although to put it in this way could be said to be generous. It arises out of a (largely French) poststructuralist and a postmodern background and has certain characteristics. Its starting points are that we are a postfoundational world (the philosophical assumption that there can be no ultimate grounding of ideas), that large ideas ('metanarratives') face only 'incredulity' and that the changing face of academia presents largely a set of problematic changes. This set of starting points can generate only a limited sense of the idea of higher education. For Lyotard (1984), the university is exhibiting a lurch towards 'performativity' in its epistemologies: what is less clear is that Lyotard offers any sense of any positive operational or even conceptual options available to the university. Separately, and drawing on the metaphor of a lever, Derrida (1992) implies that the university has some leverage available to it in the modern society and even talks of its 'responsibility' but leaves it unclear as to what that responsibility would look like.

For the American, Bill Readings, the university is into a kind of post-history of its own. Readings' (1996) book. *The University in Ruins*, constitutes that rare thing—a serious attempt to offer a philosophical account of contemporary higher education. On Readings' view, having passed through the phases of 'the university of reason' and 'the university of culture' in the past two hundred years, the university is now 'the university of excellence' in an age of systematised quality systems. This, for Readings, is a non-ideological state, since this university has been emptied of all serious purpose. Excellence is a vapid concept: any institution can interpret it in any way whatsoever. This, therefore, constitutes a kind of backhand answer to Derrida: the responsibility of the twenty-first century university is to be 'excellent', with the idea of excellence standing for no purpose, no ideal and no concept in particular. Readings' answer to his own analysis is to advance the idea that the university should become 'a community of dissensus'. If there can be no agreement on fundamental frameworks within the university, at least the university can become a forum for debate and dispute and in that way open up a discursive space in a society in which conceptual horizons are being drawn ever narrowly.

Readings' analysis and conceptual proposals undermine the title of his book. His suggestion that the university might become 'a community of dissensus' implies that a positive role lies in front of the university: despite the title, the university does not need to live in 'ruins' after all. His argument is also curious in a second way. For Readings, the university is in a post-historical age, in which the state is emptied of ideology and, with it, all of its leading institutions. The university, as a result, has lost its way, shorn of any large ideas (truth, reason, culture) that could carry it forward. But then what is 'the community of dissensus' if it is not a large idea that could carry the university forward? And around what key concepts would such a community unite when those on which the university has been built for the last two hundred years have so dissolved that the university has been undermined and is now 'in ruins'?

There should be sympathy for Readings. Those who wish to sustain a positive idea of the university have a difficult time of it just now. The days when one could espouse nonchalantly a positive idea of the university (witness, for example, Newman, Jaspers, Moberly, Minogue) are over. Empirically and conceptually, the universalism contained in the idea of the university and which made possible such stories, has dissolved. Empirically, the modern university became a set of separate *academic tribes and territories* (Becher & Trowler, 2001) and the post-modern university decentred itself altogether as its boundaries weakened and as it merged with the wider society. Conceptually, the ideas on which the modern university was built—truth, knowledge, reason, communication—all stood in the dock as mere detritus. If these concepts had any mileage at all, it lay in their separate interpretation by different communities both within and without the university. The university, therefore, was—as it were—emptied out, conceptually and empirically: it was no longer clear that the university could be said to be standing for any particular set of ideas, or to have any particular set of purposes. At best, all it might sponsor were proliferating and conflicting purposes: the university was breaking apart.

Nearly 40 years ago, Clark Kerr (1972 edition) coined the term 'the multiversity' but it was just possible that, under the extraordinary range of activities that were contained in the university, there lay some common substrate that could be said to unify the university. Over the last generation or so, one vision of such a common substrate has been implied in the work of the German theorist, Jurgen Habermas. Within his approach, which contained full frontal attacks on poststructuralism and postmodernism (Habermas, 1990), the university could be said to be an institution—perhaps *the* institution—assisting in the construction of the rational society. It is able to do this precisely because it holds to the ideal of the university as a forum for sustaining 'the ideal speech situation'. In this situation, participants are treated and treat each other as equals, communication is oriented towards a collective understanding of truth, and claims are adjudicated by recourse to the better argument. Discourse itself was to be layered by a tacit adherence to so-called 'validity claims' of rightness, sincerity, and truthfulness. This vision of the rational university underpinning the rational society was, admittedly, counterfactual: Habermas was not making empirical claims about the university but offering a critical standard by which institutions wishing to carry the title might be judged.

Despite having his followers, Habermas' project of wanting to establish a binding and critical framework of *communicative action* is perhaps losing ground to the postmoderns and the posthistorians. It is not surprising that we should see a book bearing the title of *The University in Ruins*. In a fluid age—or, as Bauman (2000) brilliantly puts it, in an age of *Liquid Modernity*—our means for gaining a grip on the world are both too many and insufficient. We live (as I have termed it elsewhere) in an age of *supercomplexity* (Barnett, 2000). In such an age, our frameworks for understanding ourselves and the world around us proliferate and compete with each other. Old certainties have to dissolve. Readings is right on that point. The question is where do we go from here? Is it possible, in any sense, to sustain an idea of the university, which genuinely serves as a unifying idea? Almost the slogan of the postmoderns is that we are witnessing the end of the universal: how, then might it be possible to do justice to the idea of the university, an idea that is utterly dependent on the idea of the universal? Perhaps the idea of the university is at an end after all.

Practical matters

I said earlier that any adequate philosophy of higher education has to have its feet on the ground: in the first place, it has to start by trying to understand higher education as it is, not as some might wish it to be. There is an important role for such a philosophy to play in proffering imaginative ideas and articulating concepts and frameworks that can serve as critical standards against which contemporary policies and practices might be judged *but* such an enterprise—to gain legitimacy—has to grind, at some points, against an understanding of those policies and practices. Earlier, I offered a list of some major shifts that are taking place in higher education, more or less across the world. There are both pessimistic and optimistic readings of those changes; and some strange intellectual alliances are springing up in those responses.

Both the traditionalists *and* those who see themselves as avant-garde espouse parallel critiques of contemporary changes in academia. The traditionalists bemoan, as they see it, a loss of standards (amid cultural and epistemological relativism) and the loss of purity of mission (with the intermingling of higher education and the world of work). Those of a more radical persuasion voice concerns that the university has so taken on agendas of responsiveness to the knowledge economy, accountability and efficiency that the separateness that formerly marked off the university from the wider world and gave discursive space for it to supply an oppositional voice is being diminished, if it has not altogether vanished. (Compare, for instance, Gordon Graham's *Universities: The Recovery of an Idea* (2002) with a quite different volume appearing at the same time, *For a Radical Higher Education: After Postmodernism* (Taylor et al., 2002).)

The idea of the university as 'the critical conscience of society' now, on this more radical view, appears no longer to offer a set of ideals that can be realised. All universities have, in a sense, become corporate universities, run as businesses and engaging—so far as they can—with the business world: some are even corporations in the business world in their own right (Jarvis, 2001). The outer has become the inner: the university has taken on the agendas, the values, and the operating principles of the wider society. Under these conditions, there is and there can be no *ideal* of the university.

We may note that, in these accounts, there is an underlying unity between the conservatives and the radicals. The conservatives saw the university essentially as a form of intellectual if not exactly elite reproduction; the radicals saw it as a vehicle quite different, as a means of sustaining an oppositional discourse and even generating social change, *even* revolutionary social change. On *both* views, however, the loss of separateness and of the intermeshing of the university with the wider society—at least, as a market—are matters of significant regret. With that intermeshing arrives an occlusion of categories once clear and under the ownership of the academic community: knowledge, truth, understanding. Whether the university was to be a means of conservation or transformation, the purity of these concepts was necessary on both counts. Now, in a more fluid age, two phenomena present themselves: the key concepts that marked out the university are now contested by the wider society which seeks to offer its own interpretations and even supplant those concepts as they are understood in the university *and* those concepts are overlain—and in the process distorted—by other concepts, such as competition, accountability, markets, information processing, learning environments, stakeholders, skill and competence.

We have, therefore, three sets of layered processes: (i) significant and worldwide transformations in the character of higher education (the kinds of changes in which sociologists, organisational theorists and policy analysts will have an interest); (ii) evolving and merging discourses about higher education; (iii) philosophical matters arising out of i and ii. A key question remains: given i and ii, what is the character of iii to be? Can a philosophy of higher education be little more than a lament that such a philosophy is no more and cannot be realised? Amid diversity, fluidity and an 'excessive accommodation' of higher education to the wider society (Galbraith, 1969), especially to the corporate world, can there be a serious role for a philosophy of higher education to perform?

It might be said that higher education still retains discursive space of its own and a philosophy of higher education can identify the features of the *discursive intent*—as we might put it—that still lays open to the university. Paul Standish (2003), for example, has spoken (in picking up an idea from Gordon Bearn) of higher education as being founded upon an interest in 'beauteous intensity'. But, even if we accept an argument of that kind, these are crumbs from the poor man's table. There are some little spaces still available to the university where it can be itself and the task of a philosophy of higher education then becomes that of specifying what that might amount to; namely, a specification of the aesthetic form of the university rather than the content of its discussions.

This is a poor strategy for two reasons. Firstly, it unduly diminishes the scope of a philosophy of higher education and, secondly, it pretends to a purity that higher education no longer enjoys. A philosophy of higher education can only become a valid intellectual endeavour under the conditions that we have surveyed and *not* by attempting to identify a discursive space in which the university can be itself but by addressing the intermingling of the university and the wider world head-on. In late modernity, that intermeshing is likely to accelerate and widen. A philosophy of higher education has, therefore, to take that conjunction as its starting point and not look longingly for interstices in that conjunction in which the university can be itself.

Engaging universities

Two points emerge from this analysis. Firstly, the prospectus for a philosophy of higher education under conditions of late-modernity turn not on purity but on *engagement*. Whether it wishes it or not, the university is engaged with the wider world (cf. Bjarnason & Coldstream, 2003). We should, however, distinguish four different forms of engagement: (i) that form of engagement which is blind and unreflective—we might term this *non-reflectional*; (ii) that form of engagement which is entered into knowingly, where the major intent is *extractional*, that is, where university enters into a project only insofar as it can extract benefits to itself; (iii) that form of engagement which is entered into knowingly, where at least a significant part of the intent lies in the university realising a sense of itself in the context of imposed standards or expectations (for example, where a university accepts an accountability function within a state-imposed quality framework): call this *impositional*; lastly, (iv) that form of engagement which is entered into partly in virtue of a responsibility that the university sees itself as fulfilling *qua* 'university'—call this *realisational*.

Of these four forms of engagement (non-reflectional, extractional, impositional, realisational), only the last, the realisational, is philosophically interesting in that it invites questions as to the nature of the responsibility to which universities might come to feel that they had some form of obligation. *Just what is it to realise the university?* Does that kind of concept, of realisation of some large idea and even ideal of the university, make sense today? The realisational concept of engagement invites further questions as to what, in the contemporary era, we can feasibly take a university to be.

The first major philosophical question then turns, to pick up Derrida's concept, on that of *responsibility*. What, if indeed it has any at all, are the responsibilities of the university in the twenty-first century? What might it mean to employ the concept of responsibility under conditions of incorporation, fragmentation, liquidity and diversity? The second point is that of the status of such a philosophical enterprise. It is surely clear that, if the university is itself a set of fluidities, with many pools of activity, self-identity and conversations going on and reaching out to varied communities in the wider society, a philosophy of higher education cannot itself be a tightly bounded enterprise. The philosophers have to pool their resources with others to engage in a wider attempt to map out in general terms the character of higher education today.

Such an enterprise would amount to a *theory* of higher education. But there are a number of difficulties even with this term (broader, as it is, than the philosophy of higher education). Is it to be thought of as supplying 'a theory' or 'the theory' of higher education? Perhaps not either: perhaps the intellectual landscape is so uncertain that we should talk even more vaguely of just theorising about higher education. But a further difficulty arises over the concept of theory, particularly in this context for 'theory' has to do duty for different intellectual activities.

We can distinguish between (i) efforts to understand the changing character of higher education; (ii) efforts to look into the future and engage in 'future studies'; (iii) imaginative efforts to offer concepts and ideas that serve as a critical standard against which contemporary changes can be assessed; (iv) imaginative frameworks that seek to offer a vista of a possible form of higher education embodying certain values. Any one of these enterprises could be undertaken either modestly or grandly: the task may be local and conceptually small-scale or epic, calling for considerable courage.

These days, for understandable reasons, the latter is largely out of favour: a 'performative' world rules out of court, so some believe, large ideas, visions, and collective projects. This, at least, is the postmodern reading of our world but we should be cautious about such a story, especially in relation to higher education. In the Western world, despite their intermeshing with the wider world, and despite that wider world (through the state, the world of work, and client groups) exerting its limitations on the university—both in its self-understanding and its practices—universities continue to enjoy considerable space. They even enjoy space to articulate stories of postmodernism. In other words, by reminding ourselves about the practical space available to universities we remind ourselves also about the discursive space available to universities.

The postmodern story is not a recipe for closure but it is a recipe for restricted and local conversations. But there is an irony here for the postmodern story is itself a large story (indeed, set of stories) about the character of contemporary society, its discourses, epistemologies, cultures and identity structures: these are very large stories indeed. So the postmodern story undermines itself conceptually and practically: its very appearance demonstrates the capacity for large ideas that in themselves can take off into very large collective projects and even ideologies. In particular, its appearance tacitly demonstrates that the university is still an institutional vehicle for the production and projection of new ideas, imaginative thinking and challenging frameworks. On the surface, the postmodern story projects a picture of village conversations; at a deep level, it shows that universalism is still with us, and even in ideological form.

Prospects

The challenges of a philosophy of higher education for a fluid and complex age are now, surely, evident and, at the same time, both the role and the ingredients of such a philosophy.

The challenges are those of establishing a way of talking about higher education under the conditions that higher education faces. These conditions include those of internal fragmentation, fluid interactions with the wider society, a dissolution of identity structures (we can barely ask let alone answer the question any more 'What is a professor?') and simultaneously a squeezing of the discursive and operational space of the university *and* an opening up of those spaces (just as the state and the world of work impose new frameworks—of 'standards' and accountability and market disciplines—so new opportunities open, as the university becomes a key institution in the framing of the 'knowledge economy'). Under these conditions, a philosophy of higher education is discursively challenged. What is its role to be? What space does it have in which to work? What is the potential of its project?

The *role* of a philosophy of higher education in these circumstances can be constructed as a conceptually small-scale enterprise or large enterprise, but it is tending to take the former shape. There being no centres of educational research that focus on philosophical aspects of higher education (our opening observation), such topics have been picked up by others, not only, for example, by those working more broadly in the philosophy of education, but also by others working in the humanities, in cultural studies and in sociology. Such studies have understandably tended to be shaped by the collective understandings of those epistemic communities. Those studies tend to be technical and professional and are limited in their scope. Large visions for higher education that offer a new 'idea of the university' are unlikely to emerge from such a milieu.

The abandonment of large ideas for our understanding of the university is particularly ironic, for the present conjunction of circumstances—an empirical enmeshing of higher education and society *and* a fluidity in social and epistemological matters generally—opens up both spaces and responsibilities for the university. For the past one hundred and fifty years or so, the university has come to see itself as a site of critical reason and an institutional vehicle for enlightenment. To these two roles has been added more recently a role in furthering social democracy: agendas of human rights and equal opportunities are present now on campus. In all of this, large philosophical problems arise: how are we to conceive of the epistemological base of the university? Do individuals have a right to experience higher education? Does the university have a responsibility towards the development of 'the learning society' and, with it, citizenship in and across society? How is research to be understood and what, if any, are the responsibilities of researchers? (Most contemporary philosophical texts on higher education are almost entirely silent on science and research.) How are we to understand 'higher learning' in the twenty-first century? What principles might inform pedagogy in higher education (whose clients are both adults and often paying considerable sums for their own education)?

These are large questions, furnishing a considerable role for a philosophy of higher education, but only provided that such an enterprise is willing (i) to work collaboratively with others (in the history of higher education; sociology of education; psychology; linguistics; discourse studies; cultural studies; policy studies; philosophy of science; philosophy in general; comparative studies; organisational studies and so on); and (ii) to work concretely with a sense of higher education as a site of engagement with the wider society.

There being no academic infrastructure in which such collaborative studies are likely to take off, the prospects for such a theoretical enterprise emerging cannot be high. Just at a time when the philosophy of higher education has both the responsibility and the social opportunity to raise large issues and generate large ideas (there is an audience for such an enterprise in a way that simply could not have existed before), those who work in the area are usually happy to work within limited frameworks speaking just, as it seems, to narrow audiences (usually those who have particular kinds of technical expertise in the humanities).

The ingredients of such a large philosophy of higher education are, in one sense, simple: they are easily identifiable. But their effective use is less straightforward. For the ingredients of such an enterprise are imagination, generosity and courage: imagination to come forth with new frameworks to help us conceive of new ideas of the university; generosity to embrace other forms of scholarship and research that might inform our sense of the predicament—conceptually and empirically—of higher education; and courage, to withstand the voices of the experts who will frame their critiques from within their own limited epistemological frames, unwilling or unable to embrace the larger picture. A fourth ingredient is a foundation for the rest: it is that of attempting to develop a form of communication that reaches out to multiple audiences, those that have interests in higher education but who are not experts in its study. Large audiences await and some have yet to be formed that are or would be interested in matters concerning the purposes of the university if only a language could be constructed in which such matters were raised in ways intelligible to those audiences.

Recovering the university

The world is not just complex; it is supercomplex. This is particularly noticeable in higher education. Some say that we are witnessing the end of grand narratives. To the contrary: we are, in higher education, at least, replete with grand narratives. Is the university to be a site of democratic rights, of societal enlightenment, of knowledge production for a technological society, of inculcating skills for the workplace, of personal transformation or of critical analysis? Is it to get by through its own wits, transforming itself to take on the image of any client or state agency that comes its way or is it to maintain some kind of allegiance to a sense of an enduring entity? Are its internal processes to be characterised by tight managerial disciplines that enable it to live 'in the real world' or is it to forge, within itself, a new kind of organic community?

The sheer posing of the questions indicates something of the range of constructions of the university that are apparently permissible today (even if some are more encouraged than others). Behind these constructions lie distinct constellations of concepts—around knowledge, democracy, work, enlightenment, persons and critique—that furnish alternative ways in which the university might understand itself. In practice, of course, they are all to be found within the university, even if different universities will exhibit their attachment to these conceptual clusters to different degrees. Further, the different clusters slide across each, with connections being formed and loosened continuously. Terms—such as critical thought, knowledge, skill, and personal development—can be found in multiple clusters of university purpose, taking on nuanced meanings in each conceptual milieu.

The state of contemporary academia can be quickly summarised, therefore. It is one in which the purposes of the university are so many pools of self-understanding on the part of the university itself. These pools of self-understanding are, in turn, part of wider discursive societal currents around ideas of democracy, enlightenment, personhood and economic growth. These discursive currents continue to widen, and to become more turbulent. The currents run against each other, and the university is caught up in it all.

In this maelstrom, terms such as chaos, turbulence, unpredictability, uncertainty, contestability, and challengeability present themselves. These terms present a new conceptual cluster by which we might understand the university, namely, the cluster of *fragility* (cf. Stehr, 2001). Face with this situation, the faint-hearted shrink: for them, we can no longer think seriously about the purposes of higher education, as if there were any large purposes that it might pursue with any assurance. For those of this persuasion, the possibilities for the university's self-definition that crowd in upon it are so numerous, so conflicting and, worse still, so contradictory, that talk of unitary purposes has to be off-limits.

This is a counsel of despair and it is not the only option. A much more positive option lies, paradoxically, in the university seizing hold of the cluster of fragility as the dominant cluster for its self-understanding. If the world is characterised—as it is—by uncertainty, unpredictability, challengeability and contestation, then let these ideas become the watchwords of the university in the twenty-first century. If, in the process, other hitherto dominant concepts—such as knowledge, truth and learning—are put in the shadows, so be it. By allowing the currents of fragility into itself, by giving them a warm embrace, the university can regain a position of giving *added-value* to the world, rather than simply—as it is becoming—providing to the world that which it calls for.

In an age of supercomplexity, the crucial matter is not one of knowledge but of *being* (to resort to a term from continental European philosophy). Knowledge is not repudiated as such, but it can no longer supply the dominant *weltanschauung* for the university. The limits of academic knowledge are becoming transparent, both in its lack of reflexivity and its inability fully to supply the epistemologies that the wider world of fast globalisation requires. More importantly, in such a world—of unpredictability and challengeability—knowledge is supplanted by *being* as the key term for the university (cf. Barnett, 2003).

If we cannot be sure what tomorrow will bring, conceptually as well as technologically and organisationally, new purposes open up for the university precisely around questions of being: how are we to live personally and collectively with uncertainty? How are we to relate both to the world and to each other when all bets are off? How do we understand research and teaching as sets of intentional acts in a context of radical uncertainty? The questions supply a new set of purposes for the university, namely *purposes of uncertainty*. There are three such purposes. In a context of radical uncertainty, the university becomes an institution that i) adds directly to our uncertainty in the world (by producing imaginative and challenging new frameworks or stories by which we might understand ourselves); ii) helps us to monitor and evaluate that uncertainty (by holding up for critical scrutiny the available frameworks (created in turn both within the university and across the wider society)); and iii) enables us to live with that uncertainty, through both the operational capacities and the existential capacities that it promotes on a personal level (in its pedagogical activities). In such purposes of uncertainty, we have a set of large purposes that offer the university—*and* the wider society—unity, durability and internal integrity.

Conclusion

Higher education across the world is undergoing a set of major changes. Some of those changes bring institutions of higher education into challenging relationships with the players in their wider environment—the host state, students as consumers, the world of work and, indeed, amidst competition and marketisation other institutions of higher education. Other changes, partly as a consequence of the first set, set challenges for the university internally: managing and leading sets of largely autonomous staff; balancing the pulls of the disciplines and institutional interests; pedagogical relationships; the rights of students and academic identities. Two large philosophical questions are posed by these changes: firstly, how might we understand 'the university'? Secondly, can higher education be any longer taken to offer a liberal education?

The key term in the second of those questions, 'liberal education', stood for (i) objective knowledge and (ii) critical thought in (iii) autonomous institutions: all three elements are now put in doubt. The concept of liberal education appears to be undermined conceptually and operationally. Under these conditions—at once empirical and conceptual—the idea of the university, as an institution *for* higher education, appears also to be in trouble. The purposes for which it stood are no longer straightforwardly available to it. Many, indeed, believe that the university is in 'crisis'. Some even believe, as we have seen, that the university is 'in ruins'.

By retaining the *distinction* between higher education and university, it is possible, however, to do some justice to both ideas, even in the current situation. We have moved into an age of supercomplexity, which is characterised essentially by conceptual turmoil. We have no sure grip on who we are, how we relate to the world and, indeed, what the world is like. These are, as it were, sociological facts of our globalised world (rather than Nietzschian-like philosophical reflections). Under these conditions, the world needs the university more than ever and large purposes open up for it. These are the purposes of compounding our conceptual turmoil, enabling us internally (ontologically) to handle the uncertain state of *being* that results and assisting the world in living purposively amid that turmoil. These are large purposes for the university that provide it with integrity and a new universal purpose. They also echo with ideas of critical thought, enlightenment and emancipation and they even offer the prospect, therefore, of a higher education that is yet a liberal education.

Chapter 10

Institutions of higher education

Purposes and 'performance indicators'

(from Oxford Review of Education, 1988, 14 (1) 97–112)

Outline

Institutions of higher education fulfil different kinds of purposes, a key distinction amongst that are purposes which are set by the wider society and purposes that are intrinsic to the character of the IHEs themselves. The term 'fitness for purpose' masks this distinction, for it speaks to the extrinsic purposes of IHEs supplied by the wider society. The term, therefore, promotes an instrumental conception of higher education, and is an example of instrumental reason. In parallel with this style of thinking, IHEs are being assessed through the application of 'performance indicators', but the logic of performance indicators is such that they are unable to reveal the effectiveness of IHEs in fulfilling their key educational purposes. Four essential conditions are offered as constituting the purposes of an 'institution of higher education', and I offer some closing remarks on evaluation aimed at doing justice to the educational character of our institutions.

'Fitness for purpose'

The term 'fitness for purpose' recently appeared in the language of higher education in the UK. It was used by the Secretary of State for Education (Joseph, 1984), was in the Government Green Paper (DES, 1985) and formed the title of a set of essays by the Chairman of the Board of the National Advisory Body for Local Authority Higher Education (Ball, 1985). What are the implicit values of the term; can we give any substance to it, apart from the political argument with which it is accompanied?

In excavating the interest structure of the term 'fitness for purpose', two alternative strategies present themselves. We could embark on a textual analysis of its recent uses to uncover the underlying political metaphors and presuppositions, and so illuminate the political significance and implications of the term. For example, it may be that the surface rhetoric of the term is located in an apparent concern with 'standards' in our academic institutions; but that the actual political meaning of the term springs from a concern of the state to define a particular set of purposes for institutions of higher education. We might also see, within that framework, a further determination on the part of the state to set even tighter frameworks of purposes for the different sectors of higher education, so legitimising the present differential allocation of resources to them.

If we were to engage in that form of analysis, we would in effect be using the term 'fitness for purpose' as the springboard for embarking on an examination of the political economy of higher education. The other possible strategy is to focus more precisely on the term in its own right, so as to bring out what might be termed its inner logic. Having revealed that, we would then be in a better position to offer contrasting conceptions of purposes with correspondingly different inner logics. It is this second strategy which I shall attempt here.

Institutional purposes: two key distinctions

We can start by looking at the idea of 'purpose' itself. Two key sets of distinctions can be made: first, the distinction between the purposes that any one institution of higher education might set itself on the one hand; and the purposes that attach to all institutions of higher education, in virtue of which they are institutions of higher education, and not, say, industrial concerns or even colleges of further education. If any serious meaning can be given to such a high sounding phrase as 'the purpose—or purposes—of higher education', it would consist of a general set of conditions that any institution of higher education has to satisfy in order to warrant the title 'institution of higher education'. (Later, I try to identify those general conditions.)

Clearly, the specific purposes that a single institution might set for itself have to be consistent with the general purposes of institutions of higher education. An institution of higher education would not normally be justified in using its funds to run a casino, since that kind of activity would be likely to fall outside the *general* purposes of what it means to be an institution of higher education. Still, *within* that framework, these institutions are entitled to choose their own way of interpreting and implementing the general conditions. IHEs have, at least in theory, a measure of freedom of choice as to the specific purposes they set themselves (Berdahl, 1985).

In fact, however, in the UK, institutions of higher education have not really taken advantage of the opportunities available to develop an individual character of their own (Burgess, 1981). This is evident in the very limited way in which IHEs in the UK vary in the extent they have publicly identified the key purposes for which they stand. The idea of our academic institutions setting down in a public document their own 'mission statements' has never fully caught on, even if there is only now more incentive for them so to do (Toyne, 1985). Institutions in the public sector have surely done this more readily, and perhaps this owes something to the Council for National Academic Awards which in its five-yearly reviews of institutions—as distinct from its parallel reviews of separate courses—has prompted institutions to produce their own goal statements about themselves, as part of their academic planning.

That, then, is the first distinction to which to draw attention: the distinction between the general purposes which all institutions of higher education need to fulfil (to justify their falling under that common description); and the particular purposes which an individual institution might set itself. (We shall return later to the relationship between these two levels of purpose.)

The second key distinction is that between purposes which institutions of higher education fulfil which are set within the academic community; and purposes which are set outside the academic community. In making this distinction, we should not assume that purposes which are set inside the academic community are wholly to the good, and that those which come from the wider community are wholly undesirable. Indeed, it is surely apparent that, ever since their mediaeval origins, the institutions of higher learning have looked outwards, supplying the state with administrators and other qualified personnel. Purposes which come from outside the academic community are not, therefore, necessarily antithetical to those which the academic community generates itself.

On the other hand, some of those purposes which come from within the academic community itself are actually of doubtful value, when viewed against the traditional conception of higher learning. For example, the increasing splintering of the academic community itself into mini academic sub-cultures (Becher, 1981) is clearly a matter of concern to those who believe that higher education should, whatever else it provides, offer a liberal education and that amongst the components of a liberal education are those of a willingness to break through boundaries of thought and to offer a breadth of cognitive perspective (Peters, 1977).

So there is a complex set of relationships between purposes set outside the academic community and those set inside. That, though, is the second distinction to pick out.

Having grasped these two sets of distinctions, we can superimpose them on each other. This generates four kinds of purposes. That is to say, we can talk of general purposes which hold across all institutions of higher education, which are either set within the academic community or are set outside. And we can also talk of purposes particular to a single institution which are on the one hand set by that institution or are set for it by bodies or agencies in the external community. This kind of conceptual framework raises all kinds of empirical questions about the degree of permeability of institutions both at the local and at the national level, which are worthy of empirical examination (Brennan, 1985). For instance, it might be that in modern society, the area of purposes set outside the academic community is growing; and the area of those set within is diminishing. If this is so, we are faced with the situation shown in Fig. 10.1:

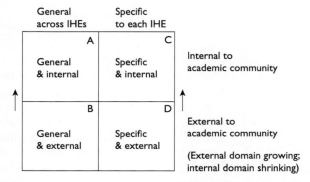

Figure 10.1 Purposes of institutions of higher education—a schema

Over time, the line denoting the distinction between externally set purposes from those set internally is moving upwards, so that the space available for internally set purposes is diminishing.

The rest of this paper will focus on the left hand side of Fig. 10.1, namely those purposes which are general across all institutions of higher education. In other words, purposes which are specific to individual institutions will be set aside. And within the range of general purposes, I shall focus on those purposes which are generated from within the academic community (box A in Fig. 10.1), although I shall also want to contrast them with purposes which are set outside the academic community (box B). Indeed, it is the argument of this paper that in demonstrating their fitness for purpose, institutions of higher education cannot neglect their internal purposes, however much they are required to fulfil external purposes.

Problems with general purposes, internal to higher education

What actually might be meant by general purposes, internal to higher education? In fact, are there any? Is not one of the characteristics of higher education that everybody knows what institutions of higher education are in business for; but that, unfortunately, we all have different views on the matter (Kerr, 1972)? It is not that we have no idea what, essentially, institutions of higher education are for; it is not that we lack any idea of their functions. On the contrary, it appears that we suffer the embarrassment of having too many conceptions of what institutions of higher education are for. This view, though plausible, suffers from two defects.

Firstly, it obscures one of the distinctions that we started with, that between purposes common to all IHEs (in virtue of which they are IHEs) and purposes particular to individual institutions or their component parts. The fact, therefore, that institutions and their departments fulfil many different purposes is not incompatible with their also falling under a general description by which we recognise IHEs. Secondly, we should not assume, without attempting any such investigation, that such a general description is impossible to pin down.

A further set of observations concerns the implementation of purposes. The first point is that if achieving their purposes is not to be just a matter of luck, then the members of an institution need to have a reasonably informed and uniform idea of what the purposes of an institution of higher education are. And it seems a straightforward—almost logical—point that its members need not only to share a consensus on what those purposes should be; they need actually to have a reasonably high level of commitment to them. It seems clear that our modern institutions of higher education, complex and large as many of them are, and faced with increasing demands and diminishing resources, are hardly likely to meet their purposes effectively unless their members—in particular, their academic staff—are collectively committed to their achievement.

So clarity, commitment, and a reasonable degree of consensus over purposes seem necessary requirements. But these reflections surely present problems. For, as we earlier remarked, institutions of higher education, by and large, have a pretty cloudy idea of what the essential purposes of higher education might be. And this is understandable, because (as we observed earlier), other than in the moment of their being founded, British institutions have, until very recently, not been obliged to think them through. In other words, institutions of higher education tend, unless challenged to review themselves, just to assume that they are remaining faithful to the essential character of higher education. It is a case of 'we exist, therefore we are worthwhile'.

'Fitness for purpose': an example of instrumental reason

So much for the single term 'purposes', at least for the moment. Let us now return to the whole phrase we started with, that of 'fitness for purpose'.

I want to suggest that there is a problem with the whole idea of 'fitness for purpose' as a way into understanding IHEs and their effectiveness. In one sense, the key term in the phrase is the smallest: the linking term 'for' is actually very powerful. It both links *and* separates the two terms. As a result, the idea of 'being fit *for* a purpose' is two ideas brought together. The linking term *for* acts to bridge the conceptual gap between the two ideas of being fit and the purpose for which the IHE is fit, or is striving to become fit.

What follows from these conceptual points? Simply this: unpacking the notion of 'fitness for purpose' reveals that, in this terminology, the institution's purpose is tacitly seen as separate from its fitness; in other words, the purpose is extrinsic to the fitness. The fitness is achieved in order to be able to do something else.

This kind of thinking contains, therefore, an instrumental conception of education. It has no allegiance with the liberal idea of higher education as being a good in its own right. In the liberal conception, we can note, the idea of being fit for a purpose makes no sense at all, since there, the process of education is intrinsically worthwhile.

It would be wrong to imply that the instrumental way of looking at higher education is irrational. In a sense, it is utterly rational. It posits an end, and asks if the means—our institutions of higher education—are so organised that they will achieve that end. It is the rationality of a technological society: it is, to use the terminology of critical theory—and, in particular, that of Jürgen Habermas—a splendid example of instrumental reason (Connerton, 1980; Held, 1983; Gibson, 1986).

What, though, is so problematic about this style of thinking? At least, so it might be thought, this approach helps to promote an informed evaluation of the performance of institutions of higher education. If we have a clear idea of their purposes, we will surely be in a better position to assess how well they are doing in achieving them. What could be wrong with that?

The answer is that from an educational point of view, this style of thinking all too often misses the main target. The actual value of institutions—as *educational* institutions—is all too frequently bypassed. It is bypassed, not as a result of some conspiracy, but as part of the logic of this kind of thinking.

What *is* the logic of this style of thinking? It has three components. First, as we saw earlier, it looks to external values and objectives. So, for example, institutions come to be assessed in terms of their financial efficiency—their so-called unit costs—or, to take another example their non-completion rates (i.e. the extent to which students fail to complete their courses). But these are the approaches of the accountant and the bureaucrat rather than the educationalist. In other words, using approaches of this kind, we come to judge institution in terms of values dominant in the wider society, rather than those in higher education itself.

Secondly, it encourages the use of numerical performance indicators. The numbers of applicants with good A levels, the proportion of graduates with good degrees, the numbers of graduates moving into different sectors of the labour market, the economic rates of return (supposedly an indication of the extra human capital generated by the student's higher education) are examples.

But this style of thinking goes even further: there develops all too easily a sheer focus on the size of institutions and the numbers of different aspects of them come to be predominant. In other words, quantity comes before quality. For example, the number of a lecturer's publications becomes more important than the quality of those publications. The number of books in an institution's library becomes more important than their quality. And when it comes to choosing who shall gain access to higher education, A level points scores gained in past school examinations are more telling than applicants' potential to succeed in the future on a degree course in higher education.

Those who want to defend this way of looking at institutions might feel inclined, at all this, to point to the way in which such measures of evaluation are becoming more sophisticated and are being developed so as to incorporate indications of quality as well as quantity.

For example, in theory, simply looking at a list of an individual's publications could give way to a citation analysis, and that analysis could be weighted so as to reflect the most important refereed journals in the field. Or, picking up the concern with the throughput of students, an effort could be made to weigh students' qualifications on entry with their degree classifications, and so generate an index of 'value added' as it is coming to be termed.

The problem with these attempts to get at quality is not that they are not worthwhile: they are. The difficulty with them, so far as higher education is concerned, is that they offer no insight into the central matter, namely the character of the educational processes within IHEs. In short, numerical descriptions of inputs and outputs tell us nothing about the specifically *educational* character of our separate IHEs.

Again, to exemplify this general statement, a disinterested observer coming to higher education solely through a perusal of such performance indicators would have no clue to indicate that a crucial issue is, or should be, the quality of the student's learning. Much lip service is paid to this notion, but in reality, very little attention is given to it (Sizer, 1982; CVCP, 1986, 1987). The UGC has admitted that it has little way of assessing the quality of teaching (UGC, 1985); at least, though, teaching is on the political agenda. On the other hand, student learning, the quality of which cannot be expressed in numerical terms, is hardly anywhere to be seen within the public debate over the future of higher education (DES, 1987a).

This brings us to the third point about the presence of instrumental reason in public discourse about higher education. It is that talk about higher education all too easily focuses on the means, rather than its purposes; so much so, that all too easily the means become purposes in their own right. For example, unit costs become not just a measure of an institution's performance, but they become a guiding light by which the institution steers itself.

Or to take another example, the, generation of research income is seen as a valuable activity in itself, irrespective of the value of the research projects to the community that it finances, or the consequent downgrading of those research efforts in the humanities which do not depend on large running grants.

Performance indicators are not, therefore, just measures which others on the outside use to judge institutions. They also become means by which the institution organises and directs itself, and judges its own performance (CVCP, 1987). And the intrinsic character of performance indicators is such that they are bound to divert institutions' attention away from their essential purposes, values and continuing processes.

'Standards' as a synonym for control

If this analysis about the growth of instrumental reason is correct, we might stop to ask why such an anti-educational style of thinking should have found its way into higher education. The answer, surely, is not hard to find. Its preoccupation with facts and figures rather than purposes and values is part of the general form of instrumental reason. It springs from, as it has recently been suggested, a motivation within society "to control and dominate, and to exercise surveillance and power over others" (Gibson, 1986). It is not coincidental, I suggest, that this style of reasoning about institutions of higher education comes at a time when the state's interest in planning higher education, and when its planning agencies, are paramount (Gellert, 1985).

A consequence of this concern with getting the means right is that the need for institutions to be 'managed' takes on a particular importance. And if they need to be managed, then they need to be managed by 'managers'. And we see this thinking coming through not only in higher education—in the Jarratt report for instance (1985)—but in our public services in general (for example, in the health service, where managers who are not themselves members of the health professions are now managing the service; and where talk of managing the service all too easily gives way to talk of managing the system).

Admittedly, some restraint should be exercised before disparaging the application of the managerial perspective in higher education. It is a salutary lesson for many academics to remember that they are the beneficiaries of what, when viewed from within other parts of the educational system, and even more so when viewed from the position of other public services, seems to be a not unreasonable level of public resource. Nevertheless, it surely makes good sense to work towards a situation in which members of an institution are not simply managed, but feel themselves to be actively participating in its evolution. This is especially the case for IHEs, in which— quite apart from the activity of research—the key activities of teaching and the promotion of effective learning require a particular level of personal involvement and commitment on the part of the teaching staff.

The instrumental style of thinking is not confined, we can note, to one side of the political spectrum. It is also to be found, for example, amongst those who believe passionately in widening access to higher education. In itself, this aim is surely uncontroversial: if higher education is a good, then in principle is should be open to all those who can benefit from it. Indeed, since it is part of the argument of this paper that higher education has its own intrinsic worth, it follows that higher education is a 'good' in its own right. Therefore, unless there are good reasons to the contrary, the general community should endeavour to reduce unnecessary constraints on access for those who can benefit from it. But this argument in itself requires a prior determination of the intrinsic good represented by higher education, and the *internal* benefits to be drawn from it.

The problem, accordingly, with unqualified pleas for wider access is that all too often wider access is conceived in such a way that it becomes an end in itself, without its proponents stopping to ask 'access to what' or 'access for what?' In other words, the means has again become an end, and the actual end—the purpose of higher education—is lost sight of, or (more often) is simply never raised as an issue.

By way of summarising this section, then, we can observe that although the surface structure of the idea of 'fitness for purpose' is that of a general interest in the maintenance and development of standards (which those who use the term are intent on protecting), its deep structure turns out to have very little to do with any interest in the quality of what is going on in institutions of higher education.

Two counter models of purposes in action

(i) Institutions of higher education as academic communities

But how else might we get a purchase on the effectiveness by which our institutions of higher education fulfil their purposes? One of the problems is that, in our modern society, we are trapped into the kind of discourse I have been describing—for it is the discourse of a technological-bureaucratic society, with its associated form of rationality. What we need, therefore, is another vocabulary with which to characterise our institutions.

For higher education, we need—I suggest—to return to a conception of what an institution of higher education is—in essence. From their mediaeval foundations, institutions of higher education have always been associations of individuals who have come together to study and learn *together*. The term 'universitas' originally referred not to the university as a forum for the study of all (i.e. universal) knowledge, but to the university as a place where all scholars could gather and work together (Cameron, 1978). In other words, institutions of higher education are essentially collaborative institutions; and the nature of interpersonal relations between individuals in those institutions is, therefore, highly significant. The idea of democracy is misleading here with its overtones of formal decision-making and representation. What is at stake is, rather, the opportunity for everyone to have their point of view heard in the continuing internal life of IHEs, and the corresponding responsibility to submit to a critical dialogue of one's peers.

Translating this idea into the conceptual framework of the social theorist, Jürgen Habermas, we can talk of an institution's communicative competence (Habermas, 1979). This might be seen in an institution's ability to break down subject barriers between different subject areas, or the collective ways in which its particular purposes are defined by its members of staff, or—and of particular, significance—the extent to which individual staff collaborate in framing the curriculum for their students with their attendant teaching and learning methods. It would also come through in the extent to which the work of an institution is seen as a corporate responsibility.

In other words, do individual members of staff by and large 'do their own thing' or do they work together, feeling that they are engaged in a common enterprise across the institution? Do they feel themselves to have a responsibility for all the work that goes on in the institution?

Underlying this set of considerations is a view of the purposes of the institution in which the formation of the institution and of its individual members are two sides of the same coin, for both are dependent on open personal communication between individuals across the institution. And if institutions of higher education take this part of their activities seriously, they will—given their size and complexity—need to find ways of developing internal processes which encourage the continual breaking down of the barriers which are generated by research and the growth of knowledge in discrete areas (Becher, 1981).

It will also be a matter for concern how far the students themselves are treated as members—albeit junior members, whose full academic development has some way to reach maturity—of the academic community. In other words, what is the character of the relationships between the staff and the students? How far is the individual student's point of view respected? How far are they encouraged, in fact, to form a view of their own? And to contribute to the institution as an institution?

This, then, is a view of purposes which looks to the internal life of institutions. It is a view which is concerned with meaning and understanding: can an institution of higher education promote a sense amongst its members—staff and students—that all its activities are in some sense united by a corporate conception of those activities? Or is the modern institution of higher education just a motley collection of individuals acting separate roles and conducting distinct activities which have nothing in common? (Kerr, 1972). At one time, they were united by a common sense of grievance against the state's budget for higher education. In future, though, even that source of commonality is likely to disappear as sources of funds proliferate, at least for those activities which are seen as providing a quick return to the market place (DES, 1987b).

It is also a view of academic institutions which recognises that individuals—whether staff or students—are or should be undergoing a continuous process of individual formation; that that process of individual formation is a responsibility of the individuals themselves; *and* that the institution—through its processes of interaction and communication—can play a significant part in assisting that process. This is the case whether we are thinking of the individual scholar or researcher who needs to expose his or her ideas to other colleagues; or whether we are thinking of the student on an honours course who needs to be brought up against the cognitive perspective offered by other disciplines, or simply needs to be encouraged to offer one of his or her productions—whether it be an artifact or an essay—for the response of other students.

What this view of the purposes of institutions of higher education is concerned with is simply the idea of institutions as academic communities and the development of students into members of that community. At the level of the institution, it therefore looks to the body of academic staff seeing both academic programmes and their planning and review as corporate activities, in which all members share an interest.

At the level of the individual student, it looks to the institution caring seriously about the experience of the individual student: does it foster the intellectual growth and maturity of the student? Is it one which, in the terminology of those researching into student learning, will encourage the student to employ learning strategies built on deep and holistic processes (Marton *et al.*, 1984), in which the student is himself determined to understand the intricate meaning of important concepts, and place it within an overarching schema of his own; in other words, forms his or her own stamp on things? Or is it one which—through a curriculum which is over-heavy with material to be got through and a correspondingly repressive assessment regime—merely encourages a passive reproducing and an atomistic approach? We are now beginning to understand some of the linkages between the way in which we present the student with the curriculum and the student's experiences (Ramsden, 1984). Consequently, from here on, the meanings that the student forms, assimilates and takes away with her are partly the responsibility of the teaching staff through the way in which the curriculum is presented to the students. No longer is it possible for staff to believe their responsibility is simply one of the transmission of knowledge, in the belief that what the student makes of that knowledge is solely his/her responsibility.

This, then, is a concern with purposes which focuses on the structures of meaning—for both staff and students—and the ways in which individuals within our IHEs feel themselves to be participating in those meaning structures, in their negotiation and in their development. It is, to draw on the terminology of Jürgen Habermas, a hermeneutic conception of purposes (Habermas, 1978). And we can also conceive of an institution of higher education evolving in this dimension (Thompson, 1984). The institution as an academic community can go on developing the degree to which members of staff and individual students feel themselves to be part of a common community. These are not in any sense 'given': an institution can always go on improving its effectiveness in these areas of its internal life.

(ii) Institutions of higher education as critical centres

So much then for the instrumental and the hermeneutic conceptions of purposes. But there is, I want to suggest, a third idea of purposes which is related to the hermeneutic conception but which institutions of higher education must not forget. This is the notion of the academic community as residing not in any kind of discourse but in a particular form of discourse. And it is a discourse characterised not by any special subject content but by the manner in which it is conducted. It is a view of the academic institution founded on a critical discourse or—in the terminology of an American social theorist—a 'culture of critical discourse' (Gouldner, 1979).

This form of internal life is exhibited in a number of ways. It comes through in the way in which the purposes of the institution itself are kept under review. It is also evident in the extent to which staff allow their own activities to be evaluated, whether it is the work of an individual participating in an appraisal of his or her teaching methods and learning experiences to which students are exposed, or whether it is a course team or the members of a department submitting themselves, or the courses they offer, to a review by their peers from other departments or from other institutions. It also comes through in the ways in which students themselves are encouraged to develop critical perspectives towards their learning and are given the conceptual apparatus to allow that to happen.

Ultimately, then, this critical conception of the purposes of higher education looks, whether at the level of the institution, or course teams or individual members of staff or the student, to the continuing development of autonomy and independence, though aided by the constructive critical comment of others. This is, therefore, to use an appropriate shorthand description, again following Habermas's terminology, the emancipatory conception of purposes (Habermas, 1965).

It is worth noticing that the kind of critical dialogue which is offered by peer review does not apply just to the fully-fledged members of the academic community and their activities. Peer review is well-known in relation to research and—at least in the public sector—for courses and institutional arrangements. But it also has a place within the efforts of students themselves, and not only in course or project work, but even in student self-assessment (Boud, 1985).

The argument so far

That, then, is a sketch of three kinds of purposes, in which the latter two (the hermeneutic and the critical) have been set against the more conventional approach (the instrumental) I started with. That more conventional approach is, it will be recalled, focused on inputs and outcomes, and assessments of achievement in terms of performance indicators which have their home in criteria which are strictly external to what institutions of higher education are ultimately about. The two alternative conceptions are quite different in both these respects. They look to purposes as they are exemplified in the institution's continuing and developing processes, and they are concerned with the internal life of institutions. In short, they are concerned with the intrinsic character of what it is to be an institution of higher education (Moodie, 1986, p. 7).

At this point, it is worth bringing into the open some claims which are *not* being made here. It is not being said, for example, that IHEs should define themselves in terms of purposes antithetical to the dominant values of their host society. Nor is it being argued that there is a sharp break between the essential character of IHEs and every other activity within society. It is not being suggested that the institutions and values of the wider society are of lesser account than those of IHEs. And, lastly, it is no part of the argument here that IHEs should attempt to isolate themselves from the 'corrupting' values and ideologies of their society. All of these propositions—were any of them to be made—are, in any case, founded on a misreading of the position of the modern academy. The modern IHE cannot, if indeed it ever could, opt out of its host society, for it is a key institution within it. Equally, if it has something of value to offer society, then it has an obligation to diffuse it as widely as possible throughout society.

The argument here is not in substance one concerned with the institutional relationships of IHEs and the wider society or even with the actual values of the academic community. It is not, in other words, an essay on the sociology of higher education. It is, rather, a conceptual inquiry into what we take to be the defining purposes of institutions of higher education. Whether we are concerned to develop a *modus vivendi* between higher education and society, or to promote a continuing dialogue, or even to disseminate the value of higher education, we need first to be clear about that for which IHEs, in essence, stand. It *is* part of the argument here that that essential character, unlike some other social institutions, lies in the particularity of the continuing internal processes of IHEs. If we wish seriously to assess the fulfilment of their purposes, therefore, we cannot succeed solely through an approach which relies on numerical indicators of their performance.

The problem with indicators of performance—used in the conventional approach—is not just that they are simply only indicators and do not illuminate the character of the performance. It is their more pernicious nature in that they never could say anything about the internal life of institutions. Capturing that would require a quite different approach to the evaluation of institutions' achievements. For they are achievements not realised in any end-point which can be pinned down by performance indicators but instead by a sensitive insight offered by participants on the spot. The illumination of a process, whether it is the learning approaches adopted by students or the way in which staff collaborate to offer a course, cannot be achieved by a judgement of outcomes, no matter how sophisticated.

In the language of the philosopher of education R. S. Peters, higher education is, I am suggesting, both a task and an achievement concept (Peters, 1967). On the one hand, institutions of higher education have to adhere to certain principles, aims and processes, by virtue of which they can justifiably be termed institutions of higher education. It indicates the fulfilment of particular, though general, criteria which any institution has to achieve to warrant the title. On the other hand, their fulfilment is achieved not suddenly at a moment in time (like the scoring of a goal), but is rather achieved through the continuing internal processes of an institution. In this sense, higher education is as much a task as an achievement. Consequently, in any evaluation of institutions' effectiveness, we would need, if we were serious about it, to find ways of getting at and illuminating its processes.

Four intrinsic purposes of institutions of higher education

But what, ultimately, does it mean to be an institution of higher education? Is it possible to set out the conditions which institutions have to fulfil in order to warrant the title 'institutions of *higher* education'? I want to suggest that whatever else an institution of higher education does—in the way for instance of providing highly qualified manpower or pursuing important lines of research or attracting a student intake from disadvantaged social groups—whatever its own purposes or those enjoined on it by society, there are four intrinsic purposes which all institutions of higher education must fulfil. These are as follows (they follow from the earlier argument): (i) a concern with the development of each student's autonomy, self-critical abilities and academic competence (evidence here would include, for instance, higher order skills such as identifying problems, marshalling evidence, seeing connections, and forming judgements); (ii) the institution as a self-determining institution, taking corporate responsibility for the maintenance of its own standards and its future development: here, the internal life would promote a self-critical and a self-learning academic community; (iii) an institution in which the life of research is important in the sense of 'a culture of critical discourse', or systematic critical inquiry on the part of individual members of staff (this sense of research would not, it will be noticed, require large research grants or massive capital equipment); (iv) a concern to make this form of higher education—essentially one of critical inquiry—available to all who can benefit from it and who wish to have access to it. This might mean that we need to take part-time higher education more seriously and give it positive discrimination. It might also mean the development of admissions procedures which seek to assess applicants' potential for *future* success. And it could mean recognising that not all applicants who hold formal entry qualifications are in fact committed to the style of life, commitment and interaction represented by the academic community.

These four are, I want to claim, essential purposes of higher education. In other words, an institution must be able to demonstrate that these concerns are built into its internal processes. They are the general conditions of what it means to be an institution of higher education. Collectively, they amount to a statement of the purposes of higher education, against which institutions should be obliged to demonstrate their fitness, for the external world to be able to accept that genuine processes of higher education are being conducted.

In other words, the essential purposes of institutions of higher education and the fitness of institutions in relation to these purposes, are going to be demonstrated more through the character of institutions' continuing internal processes than through any particular achievements—and 'achievements' here include the proportion of first class honours graduates and the number of Nobel prize winners as well as student:staff ratios and unit costs. Ultimately, we shall only properly know our institutions of higher education by the character of their internal living processes and the daily experiences of both students and staff. In short, we should ask of an institution: is it a collaborative, exciting, critical, alive institution in which to develop intellectually?

The four conditions are, then, fundamental: there can be no escape for genuine institutions of higher education. But they are not completely binding, for they leave open to each institution how they are to be met. And institutions will vary in the relative importance they give to each of them; some will want to give particular importance to access, to ensuring that their admissions processes are genuinely open. Others will want to give attention to the student experience, perhaps experimenting with ways of promoting the individual student's autonomy through open learning strategies and learning approaches which foster the student's conceptual understanding. And still others will want to build up the corporate aspects of the institution, finding means of encouraging cross-fertilisation between disciplines and encouraging members of staff to give up time to assist in the review of other colleagues' courses.

Any of these is a legitimate response for an institution to make to the four conditions I have outlined, as an autonomous self-directed community. But all four conditions would need to be met to some degree: institutions would need to show that each was being taken seriously, and that none of them was considered as so important that any of the others is neglected.

Institutions of higher education are not ivory towers

There should be no misunderstanding that these should be an institution's only concerns. We began, after all, by observing that institutions of higher education will wish to fulfil all sorts of purposes, some of their own choosing, and others supplied by the wider society which grants them their funds. This is entirely acceptable, provided the four internal purposes are maintained.

It has always been one of the functions of higher learning to supply cohorts for the professions; and professional education is perhaps the almost unnoticed dominant characteristic of modern higher education, with UK IHEs interacting with nearly one hundred professional bodies. And indeed, if an institution designs a course to fulfil certain professionally oriented objectives, its effectiveness must be tested against that programme. But such extramural considerations come into account in appraising institutions, not as an *ex cathedra* requirement, but because the institution has chosen to fulfil its fundamental purposes in that way.

Similarly, it is not being said here that institutions of higher education, which are in receipt of public monies, do not need to concern themselves with the efficient use of those monies; performance indicators such as unit costs, non-completion rates, and patterns of degree classifications do, therefore, have a part to play in assessing the performance of our institutions. But it is only a part. And ultimately, it is only a minor part. For the elements of an institution's performance that they illuminate—largely matters of the institution's efficiency as an organisation—do nothing to illuminate the nature of the internal processes and interactions which are the real exemplification of an institution's claim to be an institution of higher education.

Institutions of higher education will demonstrate their fitness for purpose, therefore, by the ways in which they can show their adherence to the four fundamental conditions of their internal processes (set out above), and by their success in implementing them and the different weight they give to each.

To whom is the institution supposed to demonstrate its achievement of those purposes? Is it just a matter of demonstrating to its own satisfaction? Or is the institution supposed to do the demonstrating to—in the familiar term of our time—its peers? In other words, through some kind of peer review process, operated in conjunction with the validating bodies? Or is it again that the institution is going to be expected to demonstrate its fitness to some more or less external body or interest group? Here, I have in mind not only quasi-governmental planning agencies (such as the UGC and the NAB) or monitoring agencies (HMI), or even professional bodies, but also wider and more nebulous groupings such as industry and commerce, and—most nebulous of all—the pool of prospective students.

These questions are not unimportant, but they are second-order. Far more fundamental is that we should be clear about what it means to be an institution of higher education as such, and that within that framework, individual institutions should be encouraged to work out their own identity (their specific purposes). When, and only when, those conditions have been met, we will be in a position to adopt an evaluation methodology—preferably in collaboration with each institution (Adelman, 1984)—which is appropriate to the purposes of institutions of higher education. Since those purposes, on the argument here, reside partly in the character of an institution's processes, it is clear that externally applied assessments of numerical indicators cannot play a major part. Instead, an in-depth examination of an institution's internal character would seem to be a necessary condition, involving at least some external evaluators (but who have a sensitivity to the particular character of the individual institution). It may turn out that a properly informed evaluation can only be accomplished through some kind of participant observation over a sustained period (e.g. Adelman & Powney, 1984).

The conclusion here is obvious. If we are clear about an institution's purposes (both general and specific) and if we have an appropriate evaluation methodology, the results of the evaluation will stand both as a guide to the institution itself, and to any third party to which the institution is accountable. Admittedly, the likelihood exists that an evaluation of this kind will be problematic for external agencies concerned with national planning and funding, since such an institution-specific evaluation is unlikely to facilitate cross-institutional comparisons. In that case, there will be—as some have recognised (Bevan, 1984; NAB, 1987)—a responsibility on those who proclaim the virtues of performance indicators to embrace the more qualitative evaluations of IHEs as a valuable supplement to the more numerical information at their command.

Concluding note

It is worth observing that in examining the purposes for which institutions of higher education might become 'fit', something else has emerged. In touching on such notions as the development of the student's critical abilities, the life of research as critical inquiry, on open access and continuing education, and on academic community as characterised by openness and constructive, collaborative, critical dialogue, we have in the process outlined a restatement of the idea of liberal higher education in modern terms.

Part III

Students and learning

Chapter 11

Supercomplexity and the curriculum

(from *Studies in Higher Education*, 2000, 25 (3) 255–265)

Outline

For some time (over 100 years), the dominant influence in the shaping of curricula has been that of the academics in their separate knowledge fields. In the contemporary world, that academic hegemony is dissolving as curricula become subject to two contending patterns of change. Firstly, in a mass higher education system, there will be tendencies towards increased diversity in the components of curricula. Secondly, and in contradistinction, as the state looks to see a greater responsiveness towards the world of work, it is possible that a universal shift in the direction of performativity is emerging: what counts is less what students understand (still less their critical insight into matters) and more what they can do (as represented in their demonstrable 'skills'). Not surprisingly, curricula are taking on ad hoc patterns that are the unwitting outfall of this complex of forces, diversifying and universalising as these forces are. Consequently, higher education curricula will be unlikely to yield the human qualities – qualities of being – that the current age of supercomplexity requires.

Introduction

This article offers some preliminary suggestions arising out of a research project that has been examining the changing patterns of undergraduate curricula in the UK. The project has been examining five subject areas in six multifaculty universities. The subject areas chosen were chemistry, electronic engineering, history, nursing and midwifery studies, and management studies; the six universities were chosen to represent a range of institutions across pre-1992 and post-1992 institutions. The purpose of this article, however, is less to offer detailed empirical findings and more to begin to develop a framework through which curricula change in a mass higher education system at the end of the twentieth century can be understood.

Curricula in UK higher education have not been extensively studied and those studies that exist are becoming dated. The major works by Boys *et al.* (1988) and Squires (1990) most closely approach the topic, but their datedness alone points to the desirability of examining curricula within the contemporary higher education system and of attempting to incorporate contemporary social theory.

Situating curricular change

Curricula are offered by institutions of higher education which themselves are located in a world of change. The extent to which those institutions perceive such a world of change and the extent to which they choose to respond to those changes will inevitably vary. There will also be variation, we may hypothesise, across disciplines. These simple initial observations generate some significant questions. For instance, to what extent are institutions responding to change? What are the sources of change to which disciplines respond? What are the characteristic differences in response? What is the balance of influence as between institutions and disciplines?

In relation to curricula that institutions offer, such questions prompt a more fundamental challenge: what kind of analytical framework (or frameworks) is going to be helpful in understanding curricula and curricula change? At what level should the analytical framework be pitched in order for us to gain a purchase on higher education curricula?

Since higher education curricula have not been extensively studied, we may turn to wider literatures to secure some initial bearings. For example, Clark (1983, p. 143) suggested that universities can be located amid a triangle of forces: state authority, market and academic 'oligarchy'. Translating this schema so as to illuminate curricula, we could assess, in turn, the extent to which curricula are shaped by national bodies, by the power of the market and by the interests of the academic community. Such a schema, however, presents immediate problems.

Firstly, the professions—to which many courses in higher education are oriented—would surely have to be considered to constitute a separate force of change. Secondly, the idea of a market in relation to curricula is problematic. The UK is developing a student market—and is, thereby, approaching the USA model in this respect—but the employer interests could be considered to constitute a kind of quasi-market to which courses may be orienting themselves. On the other hand, the 'labour market', in so far as it is a set of signals from employers interpreted by applicants, brings together both students and employers. The market, accordingly, has no unambiguous reading in relation to curricula.

Thirdly, the category of 'academic' is problematic. On the one hand, across the disciplines, there are significant differences in the construction of the 'academic' as a particular form of identity: across the fields of knowledge, differences are apparent both in terms of the relationships to the world of work and in terms of the relationships between research and teaching. What it is to be 'an academic' is by no means given but is a matter of dynamic relationships between social and epistemological interests and structures.

On the other hand, while there may be characteristics of curricula that are generic to disciplines (and that has to be determined), it would be uncontroversial to suggest that some characteristics at least are disciplines-specific. Furthermore, some disciplines could be sets of activity largely distinct from the world of work whereas others derive their locus from activities in the world of work (including the professions). So the category of 'academic' is problematic also in relation to curricula conjuring up dimensions of specificity and generality; and of knowledge-in-itself and knowledge-in-work.

If a schema such as Clark's—in attempting to chart the forces acting on curricula—runs us into difficulties, an alternative tack might be to turn to a framework such as that of Bernstein. His concepts of framing and classification (presented in his earlier work but developed in his more recent work [1996]) could be potent means of analysing curricula in higher education. They can help to illuminate, for example, the extent of boundaries both between lecturers and students in the pedagogical relationship (the tightness of framing) and the boundaries between the curriculum contents (the tightness or looseness of its classification). There is a difficulty, however, with such an approach in that, while it illuminates the internal characteristics of the curriculum, especially the character of the pedagogical relationships and identities, it glosses over the dynamics between the curriculum and its total environment. Indeed, the notions of power and control, which lie behind Bernstein's framework, cannot be properly understood in the curriculum setting unless we situate the curriculum within its total context.

There is a fundamental dilemma, then, before us in attempting to understand curricula in a mass higher education system in the modern world: either we focus on curricula as sites of social processes in their own right, and in doing so neglect the ways in which the wider world interpenetrates higher education, *or* we attempt to include the wider world in so far as it affects the curriculum and, thereby, run into the difficulties of attempting to form analytical frameworks that can do justice to the complexity of those relationships (across, in the UK, around 100 university institutions and 40,000 courses).

Only the latter strategy could be said to be intellectually and practically adequate to the situation that confronts us. We need to situate curricula amid the wider social and even global context. The curriculum *is* likely to be influenced by many factors external to higher education. In turn, manifold dynamic relationships are developing between those external factors and knowledge fields on the one hand and institutions of higher education on the other as they take up their own place in the wider repositioning of higher education in the wider world (Coffield & Williamson, 1997). Consequently, there can be no reason to believe that there will be any definite pattern to changes taking place in curricula.

A supercomplex world

The challenges of understanding the changing patterns of the curriculum in higher education are, however, even more severe. Higher education is faced not just with preparing students for a complex world but is faced with preparing them for a *supercomplex* world. It is a world where nothing can be taken for granted, where no frame of understanding or of action can be entertained with any security. It is a world in which we are conceptually challenged, and continually so.

A *complex* world is one in which we are assailed by more facts, data, evidence, tasks and arguments than we can easily handle *within* the frameworks in which we have our being. By contrast, a *supercomplex* world is one in which the very frameworks by which we orient ourselves to the world are themselves contested. Supercomplexity denotes a fragile world but it is a fragility brought on not merely by social and technological change; it is a fragility in the way that we understand the world, in the way in which we understand ourselves and in the ways in which we feel secure about acting in the world.

This triple set of challenges—of understanding, of self-identity and of action—arises out of a conjunction of contexts that are caught in the term 'a global age' (Albrow, 1996) in which forms of life interact globally. Associated subcontexts are those of the arrival of the information age, with its compression of time and space; the so-called post-Fordist environments of work, which place more onus on individuals to take responsibility for their actions in flatter organisational structures; and an increasing multiplication of sites of knowledge production coupled with a widening of the forms of what is held to count as legitimate knowledge. A separate context germane to these considerations is that of the rise of the 'risk society' (Beck, 1992) in which society—worldwide—comes to be structured anew through 'manufactured risk', namely, those forms of risk that human beings have generated through the technological and conceptual schemas that they have wrought on the world (Giddens, 1995).

A further global change that may be characterising forms of knowledge is that of a possible shift towards 'performativity' (Lyotard, 1984). This performative shift may work at relatively subterranean levels, being evident at the level of topics and even concepts within disciplines. As disciplines are called upon to demonstrate their use-value in the global market, subtle shifts may be detected in the inner constitution of disciplines. (I return to this matter later.)

A yet further set of relevant changes is that of the changing patterns of the economy in an advanced society such as the UK. Although the economy may be falling somewhat short relative to its competitors, nevertheless the underlying intention is to develop a high-skill, high value-added economy. Two shifts are embedded in this observation. Firstly, the 'knowledge society' (Stehr, 1994) calls for increasingly differentiated knowledges (plural) (Gokulsing & DaCosta, 1997) of an increasingly elaborate form. Secondly, to technical skills is added a call for more generic skills. (Whether the latter exist is a further matter that we cannot go into here.)

This supercomplexity shows itself discursively in the world of work through such terms as 'flexibility', 'adaptability' and (more recently still) 'self-reliance' (Association of Graduate Recruiters 1995). In such terminology, we find a sense of individuals having to take onto themselves responsibility for continually reconstituting themselves through their lifespan. (Such an individualism also comes to form a new definition of 'the learning society'.) It also shows itself in the call for 'communication skills' and for 'leadership skills' since, in a globalised world, communication is made both more problematic and more urgent.

Interpreting the signals

Against this background, those in higher education responsible for offering programmes of study are faced with nigh-on-impossible challenges. Each curriculum can be understood as a set of more or less intentional strategies to produce—in each student—a set of subjectivities. But, from our preceding reflections, it is clear that the required set of subjectivities is unlikely to be made clear to higher education. Higher education is called upon to be responsive to the 'needs' of society, especially to produce skilled human capital for the labour market, but even for those willing to so respond, higher education is having to detect and to decipher the messages coming at it.

The messages are mixed, uneven, often weak, changing and even conflicting; and even merely tacit. Subjectivities for now or for an uncertain future; for the immediate locality or for the global world; for a supervisory role or for one of 'leadership'; for a particular sector of the labour market or—through 'generic skills'—for the world of work as a whole; these are just some of the decisions, accordingly, that the construction of a curriculum in higher education calls for.

A curriculum—as we have noted—is an educational project for producing a set of subjectivities; but the subjectivities are likely to be mixed in any instance. A world of supercomplexity—as I earlier termed it—implicates different dimensions of human being calling forth, in curriculum design, epistemological (knowing), praxis (action) and ontological (self-identity) elements. As a result, we may conjecture, the curriculum is widening: a broader array of subjectivities is being urged upon higher education as worthy of a place within the undergraduate curriculum. It never was solely a set of epistemological elements, but they have probably tended to dominate most curricula in higher education. The reason for such an epistemological domination is that the control of the curriculum has been—to a considerable extent—in the hands of the academics; the curriculum in higher education has been a site of so-called producer capture. Those elements are now broadening as the needs of a changing and supercomplex world exert themselves.

A further set of signals affecting the development of the curriculum is constituted through the growth—as a matter of state policy in the UK—of higher education as a market. The Teaching Quality Assessment exercise (now termed Subject Review) in the UK has, as part of its purpose, the publication of the assessments so as to stimulate a more informed set of consumer choices. The setting of course fees is doubtless stimulating more of a market. The market, however, is not just local (within the UK) but is also global. Many institutions see their competitor institutions as those in other countries as much as, if not more than, in the UK. Some institutions—or, at least, some departments—may declare themselves to be immune to market considerations, apparently secure in the knowledge that they are assured of a ready supply of well-qualified applicants. The extent to which such self-assurances are reflected in perhaps slowly changing curricula practices remains a matter for investigation.

A yet further matter affecting the form and character of curricula in higher education is that of the injection into universities of a more corporate style of management. 'Top-down' signals about the kinds of 'skills' to be developed might be mirrored, for example, by the establishment of modular degree schemes, designed both to offer efficiency savings and to inject something of an internal student market. Institutional learning and teaching strategies—now required by the Higher Education Funding Council of each institution in England—may also influence curricula as well as pedagogies; for instance, in looking to inject action-oriented elements and elements that look to students to extend their own selves.

For now, a final set of signals requiring interpretation by curriculum providers is that of the effort on the part of the state to bring about more of an equality in status between the two major functions of a university, namely, research and teaching. In a mass higher education system, it is felt both that teaching has to be more effective and more efficient (especially given the lower unit of resource provided by the state itself) and that research cannot offer the main basis of teaching, given the selectivity towards research that a mass higher education system brings. Accordingly, the state is attempting to encourage innovation in the teaching function, both technologically (especially through the greater use of information technology) and educationally, through experimentation and dissemination of 'good practice'.

Wittingly or unwittingly, such pedagogical innovation will have implications for the curriculum, in the most general sense of that term.

Mixing the currents

A curriculum, then, is going to represent a mix of dimensions and elements embedded in such media as disciplinary developments, state-sponsored debate, the student market and increasing academic–employer discussions. Extending a little beyond our discussion hitherto, nine dimensions can be disentangled, each with its own elements:

   (i) internal and external;
  (ii) epistemological, practical and ontological;
 (iii) truth and performance;
 (iv) managerial, academic and market;
  (v) local, national and global;
 (vi) past, present and future orientation;
(vii) context-specific and context-generic;
(viii) endorsing and critical orientations;
 (ix) reflexivity and the promotion of self.

These dimensions and elements cut across each other. For instance, 'skills' can be evident under several of these dimensions (ii, iii, vii, viii); markets (iv) can be local, national or global (v) in character *and* they can be internal or external in character (i); knowledge (ii) can be truth-oriented or performative (iii) in character. Many more such cross-cuttings can be observed.

The ways in which these dimensions and elements might enter the curriculum are likely to be numerous and inchoate. For the most part, we may conjecture that decisions are not taken deliberately. On the one hand, lecturers offering a course will be unlikely to possess the conceptual background in order to be able to make such decisions explicit to themselves. That is to say, they will not necessarily be aware that they are making decisions along these dimensions. But, in addition, *these* matters of curriculum design may not be voiced at all; they may not be matters for discussion. There may be no local forum where such matters can be raised; there may be no course team where such issues could be identified, addressed and made problematic. To do so would, among other things, make public and explicit a curriculum that stands outside of the lecturers as individuals and, therefore, might appear to impinge upon their academic freedom. Curricula in higher education are to a large degree *hidden curricula*, being lived by rather than being determined. They have an elusive quality about them. Their actual dimensions and elements are tacit. They take on certain patterns and relationships but those patterns and relationships will be hidden from all concerned, except as they are experienced by the students.

The end of purity

It is unlikely that there remains any complete *singular* (Bernstein, 1996). The arrival of mass higher education, the lowering of the unit of resource, the desire of the state to move curricula in the direction of *enterprise*, the increased pull of the labour market, the bargaining that students may come to exert on their curricula, the greater interest of the professions in their educational functions: all these developments are society-wide in their manifestations. Some institutions and some knowledge fields will be able to resist changing to some extent but it is unlikely that any pool of purity will remain. *Every curriculum will exhibit some form or even forms of hybridity.*

Emerging models are, therefore, likely to be constituted through amalgams of different components (see earlier). The key question, then, is twofold: what are the principal components of emerging curricula? What are the emerging dominant combinations (models) of curricula? Despite the likely omnipresence of differing forms of hybridity, might we also be witnessing contemporaneously the emerging of a new universal in the patterning of curricula? Is it just possible that we may be in the presence of a multiplying differentiation *and* a common thread? Such a set of contending forces may be precisely to hand. Of course, if there is a unifying thread, it will not come neatly packaged, readily visible; it is bound itself to exhibit internal differences.

The performative slide

Following Lyotard (1984), we can hypothesise that curricula are exhibiting a general tendency of *performativity*. Performativity comes in a number of variants, of which I would identify the following.

(a) *Epistemological*. The intellectual base of a knowledge field may itself take a performative turn, in which pragmatic interests directed to problems in the world come to be embedded in the inner structure of the field. Subfields, topics, frameworks and concepts may all have their locus to a significant degree in the world of action. Problems-in-the-world call for solutions. It may be, of course, that the problems are technical in character and are themselves the result of earlier technologies, themselves underpinned by knowledge fields. In other words, the new problem-solving is called for as a result of the 'manufactured risk' (Giddens, 1995) begotten by knowledge already-in-the-world. Mode 1 knowledge (in the academy) is called upon to transmute itself into Mode 2 knowledge in the world (Gibbons *et al.*, 1994). For example, lasers have been spawned by Mode 1 knowledge but in turn cause Mode 1 knowledge to turn into Mode 2 knowledge as lasers come to constitute part of the intellectual fields of physics and electrical engineering. This performativity is epistemological because we are here witnessing a slide in the epistemology of knowledge fields. Subtly, and unnoticed, they become operational and pragmatic in character.

(b) *Corporate-instrumental.* Many sectors of the corporate world are presenting with clusters of problems to be addressed which may be taken up as research topics and which, therefore, again bring a reshaping to the knowledge field. Such *problem nets* do not just emerge from industry (such as the electronic, pharmaceutical and engineering sectors) but may arise from the professional or service sectors (such as the transport, architectural or social work settings). In turn, such problem nets may serve as pedagogical devices.

(c) *Pedagogical—technological.* The technologies of the pedagogy may not just change but come to take on a performative aura, in which the performance becomes objectified, split apart from the substance of the educational transaction. With computer technologies in particular (such as Powerpoint), the lecture becomes an event to be consumed by passive spectators. This mesmerism works a new magic, not of ideas and concepts but of glitz and show as such.

(d) *Pedagogical—educational.* In a mass higher education system, there emerges a drive to produce 'independent learners', such learning being apparently facilitated by new technologies, especially the computer. The computer both captures and sets free, as it seems, at the same time. It also calls forth new performativities, requiring (in some forms of computer modelling in engineering and chemistry) the coordination of eye, hand and brain in new interactions and new systems.

(e) *Educational—disciplinary.* Partly through the press of a heterogeneous intake of students (amid 'massification'), efforts are made to find ways of increasing the students' understanding of topics. Understanding, in other words, can no longer be taken for granted but is now focused upon the conditions of entry into a disciplinary domain. 'Problem-solving', accordingly, has entered the more technical curricula but now takes on a particular hue, namely that of cementing basic routines within the discipline.

(f) *Educational—corporate life-world.* Increasingly, students are being asked to take on the general capacities ('core skills') required by the corporate world. They are required to give oral presentations on their projects, engage more in group projects, and attend to their written communicative 'skills' (which themselves are expected to be more iconic in character). Within curricula, students are being asked thereby to assume more performative identities alongside their cognitive personae.

(g) *Self-monitoring.* Both in the humanities and in the vocational disciplines, students are being required to develop self-monitoring capacities. These may be largely internal and educational in character, calling for the development of reflexive capacities of various kinds (and in this sense could not sensibly be said to be performative in character). But, and especially in the vocational fields (nursing being a good example), self-monitoring may take on a performative character, where students are asked to demonstrate publicly their powers of self-monitoring. The pedagogical technologies widen, for example, to include 'learning logs'.

As these features come to be ever more commonplace, as they become evident—doubtless to different degrees and with separate nuances—across knowledge fields and institutions, so there arises a near-universal shift towards performativity. From a curriculum for inner contemplation to a curriculum for outer performance, there appears this recurring pattern. Partly, this transition is an unintended consequence of responses to a 'massified' pedagogical situation. Partly, it is a reflection of an underlying pedagogical shift: knowledge itself is taking a performative turn. But partly, too, it is symptomatic of closer relationships with wider stakeholders so that the external is assimilated within and becomes constitutive of curricula and pedagogies themselves. The external becomes the internal.

The results, we might hypothesise, are likely to be profound for the formation of student identities. At one level, students are likely to be more adept at handling themselves in the world in the domains of performance itself but also of cognition and self-identity. At another level, however, understanding may be contained, held back at levels which simply ensure a satisfactory performance. No longer can we look forward to informed action; what emerges is behaviour lacking an underpinning in deep and wide understanding. The mass higher education may be producing accomplished technicians, able to deal with real-world problems, interweaving within and between teams and presenting themselves to effect. They may even produce transformations (Harvey, 1996) in their environment. But the verbs in those sentences—'deal', 'produce', 'interweave', and 'present'—indicate that we are in the presence of instrumental and technical reason as distinct from reflective and communicative reason. In attempting and in apparently succeeding in helping students to live in the here-and-now, curricula may fail to impart to students the ontological and epistemological resources for engaging meaningfully with others in a world in which nothing is certain.

Directionless transitions

Curricula in higher education, I have been implying, take different shapes as a result of separate sets of negotiations between contending forces. The state, the labour market, students, knowledge fields and institutions exert their influence in varying proportions across curricula. At one level, this heterogeneity is valuable. The labour market and society more generally require a diversity of subjectivities. This unplanned free-for-all has a logic to it. In the UK, moves by the Quality Assurance Agency (QAA) to develop common threshold standards by benchmarking curricula in different subjects can be read as a means of clarifying the messages in the 'relays' (Bernstein, 1996) between the higher education system and the labour market. But they can also be read as an inappropriate effort to limit diversity at a time when more diversity is required (Brown, 1999).

But the QAA strategy can also be seen as problematic in another sense. Graduates are having to make their way in the world, a world that exhibits global features of challenge, uncertainty, turbulence, unquantifiable risk, contestability and unpredictability. That curricula are the haphazard fall-out of largely unreflective interactions between a multitude of influences is not going to produce subjectivities that are appropriate to this world of supercomplexity (Barnett, 2000). This is so at two levels. Firstly, the range of subjectivities that emerges from universities in a mass higher education system can hardly be adequate to global features: particularities are no match for global features. Secondly, higher education remains largely amateur in the construction of its curricula. By and large, many departments—even in pre-1992 universities—have teaching committees but they lack the conceptual resources to construct curricula on an informed basis. (It appears that the newly established Institute for Learning and Teaching is likely to focus its attention on teaching activities. There is no sign as yet that it will seek to develop an agenda for curriculum matters as such.)

Putting it charitably, we can say that the changes that are apparent in undergraduate curricula are evidence of a search for curricula that are appropriate to a supercomplex world. Gradually, curricula are showing signs of providing students with powers of reflection, capacities to act in the world, a greater awareness of self and metacapacities that generate personal and interpersonal resources not just for coping with supercomplexity but also a mode of effective being within it.

That the competence ideology is unable to secure a firm foothold in higher education, that skills are to be 'embedded' in curricula (National Committee of Inquiry into Higher Education [NCIHE], 1997) rather than being an adjunct to them, and that 'breadth' is still encouraged indicates that segregated competences are not required from higher education. Higher education is called upon to develop meta-qualities of 'self-reliance' (Association of Graduate Recruiters, 1995) that will enable graduates not just to survive amid supercomplexity but also to prosper in it and even to go on contributing to it. The difficulty is that it will only be sheer happenstance as to whether any one curriculum is likely to yield the subjectivities that are appropriate to a world of supercomplexity.

Under what conditions, then, is a curriculum for supercomplexity likely to be forthcoming? The challenge is to produce a set of experiences that in turn encourage the formation of human qualities able to engage effectively with multiple frameworks, contesting value systems and open-ended action situations. A curriculum for supercomplexity has to be an educational project at once embracing the domains of being, knowing and action; in other words, a project of ontology, epistemology and praxis. Otherwise, the resources for coping with and continuing to prosper under conditions of supercomplexity are likely to be lacking.

At most, curricula are edging forward in this direction but sluggishly; and, all too often, the development of curricula in this direction has actually been arrested if not reversed. Limited degrees of reflexiveness are exhibited both by the elite universities (especially in science disciplines) and in the new universities (under the press of high student–staff ratios). Limited degrees of exposure to the world of action are evident in older universities. Limited metacompetences are evident in the newer universities. The sciences remain characterised by a lack of reflexivity across the system. The newer vocational areas, especially in the newer universities, are intent on delivering competences for the here-and-now. Pedagogies, in a mass higher education system, may have the surface structure of promoting independence but contain a deep structure of confining subjectivities within given frameworks. Disciplines in the older universities remain highly classified, separated from each other, so denying students the powers both to develop multiple perspectives and the powers of self-critique that such multiple perspectives could offer.

Some hypotheses

We can now venture some hypotheses that might be tested empirically:

Hypothesis 1: In higher education, no curriculum will be devoid of change. However, no definite pattern of change will be detectable.

Hypothesis 2: The form of a curriculum will reflect the dominant sources of influences.

Hypothesis 3: Curricula will be inward looking, reflecting a project of *introjection* where they are largely the outcome of academic influence, and will be outward looking, reflecting a project of *projection*, where they are subject to external influences.

Hypothesis 4: The dominant change in higher education is that of an orientation towards the world of work. Accordingly, change at the macro-level will be particularly evident in the direction of *projection*.

Hypothesis 5: All curricula are mixes. (The issue, for any one curriculum, is what mix and in what proportions?)

Hypothesis 6: Partly as a result of an institutional dimension becoming more significant in the shaping of curricula, the *singulars* of disciplines are giving way to *regions*, formed either by multidisciplinary combinations or by modularisation (Bernstein, 1996). (This hypothesis is a development of hypothesis 5.)

Hypothesis 7: Institutional policies connected with the curriculum (for example, of modularisation and of 'transferable skills') are rhetorical statements, reflecting the managerial and market discourses; but actual changes in curricula reflect the extent to which disciplines within institutions are yielding their insularity.

Hypothesis 8: Despite changes brought about by influences beyond the knowledge field (hypotheses 4 and 6), the discipline (or knowledge field) constitutes the largest claim on the identity of academics. Accordingly, curricula changes at the micro-level will continue primarily to reflect changes in the field of inquiry.

Hypothesis 9: Comparing the influence of knowledge fields and institutions, knowledge fields will exert the larger influence. Institutions will exert their claims where disciplines are weak; especially where the research domain is weakly developed. (It follows—also from hypothesis 8—that institutions are not yet major determinants of curriculum change *per se*.)

Hypothesis 10: Where institutions are weak in relation to their knowledge fields, curriculum change will result from non-institutional influences. Apart from change within knowledge fields itself, curriculum change will be mainly subject to three sets of potential influences: the student market, the labour market, and professional body requirements.

Hypothesis 11: In response to the diverse influences now acting on the curriculum, especially its being situated in a global world of unceasing change, the curriculum as a project will come ever more to embrace three domains of human *being*, those of *episteme* (knowledge), *praxis* (action) and *ontology* (self-identity).

Hypothesis 12: The pattern that these three domains will exhibit in structuring the curriculum will be a function of the differential power of the knowledge field and the positioning of the host institution within the higher education system.

Conclusions

Our conclusions have, in the first place, to be both empirical and theoretical; and, at this preliminary juncture, they are bound to be somewhat jejune. Empirically, we lack a proper understanding of the basic shape of contemporary curricula in UK higher education, we lack an understanding of their general patterns and directions of change and we lack an understanding of the emerging dominant models of curricula and their respective sources of change and durability (or even resistance). Theoretically, we lack a body of concepts with which to place such changes and gain significant insight into them. Here, amid the many concepts invoked in this article, I have suggested that the concepts of performativity and supercomplexity in particular offer a way forward.

Those two concepts, we can note, work in differing ways; and they speak to contending presences within contemporary curricula. The concept of performativity suggests that, amid growing differences across curricula, a new universal may just be in evidence; *and* it offers a critical commentary on such a set of emerging trends. The concept of supercomplexity takes a wider perspective and offers us a more positive perspective. It points us towards new forms of curricula that are in themselves at once critical of the emerging performativity *and* emancipatory (so far as the idea of emancipation can itself have purchase in a supercomplex age). Supercomplexity opens a vista of a new 'breadth' in curricula that is grounded in global changes which in turn call forth wide dimensions of human being; indeed, almost for the first time since the Middle Ages, makes legitimate a sense that a curriculum in our universities is connected with the promotion of human being as such. Qua concept, performativity carries a legitimate pessimism; supercomplexity offers a plausible optimism.

But, in addition to these empirical and theoretical points, a policy perspective has opened up, too, in our discussion. Curricula, I have suggested, are in a state of transition but they are not necessarily moving in any clear or even deliberate direction. Such dominant directions of change as there are—towards performative modes—are inappropriate to conditions of supercomplexity. Accordingly, a new responsibility is falling on universities to demonstrate that the education that they offer is likely to be adequate to the challenges of a supercomplex world. It is a responsibility—and an educational project—that most universities and most curricula are failing to meet.

Note

It may be observed—and, possibly, with some surprise—that, in this article, I do not invoke the concepts of postmodernity or postmodernism. For me, there are grave difficulties attaching to these terms, not least being that of the fundamental differences, as I see it, between precisely those two terms. For a fuller set of reflections along these lines, see my book, *Realizing the University* (2000).

Chapter 12

Learning about learning
A conundrum and a possible resolution

(from London Review of Education, 2011, 9(1) 5–14)

Outline

What is it to learn in the modern world? We can identify four learning epochs through which our understanding of learning has passed: a metaphysical view; an empirical view; an experiential view; and, currently, a learning-amid-contestation view. In this last and current view, learning has its place in a world in which, the more one learns, the more one is aware of counter positions and perspectives. Here is a conundrum for learning here becomes a kind of un-learning. This learning calls for the development among students of certain kinds of dispositions and qualities. These dispositions and qualities provide resources that enable students to venture forwards to enquire in a world in which every position and every perspective is subject to contestation. Learning here becomes the formation of a radical-but-active-doubt. Such a view of learning for the twenty-first century points to a poverty in the notion of 'learning outcomes', if learning is incessant but self-doubting enquiry. This learning has no outcome except the continuing formation – largely a self-formation – of the student's being. This view of learning opens the way for possibilities in curricula and pedagogy, possibilities that both unsettle students but which also help them to develop the inner resources to go on learning in a difficult world.

Introduction

What is it to learn? The question has always been fraught with difficulty but perhaps it takes on particularly added layers of difficulty in the modern age. One aspect of the concept of learning is that, through one's learning, one can go on better than before. One understands the world anew (or at least some aspect of the world) and so is better placed to negotiate one's way through the world. Learning, on this view, is epistemologically efficacious. But this aspect of learning is in jeopardy. For the modern age is replete with challenge, competing values and unpredictability. Consequently, it is by no means clear that learning, understood as a means to negotiate the world more effectively, holds the educational legitimacy it once held.

What, then, against this background, might we make of the concept of learning? Can it still do work for us today? If tomorrow is not going to be like today, and if even today is presenting us with incommensurable sets of readings of the world, some of which challenge not just our actions but our identities, then the concept of learning can only be saved by some major surgery. The idea of learning as a means of securing better guides for negotiating the world has to be put in the dock if not repudiated altogether.

At the same time, learning – especially in the form of *higher* education – was held to be edifying. Through enquiry, one was elevated into a higher plane of being. Newman, after all, spoke of an 'ascent' into a 'philosophical outlook'. The German concept of Bildung, too, has connotations of a personal movement through study, into a different order of human being (cf. Lovlie, Mortenson, and Nordenbo 2003). But this idea, that learning is of personal value, is also now in difficulty in a world in which the idea of learning is problematic. In a world of contestation, who is to decide which learning is of value? How is it possible to determine which learning might be personally edifying?

Learning is in double jeopardy, therefore. On the one hand, it is not obvious that learning can provide us with a secure basis on which to move forward in the world. On the other hand, it is not clear how it might be that learning can be personally edifying. Learning about learning seems, as a result, to produce a conundrum. Learning suggests a moving forward, and an improvement in understanding; but here, learning seems to have run into a cul-de-sac.

I want to address this conundrum by following a course of reflection on what it is to be – and to become – in a complex world. I shall introduce the three terms 'hope', 'faith' and 'venture'. I shall also want to draw on, and distinguish between, dispositions (such as 'a will to learn') and qualities (such as 'fortitude'). And, I shall critique (albeit only as a side commentary) the idea of learning outcomes. I shall argue that it still makes sense to talk of learning in the contemporary world, but only if we broaden our sense of learning to include that of going on in a world in which there are no rules for going on. Admittedly, this is a large canvas to traverse in the course of a single paper but perhaps I can be forgiven for attempting a synoptic view now. Perhaps there will later be occasions for more detailed exploration of particular features of the landscape sketched here.

Four epochs of learning

The concept of learning has undergone three revolutions, so producing four *learning epochs*, with each epoch reflecting different sets of presuppositions as to the value of learning and the learning journey it afforded. Initially, learning was a matter of departing this world and moving into a different world. This learning was metaphysical, giving one access to a meta-reality. In Plato's imagery, one was able to escape the cave of illusions and see the world totally anew. In the language of John Henry Newman (as we have seen), one was involved in an 'ascent' into a philosophical outlook. This *metaphysical view of learning* constitutes learning epoch 1.

In learning epoch 2, largely since the emergence of science and the enlightenment, learning was seen as efficacious. Through learning, one put oneself into a better position in the world. There was a real and definite world and learning enabled one to know it better. One not only knew more about the world; one was able to do things one hadn't done before, whether in relation to the physical world or the human world. This learning, this *empirical learning*, constitutes epoch 2.

Then we recognised – learnt, indeed – that the world was changing; and partly as a result of changes to the world made possible by epoch 2 learning. What we learn today won't necessarily equip us for living effectively in the world tomorrow. Consequently, learning became a matter of moving with the times. Terms such as 'the reflective learner', 'action learning' and 'work-based learning' came to the fore. There were no fixed or universal rules for learning. Learning had to be *in situ*, taking place in discrete contexts. Our learning had to adapt as we went along. Our learning skills had to be 'transferable', enabling one to shift easily from one situation to another. This *learning-on-the-hoof in an unstable world* constitutes epoch 3 learning. It was – we may note – learning brought about as a result of learning about learning.

But a further cycle of change in the concept of learning is upon us. For now, we recognise not merely that the world is changing but that it holds within it proliferating and competing frameworks by which we might understand the world. In other words, it is now no longer clear how our learning is to proceed. This is a supercomplex world, a world characterised precisely by confusion as to what is to count as learning. What counts as learning for one group or society may not at all be what another group or society sees as learning; and there is no obvious way of choosing between the two views. We may note en passant that this state of learning anomie arises partly as a result of learning across the globe in different milieux and different cultures. And new definitions of learning are arising all the time, not least through the possibilities of Internet interactivity. This learning-amid-contestation constitutes epoch 4.

Each of the four learning epochs poses its characteristic problems. Or rather, there is a single dominant problem, and it takes on different forms across the four epochs. The dominant issue is always this: what is to count as effective learning? In epoch 1, in metaphysical learning, the test is one of personal transformation: has one been transported into a new order of being? In epoch 2, in empirical learning, the test is in learning, is one's understanding of the world-in-itself advancing? In particular, has one arrived at secure understandings of the world? Does one's understandings correspond to the way the world actually is? In epoch 3, in learning in an unstable world, the test is that of performative efficaciousness. Is one's learning about the world and about one's learning in the world enabling one to maintain one's effectiveness in the world?

In epoch 4, however, it is by no means clear how to answer the dominant question – 'what is to count as effective learning?' For now, there are proliferating and rival accounts precisely over just that matter. Now, there are all manner of ideas as to what is to constitute learning. There are no agreed criteria of learning. Some say it is getting by in the world; some say it is making money in the world; some say it is learning that is going to save the Earth from environmental degradation; some say – or believe – that it is a matter of serendipity, of what emerges spontaneously from unfettered instant and global communication; some believe that it is what is constituted in practice by 'communities of practice'; some – such as the reikians – believe that it is about coming to find new energies for oneself in a troubling world. At the same time, representatives of each of the previous epochs – the metaphysicals, the empiricists and the performativists – are still with us, pressing their own viewpoints, as competing discourses of learning in society. (For older learning viewpoints never die; they only fade a little.)

This situation is a nice cameo of supercomplexity (Barnett 2000). That is, it is a situation of proliferating and often competing viewpoints over fundamental descriptions of the world before us. If we cannot agree as to what counts as learning, we certainly cannot agree as to what is to count as effective learning. And there seems to be no way through this impasse. On the contrary, the maze seems daily to grow more impenetrable as new definitions of learning arise.

Learning conundrums

It has been remarked that the more we come to know, so our ignorance in turn grows. In parallel to a knowledge explosion has arisen 'an ignorance explosion' (Lukasiewicz 1994). It is not just that we become aware of 'known unknowns' but that our knowledge has made possible interventions in the world such that it changes continuously and so our knowledge of the world is always behind the game. Our knowledge of the world has put the world beyond our full understanding for it permanently recedes before us.

A corresponding situation has arisen in relation to learning. The more we have learnt about the world, so our relationships to the world have grown more complex. And the challenges on our learning continue to mount. After all, human beings are part of the world. So our learning is in part learning about ourselves; and that in turn includes learning about our learning itself.

Here lie conundrums. The more we learn, the more learning becomes more difficult. Learning has an incessantly recursive quality. It cannot help but learn about itself. And that becomes ever more complicated as the world becomes more complex and so too our relationship with and in the world.

A second conundrum is this. Learning was supposed to have edifying properties. It was supposed to lead to a better life or to a better world or to a better state of being. Now, crudely, the reverse is the case. Learning too often leads to a more troubled state of existence or to a more fractious world. 'Better Socrates dissatisfied than a pig satisfied' was the justification for the problematic consequences of learning. But now, in this interdependent age, it seems that it is not just Socrates that is dissatisfied but being as such. Being is now aware that it is dislodged from a satisfied state. A dissatisfied world rests on the shoulders of being. Learning is turning out to be unduly and wearisomely troubling.

The very value of learning is here in double jeopardy. Learning about learning has run us into an epistemological cul-de-sac: we no longer know how satisfactorily – with any degree of consensus – how to learn. And learning about learning has run us into an ontological cul-de-sac, no longer helping to take forward what there is in the world. The value of learning is no longer clear. It seems to have neither personal nor worldly warrant.

Accordingly, the legitimacy of learning is in doubt, beset as it is by its conundrums and cul-de-sacs. Is there a way forward?

Being and becoming

The contemporary world is radically unstable. It is 'radically' unstable because the very categories by which we relate to the world and through which we seek to understand it are contested. Disputes, accordingly, are not so much about empirical evidence – do we have sufficient evidence? Is it of the right quality? Has it been produced through rigorous methods? – but are much more to do with the frameworks through which we comprehend the world. And there is no way of deciding between the frameworks.

Three objections are lodged against this set of claims. The first is to suggest that we can bracket some frameworks while we examine in a piecemeal fashion individual frameworks. This idea led Popper to speak of the myth of the framework (e.g., Popper 1970): he felt that in this way, he could dissolve the point about incommensurable frameworks. The trouble with this idea, though, is that it presumes some consensus over the value background by which one might test a framework; and it is that that is in dispute.

A second objection is that characteristically we don't have hang-ups about our understanding of the world. Certainly, we can and do go on refining it but, by and large, we are in agreement about how to go on in the world. The world exists, we know it exists and we press on in it. This is the Samuel Johnson line: I refute it (the antirealist view) thus! The trouble with this viewpoint is that it is an ostrich viewpoint: it refuses to acknowledge that there are different viewpoints, different frameworks indeed, and that one's own world is not necessarily shared and, in fact, is not shared by many others.

The last objection to the multiple perspectives line is that it is perniciously a relativist point of view and solves no problems. There are disagreements in the world: very well, let us debate them and work them through. In their different ways, Gellner and Habermas were both of this persuasion. This is the 'reasonable people know how reasonably to reason' line of argument. The trouble with this line of thought is twofold. Firstly, there is disagreement over the rules of fair engagement. Secondly, the very idea of rational dialogue presupposes arbitrary constraint on reason itself. Nietzsche, Derrida, Lyotard and Foucault have all put themselves into this latter camp.

Here, we do not have to delve into the details of these debates. The point of these reflections, for our purposes, is to emphasise that learning is fraught with difficulty, for there is dispute over our relationship with the world and for coming to an understanding about the world, *and* for finding agreement or even over the rules of dialogue in the world.

A further troublesome dimension opens up here. It has long been held to be part of higher education that it offers opportunities for human being to flourish and so for human becoming. On this view, a university is a space for students to realise themselves in worthwhile ways; and authentically to become themselves. In a higher education worthy of the name, individuals not just learnt about some aspects of the world – in disciplinary study – but they also came to learn about themselves. In their programmes of study, and through their wider university and student experiences, students are called forth, called out of themselves, to give of themselves in unfamiliar and stretching circumstances.

Characteristically, the situations that comprise the student experience have standards written into them, such that there are limits to what can be done or said, and there is a certain degree of difficulty or personal challenge; and there is a certain durability attaching to them. These features are certainly to be found both in curricula situations whether on or off campus (in laboratories, in essay writing, in group tasks and in studios); and would include off-site situations, including fieldwork and work and clinical situations. These features are even also to be found in somewhat more informal settings, outside the formal curriculum, such as helping with student newspapers, sports teams, student associations or debates and in action in the community. Not infrequently, too, students are brought up sharp against the contestability of the rules within which their activities are placed – again whether in their chosen disciplines and professional settings or in their extra-mural activities.

Students, accordingly, are being obliged to understand and live with the tenuous nature of the frameworks in which they have their being as students. Student becoming, therefore, has a dual character. On the one hand, students come to see the world through new perspectives; the familiar world is made unfamiliar before becoming familiar through conceptual and experiential frameworks. Students move into new spaces. This is an essential part of higher education. On the other hand, students come to realise that the very frameworks that have imparted new perspectives are themselves sets of conventions. It is not just that there are disputes within the frameworks but that the validity or worthwhileness of the frameworks are themselves in dispute.

Student becoming, then, has a Janus-like appearance. The student lives in a new place, and acquires a new identity even; but is aware, even if only dimly, that things could be yet other. The student is here and yet not here. Here lies the 'authoritative uncertainty' of which – quite some time ago – Sinclair Goodlad (1976) spoke. The student is both sure and unsure of his or her ground. The student has hold of a rock but it is slippery. The substance of the rock is not illusory; the ways of going on – in essay writing, in the laboratory, in the studio, in the clinical situation, and even in running a student society – have evolved over time and they have a kind of solidity to them. Here are forms of life. But the student has also become aware that these forms of life could be other than they are. *Here and not-here*: this is the nature of the student's new being. This, indeed, is the becoming promised by a *higher* education.

This expression may seem strange but, in substance, there is nothing new in it. It has been, after all, for a long time part of the self-rhetoric of higher education that it encourages *self*-critical thought. What is self-critical thought if it is not thought that monitors itself? And, in this self-monitoring must come thought that recognises that it itself could be other than it is. And since, as we have seen, being a student involves action – and potentially in several domains – it follows too that the critical self-monitoring has to include the student's own actions.

So it is part of the very meaning of higher education that it looks to the formation of student being that is both here and not-here. The student has his or her thoughts and actions in the here-and-now but is always aware that those thoughts and actions could be otherwise. And he or she also accrues the capacities to stand outside that here-and-now to self-critique those thoughts and actions. To use a term deployed by Giddens (1995), we may say that the student acquires the capacities to *disembed* herself; to wrest herself out of the very traditions and forms of going on into which she has been initiated and while still living in them.

Hope and faith

But what, then, if anything, will serve as a basis on which to found this capacity to live in the here and not-here; this willingness always to displace oneself into a position from which to critique oneself? For by itself, as remarked, learning now becomes a source of unease, and even of personal destabilisation. Far from offering more and more security, now learning can only bring more insecurity. The more one learns, the more one has at one's disposal to critique. Here lies a paradox of learning: before one's learning, what one has taken the world to be was a source of security: the world is like this! Now, learning – the learning characteristic of higher education at least – brings with it a sense that one's perceptions of the world and very concepts for framing the world could be otherwise (cf. Badiou and Zizek 2009). How, then, might being be filled out such that it is more secure amid this higher learning?

The terms 'hope' and 'faith' may be helpful to us here. They are actually interlocking terms but they have their own nuances.

Of the two terms, here, faith is the more fundamental. In grappling with her experiences, in submitting herself to the challenges and the standards inherent in them, the student has to have faith; faith that things may come out reasonably well for her; faith that her tutors and lecturers will be there, prepared to give her feedback; faith that with effort and persistence, she just may come to a fair understanding of the material or be able to take on the skills expected of her. Faith here is an untestable belief and yet, despite its untestability, is a necessary condition of the student's keeping going.

The three faiths I have just identified are all to do with the student's position as a student; her place as a student: things coming out reasonably well: her tutors offering some support in a sustained way; her efforts helping her progress. They all relate to her being as a student, and that *being* being supported and carried forward. We may call these ontological faiths, relating to the student's being in the world. But there are also more epistemological faiths at work. The student has faith that there are some epistemological connections among her experiences; they are not just random experiences. The student has faith that there is some substance to the intellectual and professional fields to which she is being exposed; they tell of the world in some way. And the student has faith that validity comes into play in her own developing accounts of the world: the evaluations to which she is subject are not arbitrary but are influenced by the norms and standards in the fields in question.

Beyond such presences of faith lies hope. The two terms are, as remarked, intertwined. The student hopes that things will turn out well, both today and over the course of her programme of studies. This hope lives in the future. While her faiths can never be fully tested – or thereby even refuted – her hopes can be dashed. The lecturer may not turn up; her assignment may meet with a poor grade; try as she might, still she can't get her head round a concept or master a skill. Today has not gone too well; it may have even be 'troublesome' (Meyer and Land 2005), but perhaps tomorrow will be better. I have just 'failed my interview' for my first job but perhaps I shall succeed in next week's interview.

Faith and hope, therefore, together provide the student with resources for going on, for meeting the day with some cheerfulness. Such resources, of relying on and believing in the world (as in faith) and of thinking that things may yet come out well (as in hope), are especially valuable amid the challenges we identified earlier that a higher learning may bring. A higher learning, it will be recalled, is liable to issue in personal destabilisation. A higher learning – of the world in itself and of engagements with the world – is accompanied with critique that becomes self-critique. One knows one could learn with deeper understanding or even that there is doubt over the worthwhileness of what one has been learning; one knows that one only has a rudimentary grasp of how to handle oneself and is doubtful that anything approaching a full mastery is within one's compass and, anyway, one isn't sure that the procedures in question are ethically acceptable (the use of animals for dissection purposes).

One's learning in higher education is accompanied by self-questioning and even self-doubt. One knows, if nothing else, that one's learning could be other than it is. In such a situation, faith and hope are especially valuable. I have been suggesting that they provide the resources to keep oneself going. The matter, however, can be put somewhat differently and more strongly. Faith and hope help the formation of the being of the student so as to bring the student into a new and purposeful relationship with the world.

Together, faith (that the world that I understand has some kind of substance to it) and hope (that my learning will help me into a better place of understanding and even action) help one to *venture* forward. Hope and faith give the student the resources to tackle the world, and to learn about it, and to build on one's learning. Through this venturing, one's learning may be connected with one's sense of oneself in the world and one's life plans. Here lies the possibility of something approaching an integrated life. But this venturing, this taking on the world, is only possible through faith and hope.

Venturing forward

In these reflections, I have been implicitly arguing that learning at the level of higher education is at least as much an ontological matter as it is an epistemological matter. Learning, at this level, is in a real sense learning about oneself; and there are levels at which this learning takes place. At a straightforward and basic level, one may learn as to whether one prefers 'concrete' or 'abstract' forms of understanding; whether one prefers local objects or universal objects of one's attention; whether as to the physical world or the human world; and whether a kind of autobiographical learning (where one associates the learning with one's own projects) or a more distant unattached form of learning.

On all these dimensions of learning – and yet others – there are options; and characteristically, even in a single class within a particular discipline, students may vary in their 'learning approaches' and their 'learning styles' (cf. Ramsden 1988; Light and Cox 2001; Brockbank and McGill 2007). And a reflexive higher education will bring one's own learning preferences from a tacit into a full consciousness. There are, though, yet deeper aspects of self that come into play, aspects to which our concept of venturing points.

Venturing forward is but a shorthand for a penumbra of dispositions that carry an individual into his or her learning. In learning, one is moving oneself from one place – of limited understanding – into another place, of somewhat fuller understanding. To make this movement requires certain dispositions. These include:

- a will to learn;
- a will to encounter strangeness (for in higher education, the familiar is rendered unfamiliar);
- a will to engage (for a higher learning requires a personal engagement with the material and experiences to hand);
- a preparedness to listen;
- a willingness to be, changed as a result of one's learning;
- a determination to keep going.

To help in understanding these (six) dispositions, we may distinguish them from qualities that have a particular affinity with higher education (Barnett 2007):

- courage;
- carefulness;
- resilience;
- self-restraint;
- integrity;
- respect for others.

The dispositions are fundamental: they mark out what it is to venture forward in general but especially in an age of uncertainty. The qualities are the ways in which individuals colour those dispositions. The qualities bestow a person's character; but in order to have a character, in order to acquire his or her qualities, a person needs to be a person as such, a human being engaging intentionally with the world. And it is through his or her dispositions that a person engages with the world.

The point of mentioning dispositions and qualities is less to develop a thesis about them as such and more to point up the place of venturing in the context of learning. In order for learning to be authentic, one has to venture into learning. And for that, one has to have the appropriate dispositions – such as the six dispositions just encountered. I cannot learn authentically unless I have a will to learn, a will to encounter strangeness, a will to engage and so forth. I venture forward with some confidence through my possession of these *learning dispositions*. And these learning dispositions are both 'moral and epistemic virtues' (Brady and Pritchard 2003) and they can be a natural concomitant of appropriate curricula and pedagogies.

Here, we must return to our earlier point of departure. I argued that learning has passed through four epochs and that the current epoch is one in which learning has destablising characteristics. In such an epoch, one may easily – as Bertand Russell once put it – be 'paralysed into inaction'. In such an epoch, too, as Yeats put it, 'the worst are full of passionate intensity while the best lack all conviction'. Learning allows one to recognise that one's own viewpoint is but a viewpoint, that other viewpoints are possible and, indeed, are present. One sees all sides of an argument. Why then press just one argument? Learning, on this view, can lead to paralysis. One hesitates to proffer a point of view precisely because one senses and may even be aware that any viewpoint is partial and that there will be contending viewpoints.

It is here that lies the value of venturing. In venturing, one presses forward while unsure of what one may encounter on the way. This is no will to power but a will to explore, to engage, to enquire; and to open oneself to strangeness. It is a will to venture forward.

Conclusions

We are, I think, in a position to draw some conclusions.

Firstly, the evolution of learning has brought us to a point where the value of learning is problematic. Partly through the explosion of knowledges and critique in the world, learning is always a kind of *learning-to-doubt*, in which the qualifications that attach to learning attach to the very forms of understanding in which learning takes place.

Secondly, and arising from our first conclusion, learning is now in part an ontological matter, affecting the nature of being and becoming. Learning now becomes a matter of a development of human being that is appropriate for a learning-to-doubt. The will to learn becomes a will to live with ineradicable doubt. This is a coming into a mode of being that is continuously unstable, and yet is able to dwell there. A higher learning thus promises just this: a coming not just into a different place but coming into that place with one's eyes open, as it were. So one lives amid continuous movement; restless, never content. But not necessarily always moving forward; more a zig-zag, moving forwards and backwards, as optimism and pessimism succeed each other; as positions are taken up and then surrendered; as alternative perspectives are embraced. In a genuine higher learning, one learns to accommodate to this flux; and even acquire the resources for actively heightening this flux.

Thirdly, seeing learning as this becoming, this *coming-into-active-doubt*, has large pedagogical and curricula implications. Negatively, it points to a poverty in the idea of 'learning outcomes', in which curricula and pedagogies are so shaped as to instantiate certain skills in students. For such skills are points of closure when what is now required is a form of learning in which one is continually opening up for oneself, even amid radical doubt. More positively, the idea of learning as a coming-into-active-doubt opens up new possibilities for approaching curricula and pedagogy as projects to encourage this form of student becoming. Implications arise for the teacher–student relationship, for the 'stretching' of the student, for placing the student in situations of cognitive and experiential complexity and for the students in a cohort engaging with each other's different points of view. Working all this through would be a large and even inexhaustible project.

We may finally conclude that learning can only be given its due as a higher learning in the contemporary world if we broaden our sense of learning to include that of going on in a world in which there are no non-contestable rules for going on. As active and radical doubt, learning has to doubt itself; but then it will always find new resources for continuing that process.

Chapter 13

Being and becoming
A student trajectory

(From *International Journal of Lifelong Education*, 1996, 15 (2) 72–84)

Outline

What is it to become a student? Higher education is an institution deliberately designed to sustain differentiated and public forms of human experience and seeks to enable individuals to get on the inside of those external forms of experience. The student experience of so doing is, however, a private affair. How do we make sense of this interaction of the private and public realms of the student experience? In coming into a proper relationship with an epistemological framework, the student displaces herself into that framework. With educational displacement comes a trajectory. The trajectory can continue upward, with the student gaining more confidence; or it can flatten off; or it can fall away, with the student losing interest in her studies and with her cognitive powers diminishing. The trajectory offers a form of becoming: the student becomes herself in a new guise—her own new, and authentic, person. The being of the student is achieved through a process of becoming the student.

Introduction

What is it to be a student? Currently, there is an extraordinary gap in our conceptual understanding of the term 'student'. The gap has to do with the intersection of the private and public realms of human experience, at the intersection of which stands the student. 'Stands', of course, is an inadequate metaphor. The student is both partly constituted by and actively – to varying degrees – produces that *mélange* of experience.

The key problem before us is easily stated. Higher education, perhaps more than any other social institution, is an institution deliberately designed to sustain differentiated and public forms of human experience and, in its educational task, seeks to enable individuals to get on the inside of those external bodies of experience. The student experience of so doing, the totality of intellectual and emotional experiences which constitute an unfolding trajectory, is however partly a private affair. The question before us is: how do we make sense of this interaction of the private and public realms of experience?

Does one have priority over the other? Is it that the external has to be transformed into the internal for it to have significant meaning? Or is it that the internal has to yield to the external in order for the integrity of the external to be maintained and realized in the mind of the student? Things are of course more complicated than this either/or formulation seems to admit. But simply to ask the questions plunges us immediately into conceptual difficulties. They reveal a fundamental gap in our understanding of higher education. A shorthand characterization of this gap is that we do not understand how higher education works: inside out or outside in?

Postmodernism says that anything goes. But postmodernism has not yet been adopted by the academy. The university remains, indeed intensifies its function as, a social institution for sustaining technical and elaborate discourses around sets of communicative rules. Developed by the sub-cultures of the academic community, the disciplines still stand as the cognitive capital of the university. Certainly, the disciplines are changing as the relationship between the state and its universities become closer. Even more technical, but also experiential *and* policy oriented in character, the disciplines – to a greater or lesser extent – are eager to demonstrate their appropriateness for the modern society. Performativity is the name of this game, both in personal competences and in the use-value of the intellectual capital on offer.

The character of the disciplines comes under some strain, therefore. The human competences they deliver are said to be inadequate. What is now required by the ever-changing labour market is metacompetences (Fleming 1991), capacities to respond to unpredictable situations and to renew one's cognitive capital through one's lifespan. Cognitive capital is itself an inadequate characterization of the accoutrements now to be fastened on. Nor is cultural capital a helpful alternative formulation. Culture and traditions are seen as regressive, as resistant to change. Human orientations not just to enter but to create a brave new world are called for. 'Flexibility' becomes one of the key code words of our time; and its core lies in its attitudinal aspect. This is not yet postmodernism, but an advanced form of modernism. Society both retains structure and calls for high-level expertise; but the specific structures of postmodern society and its associated expertise change with increasing rapidity.

The university finds itself called forth to assist these transformations in human capital. Currently, we are in the midst of changes and new demands on the educational functions of the university that we can scarcely comprehend. High-level disciplinary knowledge and skills, wider societal and work competences turning especially on advanced forms of interaction and communication ('transferable skills'), new attitudes to change and innovation, and even ethical development all crowd into the curriculum. The student is confronted with all of this and more.

Much, then, stands externally to the student, to be mastered, comprehended, and exhibited in performance. To academic competence have been added societal competence and work competence; to narrow skills have been added general metaskills to sustain the graduate in a world of unimaginable change.

So fulfilling the role of student is more demanding than ever. And the students, being rational persons wishing to make their way in the world, know this and respond to it. Precisely because of the press of the totality of the external demands, students may all too easily adopt coping strategies to enable them to get through. No longer is the role construed as the development, in interaction with one's peers, of an oppositional role to society. The external demands on the students are considerable. Instead, the challenge is construed as acquiring the degree, preferably with as little effort as possible. If the notion of 'student' is framed by the external world, if students are expected to become this or to do that or to acquire these competences, it is hardly surprising if students feel that their becoming is not of their making. The task of being a 'student' accordingly becomes one of meeting others' agendas as painlessly as possible.

The acquisition of the required competences is seen by the students for what it is: the demands of a real external world. 'Real' in the sense that its externality and its demands are *there*, even if those demands and the future that they represent are literally uncertain.

Yet responsiveness to external demands cannot be the full story of what it is to be a student. There are internal demands, too, at least in the archaeology of the idea of 'student'. Realms of thought and action both supply internal demands, 'internal' in the sense of being internal to the forms of thought and action which partly constitute student being.

Thought, for example, is itself a complex so far as the student experience is concerned. Learning, cognition and understanding are only some of the relevant concepts. Each is an achievement term as well as having task components (Peters 1967). They point to processes which are intellectually demanding in themselves; they may be painful, arduous, even perplexing. But they also point to processes which have their own inbuilt standards.

We can point to mental processes as involving learning, cognition or understanding when certain kinds of states of mind are achieved. We could not talk of understanding if the student was not able to form ideas and propositions which had some kind of verisimilitude. We could not talk of learning unless the student had changed his/her state of mind and was now able to say new things coherently or do things anew. We could not talk of cognition unless the insight that accompanied it had some kind of internal anchoring and structure.

So forming an understanding of the kind appropriate to higher education is to yield to epistemological demands. Even more active forms of demand bear in on the notion of student, however.

While not a logical part of the mental states they pick out, understanding, learning and cognition reveal themselves in time and in action. I mean action here in a particular sense. Expressing a point of view, analysing a compound, interrogating a text, bringing together different theories in a synoptic offering, critically examining one's own utterances and coming up with a counter claim: all these – and many others – are forms of action. They require the student to act, to say implicitly this is where I am in my understanding and to offer personal significations for possible evaluation. These acts are interventions in the world: in making utterances of this kind, propositions are formed and offered to the world.

Originality has nothing to do with this point. What is at issue is that the act of making a statement is itself to intervene in the world. The student becomes active, more fully herself and no longer a passive recipient of encountered experiences. There is difficulty here for the student, since to make a statement of one's own requires a certain toughness. It is to take a risk.[1] No longer willing to hold onto others' quotations or computations, the student does it or says it for herself.

These difficulties are not the intellectual difficulties mentioned a moment ago. These difficulties are personal, and ontological. They arise out of the nature of truth telling. Following Habermas (1991), we can say that participation in a truth-orientated discourse imposes a range of ethical demands. First, in offering a proposition of her own, the student is submitting herself to others' evaluations. Second, the proposition has to be offered in such a way that it can be understood by the prospective listener or reader; there has to be a receptiveness to the discourse at work. Third, there has to be a coherence or orderliness about the interventions; *ad hoc*cery or a sequence of unconnected offerings will not do. Lastly, the student has to have a degree of personal commitment to what she says or does; there have to be components of sincerity and ownership at work. Otherwise, we could say at best that we were in the presence of duplicity; at worst, in the presence of plagiarism or cheating.

In short, being a student in its fullest sense imposes internal demands on both thought and action which arise out of entering and beginning to participate in a truth-orientated community. No wonder that students, especially when faced with the external demands we noted earlier, opt for the easy life. Playing the game, getting by, engaging in conspiracies to buck the system, toeing the line, and simply doing the necessary to acquire the degree award: these are understandable stances of students in the modern age.

There is, therefore, both an internal student and an external student. On the one hand, we have the student grappling with the interior demands of understanding, of inner conceptual struggle, of formulating coherent thoughts and ideas, and of definite and bold expression. This is a virtually invisible student. Sometimes, we catch such students as they show themselves in their hesitant responses and uneasy formulations or, indeed, their silences. On the other hand, we have the external student, the student picking up the messages of the wider world and responding more or less to them. This is the student occasionally mentioned in policy documents, whether of the state or even of the university itself. This external student also has, we should note, an invisibility about it; or rather, a fictive character. It is a hypothetical student, an assumed student, a two-dimensional student largely passive in the face of the external demands which press themselves forward, simply acquiring uncritically the prescribed transferable skills and providing the sought-for human capital for the economy.

Inside out or outside in? How can we bring these two images of 'student' into a relationship with each other? What *is* their relationship? Does either side of the relationship have priority? Is it a case of the external world impinging on an otherwise pure inner life and distorting it; or is it a case of the inner life taking its bearings and, indeed, shape from the external world? To reply that it is neither of these and that the relationship is much more subtle, or dynamic or dialectical is no answer at all. Responses of that kind are evasions unless they can give us some insight into the structure of the relationship.

On understanding 'the student experience'

It should be noted that what is in question here is not in essence an empirical matter but a conceptual matter of what we take the nature of 'student' to be. What is at issue here is the doubtless perplexing issue of what it is to be a student in its fullest sense. Certainly, we can conduct inquiries into 'the changing student experience' or 'student satisfaction' or 'students' approaches to learning' (to cull some contemporary examples from the current scholarly and policy discourses).[2] But empirical inquiries of this kind do not and cannot shed light on the fundamental issue before us. Indeed, those empirical inquiries are largely groundless unless we have some answer to the conceptual question here.

We can hardly mount a serious empirical inquiry into student life and consciousness unless we have a prior notion of 'student'. First, we shall not know what to look at. And second, we shall be devoid of any critical standard against which to assess our findings. That empirical inquiries of the kind just mentioned do usually end by making implicit critical evaluations (of the character of the learning or of the experience) and yet have not usually embarked on a prior conceptual examination of the kind being suggested is an indication that prior and implicit judgements have been entered into about the ideal nature of 'student'. This absence – of an explicit conceptual inquiry – is not an indication that it is not necessary.

The inquiry required here, however, cannot be purely conceptual. If it is to be adequate to its object, it has to take into account the dominant features of the external world. If it is to say anything of substance about the interplay of the inner life with the outer world, it has to be sensitive minimally to the character of that external world with which the typical student has to cope. In understanding higher education, philosophy does real work only when it is sociologically informed.

Two worlds

Let us start in an entirely schematic way by picking out, without any pretence at comprehensiveness, features of the internal and external worlds of being a student (Table 13.1). The 18 pairs of terms in the two columns are not intended to be polar opposites. If they appear to resonate with each other across the columns, that is an additional value in the table; its first purpose is simply to put flesh on my earlier claim, that there are two students before us, the external and the internal and that they are different from each other. It is possible to weave an apparently coherent story about a fictive student drawing only on the terms in one of the columns, even if it would be an impoverished account of what it is to be a student.

In fact, most policy documents – in so far as they do mention students – limit themselves just to the sense of 'student' drawn from the left-hand

Table 13.1 Features of the two worlds of a student

External	Internal
Higher education structures	Person
Policies	Self
Universities as organizations	Personal projects
Disciplines	Beliefs
Research	Meaning
Objective knowledge	Personal knowing
Received 'truths'	Own effort towards verisimilitude
Institutions	Ideas
Institutional culture	Own values
Courses	Experiences
Staff	'I'
Libraries	Own struggles at articulation
Teaching	Understandings
Institutional resources	Inner strength
Discourses	Making sense for oneself
Outcomes	Personal achievements
Competencies	Meeting one's own targets
Degrees and awards	Becoming

'external' column. The public accounts of what it is to be a student are fictive in a double sense. First, they imply that a student is just an amalgam of the external requirements of students called for by modern society: if a student can respond positively to all those demands represented by the left-hand column, the task of being a 'student' is complete.

The second fiction is even more serious. It is the implicit characterization of 'student' as merely responsive, as fulfilling others' agendas. The fiction is that, as we have seen, this view is epistemologically naïve. Entering actively a truth-orientated discourse calls forth action. This fiction is no accident, however. It buttresses an ideology, a view that this is how the life of the student should be construed. The ideology at work is a silence: no longer is the prospect entertained that the student might offer an oppositional source in the shaping of modernity. The outcomes are defined in advance. The task of the student is to fall in with the specification.

But silences are to be found in notions of student which stand essentially on the other side of the table. Notions of andragogy, of experiential learning, of reflection, of group-based learning and of learning contracts are, in certain formulations, attempts to be sensitive to the inner world of the learner and can result in curricula which are largely based in the right-hand column. Adult learning and some forms of professional education exhibit this *Weltanschauung* among others. The starting point is the student as learner with experiences which are valuable in themselves. The next claim is that learning has personal meaning and, therefore, personal power and longevity, when based on experiences in the curriculum which are owned by the student herself. *En route*, it is suggested that peer interaction – and, thereby, a minimization of the presence of authorial presences – is a key to enabling this concrete learning to become embedded in one's cognitive strata. The concluding destination is that of particular kinds of personal development marked out by such terms as authenticity, self-realization, empowerment, transformation and even emancipation.

This, too, despite its best endeavours to do justice to the real, to the inner struggles of students, to their human-ness, is another set of fictions. It pretends that students and their learning can seriously be understood independently of the external world in which they are placed. Here, the task of teaching is construed as enabling, as facilitating and as supporting. Mentoring, for some time a term with currency in professional fields and in adult education, now makes its appearance in higher education proper. Indeed, the idea of teaching is itself skewed. Command over a discipline, a national or even an international reputation in scholarship or research, are not to be paraded. Authority arises out of skill in interactions which produce self-becoming and self-authorship on the part of the student.

It will be said that this is to confuse two things: the internal experience of being a student, as caught in the right-hand column of our earlier table, and a certain *Weltanschauung* coming into higher education from adult and professional education in which the student's pysche takes centre stage.

The point being made here, however, is that the latter, the consciousness-focused *Weltanschauung*, finds a home in higher education today because of the new receptivity that the emerging curricula offer. The ideology of life experience is welcomed precisely because of its resonance with the new internalism in curriculum thinking now arising as higher education becomes a quasi-market. Both exhibit a sensitivity to the student as a human being with an internal consciousness of her own, as someone engaged in a personal struggle to make sense of the world, and as someone with her own legitimate offerings. The incoming ideology adds a sensitivity to feelings, experiences, worthwhile beliefs and personal values. In other words, the ideology tells us that students are adults with full personalities of their own and not just an assembly of cognitive processes.

And never the twain

We have, then, two rival versions of what it is to be a student: one that takes seriously the necessary personal components of participating in a truth-orientated discourse; the other that underlines that participation in higher education itself in the modern age is not just a personal whim but is a deliberate result of state policy. The one requires individuation; the other treats students – as the term makes clear – simply as a unit within a largely undifferentiated mass.

This double vision of the student is hardly new. According to Kant [in *Understanding the University*], 'a sharp distinction was to be made between the private and the public spheres' (Liedman 1993: 76). What is new are the tendencies towards polarization of the two spheres. Whereas the German concept of *Bildung,* in its combination of personal development and intellectual acculturation, offered a bridge between the two senses of 'student' (cf. Rothblatt 1993), now we are seeing signs of the two senses splitting off from each other with little apparently to bring them together.

On the one hand, the planners, in their eagerness to forge a mass higher education system to meet the requirements of the economy within an ever leaner resourcing envelope, forget that even to have the capabilities sought by modernity calls forth deep personal qualities. On the other hand, the experientialists implicitly deny the brute facts of the external world. And they do so not only by neglecting the policy framework which has led to the students' presence; they also even downplay the reality of the academics' discourses and the fine-grained conceptual worlds already constructed and which students have to come to inhabit if they are to make any serious sense of the academic world.

I said that the gap between these two worlds, the public and the private, is growing. The reasons are clear enough. As the higher education system grows, so it becomes internally more differentiated. To the sub-cultures of the academics are added the interests of the wider society – mediated in more or less benign ways by the new corps of university managers – and the claims of new constituencies such as the adult learners. In some of its forms, notably mid-nineteenth century Germany, the traditional gap between teacher and learner was slight. All were learners on a philosophical journey. That gap has become more pronounced in an age of mass higher education and has been compounded by the new interests that have emerged. In some perceptions, the student simply is a product of the system that enters or does not enter the labour market; in others, the student is a pure centre of consciousness, engaged on a journey of self-discovery.

How, conceptually, might these two worlds be brought together? Or, to phrase the question differently, how is higher education possible? What is the relationship between the internal and external worlds of becoming a student?

The use of the term 'worlds' in the last sentence may seem to point us in a helpful direction. Both Popper (1975) and Leavis (1969), for example, spoke of the different worlds of World I, the external world of spatio-physical objects; of World II, the world of the inner consciousness; and World III, the world of objective knowledge. But, unless we can begin to fill in the ways in which those worlds interrelate, we are no better off. Admittedly, both made some schematic remarks on the matter. Popper insisted that World III acts on World I, but only through World II; but he left the nature of those interactions elusively open.

The matter is of some practical importance. What is it to teach in higher education? The teacher has to have some conception of the kind of integration being aimed at between the internal and external worlds if the necessary integration is to be brought about. The practical motivation suggests less a philosophical inquiry into the concepts of either 'teaching' or 'learning' but a more psychological path. Talk of integration perhaps points us towards a Piagetian schema of assimilation and accommodation (1971). There, surely, we find the makings of a conceptual framework for comprehending how the two worlds come together. But even if the ideas of assimilation and accommodation can be filled out, that does not help us in the present situation. For we would only have insight into the internal psychological processes at work.

What is at stake, to repeat, is the relationship of the external and the internal. And the relationship in question here is a conceptual one. What is implied in our conception of 'student' for the external and the internal to come into a relationship with each other? How can personal becoming and external frameworks have *any* fruitful relationship with each other?

Perry's stage theory of ethical and epistemological development looks a promising candidate (Perry 1970). There, we see a model of student becoming which precisely involves the internal world of student consciousness and the external world of cognitive structures with which the student is struggling to come to terms. That theory, of progressive cognitive independency from epistemological frameworks, *is* helpful. There, we have a sense of an internal struggle over time, and a progressive process of student becoming. Ultimately, the student reaches a point of hard-won independence, an independence built on the epistemological frameworks which are now internalized but yet are objectified. In the end, the student declares and commits herself, makes the quasi-ethical stand of saying: here I stand.

Elsewhere, I have suggested that Perry's stage theory needs to be carried further if the student's independence is to be maximized (Barnett 1994). Stages of critique and displacement have to be added, to allow the student the space to see through both the framework's ideological and other limitations so as to have the personal power simply to call it up as a resource as and when required. The framework is *deployed* with a sceptical and even playful detachedness.

Yet such refinements of the Perry model carry us only so far. The Perry model is still, ultimately, psychological. It is concerned with the internal states of mind, albeit states of mind which are wrestling with the external world. The external world is taken as given.

The possibility, therefore, begins to arise that the problem is insoluble. The internal and the external worlds of the student are two worlds and we can give no coherent account of their relationship. Indeed, it could be argued that there is no relationship. The argument could run like this. The external and the internal worlds are separate in several senses. The first world is epistemological, economic and policy-driven in character; the second is private, personal and psychological. We understand these worlds, live in them, constitute ourselves (as teachers, policy makers and students) by resorting to different discourses in relation to the life of the student. There is a difference, then, in their logics. The inner and the outer worlds cannot be brought together. The twain does not and cannot meet.

On splitting the difference

Yet, we know they do come together. Whether in grappling with tedious lectures, in coming to terms with insufficient material resources, or making sense of the host institution which is termed 'university', students do in their mental states normally negotiate some kind of equilibrium with the epistemological, economic and policy worlds which they are obliged to inhabit. Their outer and inner shells fuse, even if they do not become one. And many are able to show their Perry-like independence from it all as well.

How is this possible? Unless we have some notion of how it *is* possible, we are devoid of any satisfactory account of what it is to be a student. One way forward may lie in beginning from the fact that, at least pragmatically, students do seem to be able to live both in the internal world which they construct and the external worlds imposed on them. But that, of course, in the absence of the empirical work, remains supposition. We just do not know to what extent students do in fact bring the internal and external worlds together coherently.

It should be clear that there is no easy middle position open to us. We cannot split the difference. There is no half-way house or world which students could be said to inhabit. It may be that students live uneasily in both their internal and others' external worlds. But there is no happy resting place between them. It would have no discourse, no language community and no inhabitants. There would be no home for it. We are back, therefore, to puzzling out the internal/external relationship.

On living in the third world

In this section, I want to proffer the outlines of what I believe is a solution to the problem I have been discussing. The solution lies in the idea of displacement. I raised earlier the idea of displacement in discussing Perry's stage theory of cognitive and ethical development. The ultimate stage, on that theory, is one in which the student effectively is able to stand aside from the disciplinary framework, because she can see it for what it is, warts and all. Here, though, I want to develop a contrary sense of displacement, in which the student displaces not the external framework (in forming a relationship to it) but herself. In coming into a relationship with an epistemological framework, in becoming intellectually independent, the student displaces herself *into* that framework.

Talk of a single framework is misleading here. There are at least two frameworks, one at a disciplinary level and the other at a meta-disciplinary level. One concerns the discourse, the concepts, the conventions, the paradigms, the traditions and, indeed, the ideologies which constitute a particular disciplinary framework. The other concerns the way of going on that constitutes what it is to engage in any rational discussion. It involves a determination to reach towards truth, a willingness to yield to the better argument, a personal commitment to one's statements in time, and a preparedness to formulate one's utterances in a comprehensible fashion.

This distinction, between disciplinary and metadisciplinary frameworks, is profound and I shall return to it; but it is not of the essence here. The idea of displacement applies to *both* levels of discourse.

Displacement carries the idea of movement from one place to another. But it also carries a sense of taking up some kind of home in the new place.

Admittedly, there is a slightly perjorative edge to the term; one is not usually displaced willingly. All of these senses come into play in an educational setting. In the end, the student leaves her life-world cognitively speaking and enters the new world of the intellectual framework.[3] The leaving and the entering are not without difficulties and, being new, may generate anxiety. But *this* displacement, to be effective, has to come under one's own volition in the end. Otherwise, reproductive learning is likely to be the result rather than meaning-orientated learning (Marton *et al.* 1984).

The leaving of one's life-world need not be permanent. Indeed, the educational value of the displacement being suggested here is likely to be enhanced if, having entered the new world, the old can be revisited with the perspective of the new. Of course, such a revisiting is not straightforward. In such a situation, one is inhabiting two discourses at once: the discourse of immediate experience of the life-world; and interpreting that life-world in a theoretical discourse. There is an awkwardness in inhabiting two worlds at once; but there is also a wisdom that comes with informed detachment.

Trajectory: its rise and possible fall

Richard Peters talked of education as initiation (Peter 1970); Michael Oakeshott of education as entering a conversation across the generations (Fuller 1989). Each of these metaphors is highly instructive. In each, we have a sense of traditions of thought and understanding standing outside of individuals; education is then the development of the capacity to participate in those traditions. 'Conversation' reminds us that knowledge is alive and is maintained through continuing dialogue, a dialogue that is being conducted now. 'Initiation' focuses on the transmission of the individual into those external traditions.

To repeat, both metaphors are helpful. But they are misleading in that they fail properly to recognize that the student is *already* engaged in her own conversations. They imply an unformed consciousness whereas educators, especially those of adults, are confronted with well-developed centres of consciousness among their students. These metaphors, instructive as they are, oversimplify the educator's task. But they also oversimplify the challenges in front of the student. It is not simply a matter of coming into a form of life mapped out for one. It is the much more challenging task of bringing one's own framework into some kind of relationship with a different one; and, in its conceptual integrity and procedural demands, markedly different at that.

The idea of displacement recognizes this challenge. The student has to displace herself, has to leave her home, in order to come fully into the new one. This need not be a permanent separation. On the contrary, as I mentioned, there might be continual movement between the student's life-world and her new theoretical systematized world. But there is no simple regression available. Once displaced, the life-world is liable to shatter. It will be seen anew.

With educational displacement comes a trajectory. Trajectory carries the sense of velocity and direction and taking off. All these are present in student becoming. The student comes into the role of student by displacing herself into particular forms of interaction, inquiry and truth-telling. Ultimately, the student comes to stand on firm ground, knows the intellectual territory, is at home in it and feels confident enough to strike out on her own. The student becomes herself, albeit within the epistemological and interactional framework which marks out the discipline or field of study. Here, there is a personal dynamic, a movement of self; but it is progressive, giving the student increasing power. It is a trajectory.

The trajectory can continue upward, with the student gaining more and more confidence, and acquiring more and more conceptual resource and veridical leverage. The trajectory can flatten off, with the student 'coasting along', secure in the knowledge that she has 'done enough to pass'. Or, even while on the course, the trajectory can fall away, with the student losing interest for some reason and failing to maintain her cognitive powers. This is a particular problem on part-time programmes or research degree programmes which are necessarily spread over a time-frame, and where other happenings in the life-world can intrude to command the student's attention.

The 'taking-off' implied by the idea of 'trajectory' is of two kinds. On the one hand, the cognitive journey is such that it gives the student a new view from above, as it were. The notion of a '*higher* education' itself implicitly conveys this sense of a higher order of cognition. This metaphor of height has a long history in thinking about higher education. Newman considered that 'if we would improve the intellect, first of all we must ascend' (Newman 1976). The 'ascent' here is of a logical not a social kind; social superiority is not at issue. What is being alluded to is a level of conceptual inquiry, interrogation and reflection which enables the student to form a view of her cognitive experience.

We are in the presence of a higher learning when the conceptual resources have been acquired which impart this higher order capacity. In exercising it, the student is at a distance from her immediate experience in the domain in question. She has displaced herself and followed a trajectory in which the experience can be marshalled and examined. We are here in the presence of a hierarchy of cognition in which the elaborated form of thought yields the power to scrutinize, and so free one from, one's immediate experience.

The second sense of 'trajectory' which is at work here is that already implied. Thee is, ultimately, a sense of taking off and of flying under one's own power. Student becoming takes place in two modes. First, there is the coming into the formal structures of thought and understanding which mark out not just the territory but the ways of going on characteristic of the student's field or discipline. Second, the becoming has a personal aspect. The student becomes herself in a new guise. The academic who is a physicist or who is a historian is so in a continuing sense: she defines herself as a physicist or a historian. Those descriptions – 'physicist'/ 'historian' – describe persons. In coming to see the world as a physicist or a historian, the student is not alienated from herself but becomes that self more fully.

Admittedly, as an undergraduate, the student's trajectory may not take off fully. The student reaches simply the stage where she can understand fairly comprehensively the discourse, and is able to show a minimal mastery of it. But students' accomplishments are relatively reactive to experiences put their way on their course of studies. They do not reach the stage where they take off under their own power. Perhaps they just lack the personal confidence to open the throttle and attempt to take off. After all, taking off is dangerous; if things go wrong, one is in rather an exposed position. Mistakes are serious.

Conclusions: the disappearing gap

We began by suggesting that the central problem in front of us in this paper was straightforward. What account might be given of the relationship between the internal and the external domains in the making of a student? A student is a person, with her own life world and consciousness attaching thereto. But that same student is also, *by definition*, someone who is studying something external to herself.

In getting to grips with this relationship, we have *en route* indicated that there are separate externalities which impinge on the student. There is the world of objectified knowledge and the discipline(s) in which it is anchored; the programme of studies, which itself has course, departmental and institutional aspects; and the wider world of educational policy making and governmental decision, which frames the student's wider environment (but which has a very real impact, for example, both through the accessibility of staff within the course and the student's general financial and accommodation situation). It is precisely because the student intersects with these external frameworks that the idea of 'student' has public and semi-formal aspects. There is no job description but we can still legitimately talk of the role of student because of these social structures which have to be inhabited.

'Student', in the discussion here, has turned out to be a multi-layered construction. At its centre is the student struggling to bring her cognitive experiences into a coherent form and to understand them; then there is the organized programme of studies and, beyond that, its institutional context; and, beyond that still, the sphere of policy making. This paper has concentrated on the first layer in the onion ring, that of the student coming into a relationship with the ideas, concepts, theories and intellectual structures central to her programme. In short, the problem before us has been 'how is understanding possible?'

The temptation might have been to conceptualize the matter of a student and an intellectual framework separately from each other, with the student in some way having to jump the gap to get on the inside of the form of thought. That has turned out to be a misleading way of construing the situation the being of the student is achieved through a process of becoming the student.[4]

Duties and responsibilities fall on one who is a student. The student has to yield to the givenness of a form of thought or principles of right reason, even if she is to make her mark on it and perhaps develop it. Logically, there is something misleading about calling someone a student simply because she has registered on a programme of study and has just received the first grant cheque. The role of student is an achievement: 'student' is an appelation won as a result of coming into a form of thought.

Nor is the student constructed from without. The student is not simply one who assimilates the experiences put her way. The student constructs herself; comes into herself more fully. She does so through yielding to the demands of the discipline. Although the process can reasonably be called a displacement of the self, the student remains a self, in command of herself. She is starting on a trajectory over which she has control.

There is no gap, therefore, either existential or epistemological, between the inner and the outer student. It is a gradual but a definite process of becoming. The butterfly emerges from the chrysalis; and the butterfly *can fly*.

Notes

1 The notion of risk as employed here is not to be confused with the notion of 'risk' as currently being deployed in social theory (for example, in Beck 1992). The 'risk society' is a society peculiarly characterized by risk. The risk in question here is a personal form of risk. More importantly, it is a risk willingly entered into, whereas the risks inherent in the 'risk society' typically do not enjoy any underwriting from citizens. A learning community is one in which participants willingly enter into situations of risk, since the response from the other participants cannot be predicted. On the other hand, since the utterances are offered in a framework of mutual listening, reflection and learning, the risks are limited. Utterances are preferred knowing that they will not be met with invective or even worse kinds of violence.
2 'The changing student experience' is the title of the 1994 annual conference of the Society for Research into Higher Education; 'student satisfaction' is the term given to an internal survey conducted by the University of Central England at

Birmingham; students' 'approaches to learning' is a term used by Marton and others in developing a 'phenomenographic' research strategy in the 1970s and is still much in use today (Marton *et al.* 1984).
3 The concept of 'the life-world' I take from the work of Jurgen Habermas.
4 Implicit in this argument about education-as-being and as becoming is a repudiation of education-as-having as a form of 'education' (Jarvis 1992).

Chapter 14

Learning for an unknown future

(from Higher Education Research & Development, 2004, 23(3) 247–260)

Outline

What is it to learn for an unknown future? It might be said that the future has always been unknown but the matter surely takes on a new pedagogical challenge, if not urgency, in the contemporary age. The preposition 'for' in our opening sentence carries weight here. It implies an education in which a sense of an unknown future is evidently present, or at least serves as a major organizing principle in the design of the curriculum and in the enacting of the pedagogy. Generic skills may seem to offer the basis of just such a learning for an unknown future, for they are proffered as holding across manifold situations, even unknown ones. I want to suggest, however, that the idea of skills, even generic skills, is a cul-de-sac. In contrast, the way forward lies in construing and enacting a pedagogy for human being. In other words, learning for an unknown future has to be a learning understood neither in terms of knowledge nor skills but of human qualities and dispositions. Learning for an unknown future calls, in short, for an ontological turn.

A logical conundrum

If the future is unknown, what would it mean to learn for it? There is the makings of a logical conundrum here. The unknown cannot be anticipated so how can a learning take place that is adequate to the unknown, to the unanticipated? Whatever else it points to, 'learning' implies a change in understanding and a change in one's relationship to the world; but an unknown world places questions against appropriate changes in understanding and in one's relationship to a world that is unknown.

It may be responded, as we noted in our introduction, that there is nothing new in any of this: the future has always been uncertain. Learning has always, then, been a matter of learning for an unknown world.

There are a number of rejoinders to this response, so as to substantiate a claim in favour of learning for an unknown future. In the first place, the unknown-ness may be of a kind that we have not seen before due to the rapidity in which a new world replaces the old; the *sheer* pace of change. In the second place, it may be that the sense of an unknown world was never as vivid as it may now be. As a result, a sense of an unknown world never entered into curricula and pedagogical decision-making, *even if it could and should have done so*. Third, it may be that the kind of world that we are now facing is—as it were—qualitatively different from former worlds. Former periods of history may, for instance, have seen quite profound changes taking place but, it could be argued, they were changes in the infrastructure of life; they were changes to ways of engaging with the environment (the agrarian and industrial revolutions), or were changes in social institutions (the rise of democracy and personal freedom). Now, what we are witnessing is a new kind of world order in which the changes are characteristically internal. They are primarily to do with how individuals understand themselves, with their sense of identity (or lack of it), with their *being* in the world; this is a world order which is characterized by ontological dispositions.

There is a fourth kind of response to the suggestion that the world has always been one of change and uncertainty, and that is to rebut the suggestion head-on. The counter claim here would be that the world has by no means always been one that has been saturated by change and uncertainty. On the contrary, it could be argued that, seen from an anthropological perspective, what characterized society until quite recently was precisely a sense of order, of stability, of relentless predictability (cf. Gellner, 1991). For the primitive mind, the universe was largely unchanging and, too, man's place in the universe. One's ancestors and one's successors would experience largely the same world. A sense of change, particularly within the horizon of a single lifetime, is a relatively new phenomenon. I believe that there is validity in this argument but I want to set it aside, if only because it is the arguments that accede to a long-standing sense of change that are particularly interesting for our purposes here.

I want to suggest that the other three rejoinders to the comment that the world has always been uncertain each carry weight and that *all* are co-present features of the condition of our current age. Together, they make for a world that is nowadays often described in the literature as one of 'fluidity', as a 'liquid modernity' (Bauman, 2000) and as an age of 'fragility' (Stehr, 2001) or 'risk' (Beck, 1992). A number of associated terms, such as 'chaos', 'complexity' and 'fragmentation', are also often summoned in such a discourse. What is distinctive about the modern world, from this point of view, is not change per se but its character, its intensity, its felt impact.

In short, while we might concede that the world has always been changing (a point that has some dubiety), the challenges that the world now brings are of a new kind. They are changes that bear in upon our sense of our own being; they are, in sum, ontological challenges.

We can see the point that I am making here by tracing a distinction between 'complexity' and 'supercomplexity'. Complexity speaks especially to a feature of systems, such that the interactions between their elements are unclear, uncertain and unpredictable. It is not just that situations may be captured in an image of intertwined spaghetti strands such that their patterns are indeterminable; it is that the spaghetti strands are so interwoven that any attempt to engage with any one strand will have repercussive and unforeseeable impacts on many, if not all, of the other strands. This is a relatively formal description of the situation that faces most individuals in professional life. One is faced with competing claims on one's attention, with an overload of entities, but any effort to satisfy one set of claims may lead to indeterminable effects elsewhere. Such a situation of systems complexity leads to real stress; not just an overload of entities that exhaust the resources available but a situation in which the very engagement with such a set of entities is liable to set off a chain of incalculable events.

Contrast that situation with what I would term 'supercomplexity' (Barnett, 2000). Amid complexity, as just described, at least one could be forgiven for believing that its challenges could, in principle, be dissolved. If only one had more time or more resources, to a large extent the complexities facing one would untangle. The students would be taught more effectively, the patients would be treated more quickly and even more humanely *and* the interests of the various stakeholders would be met. The challenges of complex systems, even if they could not be altogether unravelled, could be dissolved to a significant degree. The challenges of supercomplexity, in contrast, could never be resolved. They are the challenges that arise from the question: what is a university? Or: what is a teacher? Or: what is a doctor? The challenges of such questions could never be dissolved, at least not in ways similar to those of complexity. For such questions, in principle, yield a multiplication of answers and further questions. And some of those answers and further questions spring from perspectives, value positions and even ideologies that are mutually incompatible. To see universities and teachers as consumers of resources, or even as producers of resources on the one hand, and to see universities as sites of open, critical and even transformatory engagement are, in the end, incompatible positions, no matter what compromises and negotiations are sought.

Questions of the kind now being identified are characteristically opentextured questions that yield, in a global and pluralist world, interpretations that are not just different but which are incompatible; and there is no straightforward way of resolving those differences. And this, in itself, marks off supercomplexity from complexity. Supercomplexity produces a multiplication of incompatible differences of interpretation.

There is, however, a further point to be made in this context and it is that supercomplexity strikes home in a particularly penetrating way so far as the university is concerned. This point is that supercomplexity is intrinsic to the modern conception of the university (that is, it predates even postmodernity). It is, after all, part of the understood character of the Western university that it should produce new ideas and these ideas, inevitably, will startle; they will offer frameworks of understanding that contrast with convention. In other words, the emergence of supercomplexity, as just described, is in part due to the university fulfilling its modern mission. That we have both multiple and competing interpretations of the world before us and that we have a sense that interpretations of the world are now infinite: all this, in part, is down to the Western university fulfilling the brief that has been set before it; in short, the project of critical enlightenment. Within this brief, it is part of the task of the university to add to the supercomplexity that is the contemporary world. In turn, we may judge, it is only right, only just, that the university should help to meet the bill that it has helped to land us all with. The university, in other words, should engage with the life-world challenges and, thereby, the pedagogical challenges, that arise from an age of supercomplexity.

'Learning for an unknown future': we now see that the task of construing such a learning—problematic as it was even at the outset of our inquiry—has now become doubly challenging. For learning has to cope with two forms of uncertainty. There is, first, the uncertainty that arises out of the sheer multiplication of entities in the world. It is a world of information overload, of multiplying performance indicators, and of unpredictability in the environmental response to any intervention. It is even an uncertainty that arises out of the sheer multiplication of pertinent evidence, of relevant knowledge. It is a world characterized by an 'ignorance explosion' (Lukasiewicz, 1994), even as the libraries of the Western universities groan under the weight of volumes and journals, not to mention the arrival of electronic forms of scholarly communication (cf. Ekman & Quandt, 1999). This is a world that is radically unknowable: even though we may make modest gains here and there, our ignorance expands in all kinds of directions.

Alongside this form of uncertainty, an uncertainty that arises from the complexity of the world and our knowledge of it, arises another form of uncertainty, as we have seen. It is a more personal form of uncertainty, the uncertainty that arises out of a personal sense that we never could hope satisfactorily even to describe the world, let alone act with assuredness in it. 'Anxiety', 'fragility', 'chaos': these are as much characterizations of an inner sense of a destabilized world. It is a destabilization that arises from a personal sense that we never can come into a stable relationship with the world. The descriptions of the world that are available to us—especially in a global and multicultural world—multiply and conflict with each other. This is the uncertainty that arises out of supercomplexity for supercomplexity is precisely that paradoxical condition in which our descriptions of the world are always contestable and in which we know that to be the case. Our hold on the world is now always fragile.

Learning for the unknown

We can now see, I suggest, that the educational tasks of learning for the unknown are themselves twofold. On the one hand, there is the educational task of preparing students for a complex world, for a world in which incomplete judgements or decisions have to be made; incomplete either because of the press of time or because insufficient evidence is to hand fully to warrant any particular decision or because the outcomes are unpredictable. These possible forms of incompleteness are by no means mutually exclusive: incompleteness may be manifold, even in a single situation. On the other hand, there is the educational task of coming to a position where one can prosper in a situation, of multiple interpretations. Whereas some minimal form of security is available in the first situation, here, in this second situation, no security is available at all; that is its essential character.

These educational tasks are surely quite different in character. Loosely, the first task speaks to what has recently become known as Mode 2 knowledge (Gibbons *et al.*, 1994; Nowotny *et al.*, 2001). Here, the task is that of problem-solving *in situ*. Such a form of knowledge production and knowledge use is creative and is bounded by uncertainty. Much as one may wish to fall back on formal knowledge having a universal aspiration (Mode 1 knowledge), in the end, one has to rely on one's capacity for seeing a way forward in a particular setting, with particular challenges bearing in upon one. This form of knowledge is necessarily creative, in part because of its particularity. There is always going to be an epistemological gap between the universal claims of Mode 1 knowledge and the challenges presented by a particular situation. Here, knowledge is always going to be incomplete; one can never know how things will turn out. What is called for, therefore, is a creative knowing *in situ*. And this is a form of knowing that calls for imagination. All this is implied, at least, in the idea of Mode 2 knowledge.

But, understood as problem-solving in the world, Mode 2 does not quite capture what is required, even with a heightened sense of its creative and imaginative qualities added in. For, as indicated earlier, a complex world is a world that is radically unknowable. The entities in the world and their dynamic relationships are such that we can never, as it were, freeze-frame the world. Its character must always elude our attempts to understand it; our knowledge of it, no matter how creative, how particular and how imaginative, must always fall short of it. The idea of problem-solving, so central to the idea of Mode 2 knowledge, is problematic because it implies that—with sufficient imagination, daring and creativity—a solution can be designed. But this is a world in which solutions cannot be designed, in the sense that a problem has been entirely satisfactorily met; there are always repercussions, unintended consequences and loose ends.

A Mode 3 knowledge, therefore, surely beckons, in which it is recognized that knowing the world is a matter of producing epistemological gaps. The very act of knowing—knowledge having become a process of active knowing—now produces epistemological gaps: our very epistemological interventions in turn disturb the world, so bringing a new world before us. No matter how creative and imaginative our knowledge designs, it always eludes our epistemological attempts to capture it. This is a Mode 3 knowing, therefore, which is a knowing-in-and-with-uncertainty. The knowing produces further uncertainty.

But it is still a form of knowing, a form of knowledge, albeit a knowledge which is itself a complex of personal, tacit, experiential and propositional knowledges (Eraut, 1994). The second task, in contrast, of coming to a position of some security amid multiple interpretations—of the kind opened up by a condition of supercomplexity—cannot be understood in a language of knowledge and knowing, however subtle that language becomes. For, amid supercomplexity, the world is not just radically unknowable but is now indescribable. Amid supercomplexity, we cannot even describe with any security the situations that face us. Indeed, we cannot even hold onto a language for describing the world. It is not just that, as in Mode 3 knowledge, the world recedes from us, even as we approach it. It is that we do not even know what the world is like sufficiently for us to start on our knowing activities.

Under these conditions of uncertainty, the *educational task is, in principle, not an epistemological task*; it is not one of knowledge or even knowing per se. It is not even one of action, of right and effective interventions in the world. For what is to count as a right or an effective intervention in the world? Amid supercomplexity, *the educational task is primarily an ontological task*. It is the task of enabling individuals to prosper amid supercomplexity, amid a situation in which there are no stable descriptions of the world, no concepts that can be seized upon with any assuredness, and no value systems that can claim one's allegiance with any unrivalled authority.

This is a curricular and pedagogical challenge that understands, therefore, that terms such as 'fragility', 'uncertainty' and 'instability' are as much ontological terms as they are epistemological terms. Accordingly, this learning for uncertainty is here a matter of learning to live with uncertainty. It is a form of learning that sets out not to dissolve anxiety—for it recognizes that that is not feasible—but that sets out to provide the human wherewithal to live with anxiety. To speak of anxiety here is not, it will be understood, to convey a pathological sense of psychological disturbance. Rather, what is meant is a generalized understanding that the world is forever beyond any clear uncontestable understanding. The ice is perpetually slippery but this says nothing about the individuals on the ice; only about the conditions of epistemological insecurity in which they now find themselves. But this epistemological slipperiness generates, in turn, ontological destabilization. For if the world is radically unknowable then, by extension, 'I' am radically unknowable. Especially, for our concerns here, and as we saw earlier, what I am as a doctor, student or professor is itself unclear, contested, destabilized.

Much is made at present of the idea of risk; but, as with complexity, that concept is characteristically understood in somewhat narrow terms, that is in terms of *systems risk*, the risks that are attendant on the interactions of entities in complex systems (such as the effects of multiple drugs being used together; or, closer to our theme, of a new course of action either being taken or not being taken by a university's senior management team). Such systems risk is not to be downplayed but what our reflections here are pointing to is, in addition, an *ontological risk* that arises out of supercomplexity. If there are no stable descriptions of the world, then are no stable descriptions of 'me'. The 'I' is liable to be destabilized.

Under such conditions, a double educational task arises: first, bringing students to a sense that all descriptions of the world are contestable and, then, second, to a position of being able to prosper in such a world in which our categories even for understanding the situations in which we are placed, including understanding ourselves, are themselves contested.

Pedagogical being

Our explorations to this point may have seemed unduly abstract but they point to a set of educational tasks that experienced and skilled teachers are confronting and fulfilling every day. It may be that academics, in their teaching roles, would not employ the language brought into view here but the tasks are surely being comprehended, albeit in different ways across the different disciplines. In a recent study (Barnett & Coate, 2004) of the ways in which the higher education curriculum is currently understood—in which the author was involved—a chemistry lecturer observed:

> If we go back to Dearing, what struck me is that he is saying, really, that we've got to educate people who are going to earn a living. And they won't earn their living because they know how to produce a molecule in a particular way. That's not the way people earn their living these days.

This lecturer is surely saying, amongst other things, that neither knowledge nor skills, even high level knowledge and advanced technical skills, are sufficient to enable one to prosper in the contemporary world. Other forms of human being are required.

Here is a further quotation, this time from an interview with a history lecturer:

> We have always tried very hard to assess oral presentations so if you looked at one of my third year students who has done a lot of history of art, they would be much more confident about speaking in public. They might not be terribly articulate but they are incredibly confident ... we are going to have to think less about specific course content and more about an approach to learning.

Again, in this quotation, we see a corresponding downgrading of the significance of both knowledge and skills. What is being underscored here is the idea of confidence—and the concept comes into view twice in this short quotation. Knowledge is here—in the form of history of art—and so too are skills; but both have limited parts to play in the conception of the educational task being opened to us. Indeed, skills are actually being downvalued for the students may 'not be terribly articulate'.

What is important for this lecturer is the students' sense of themselves and of their relationships with the world around them. The students have, as it were, an indwelling in themselves, a confidence in themselves, an investment in their own selves that enables them to go forth into a challenging world. They have the confidence to speak in public, even though—presumably—they are aware that those public offerings are very liable to be contested. They know, therefore, that those public utterances are contestable at every turn; but, yet, they have somehow acquired a confidence to have a go, to launch themselves forth in a world that will furnish responses that cannot be entirely anticipated.

Here is a final quotation, this one taken from an interview with a lecturer in nursing studies:

> After five weeks, one day we turned up about half an hour later than and they were doing exactly what they would have been doing with us. They were organizing a discussion and, of course, they were adults: they didn't need us for that. We became more the resource.

An implication that I want to draw from this quotation for our purposes here is that, in this reported situation, the participants were (again) exhibiting neither knowledge nor skills but a willingness to go on by themselves; and here, we may note, the going-on by themselves was collective in its nature. They were organizing a discussion: the participants were engaging together presumably with some commitment and even enthusiasm. They were intent on their own pedagogical voyage with a collective will. We may say, to put it more formally, that the participants here inhabited a form of pedagogical being that was authentic (to use a Heideggerian term). Their being lay in that which was 'present-at-hand' (Heidegger, 1962), namely themselves, and the other participants, such that there was a jointly creative endeavour underway.

To summarize our observations on these three quotations, then, we may say that experienced teachers, without necessarily having or deploying a formal language to describe their own pedagogical achievements, are engaged in more than helping students to acquire knowledge and understanding and/or to acquire skills and capacities. These forms of pedagogical accomplishments, as realized in their students, are necessary but now are understood increasingly to be insufficient for a higher education in the contemporary world. To capture their pedagogical accomplishments fully requires an additional language. At one level, that language is caught in terms such as self-belief, self-confidence and self-motivation (as mirrored in our three examples). But even a language of that kind does not quite do justice to the pedagogical accomplishments in question. For these accomplishments point us, surely, to a language of self, of being, and of such terms as energy, authenticity and will.

Even if it is granted that a higher education curriculum should pay attention to the three moments as they are unfolding here—of understanding (knowledge), acting (skills) and being (self)—it may be asked: what has all this to do with learning for an unknown future? The answer is that matters of will, energy and being come into view in learning for an unknown future because the value of knowledge and skills recede in this milieu. If, in different ways (as the outcome of both complexity and supercomplexity), the world is radically unknowable, then knowledge and skills can no longer provide a platform for going on with any assuredness. The ice, as we have observed, is thin and perpetually cracking.

Under those conditions, one goes forward not because one has either knowledge or skills but because one has a self that is adequate to such an uncertain world. One's being has a will to go on. In using such a language, we do not have to invoke Nietzsche's Overman, with its hint of cavalier self-belief, for what is at issue here is a self that is capable of having some security in the world, even as it is buffeted by the world. For that, in turn, the self has to be self-energizing and self-propelling; and we surely saw indications of such selves in our three quotations.

Pedagogical uncertainties

To say, however, that the self—in an uncertain world—has to be particularly self-energizing in no way curtails curricular and pedagogical challenges. On the contrary: the reflection at which we have arrived opens up curricular

228 Students and learning

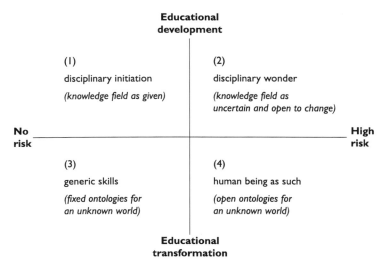

Figure 14.1 Pedagogical options: a schema

and pedagogical challenges. Of these two sets of challenges, the greater lies in the pedagogical challenges.

Let us plot the challenges in broad-brush terms. Two axes suggest themselves. One axis has at one pole 'educational development' and, at the other, 'educational transformation'; a second axis has, at its poles, 'no risk' and 'high risk'. This generates the schema illustrated in Figure 14.1.

We can chart the learning opportunities that this grid offers us in the following way.

Quadrant 1: Disciplinary Initiation

Let us say, perhaps even generously, that most higher education programmes can at least be understood as offering some form of educational development: the student advances in understanding and skills. However, the forms of educational development on offer may typically be construed as largely shorn of risk: the sheer prior specification of aims and objectives and an encouragement to frame curricula guided by the requirements of professional bodies and—in the UK, at least—against national 'subject benchmark statements' all have the latent function of producing curricula that are lacking in risk. Uncertainties are kept to a minimum: this is the educational logic at work.

Quadrant 2: Disciplinary Wonder

To be fair, academics who take their teaching seriously have long found spaces to do creative and generous work, imaginatively constructing curricula that help to transform students. Where such imaginative teaching is taking place, we may envisage even that students are placed in educational situations that are, in a sense, risky. These students are invited to stretch themselves, as they grapple with the challenges of developing their own take on matters.

Quadrant 3: Generic Skills

Increasingly, there is a sense emerging that such curricula are inadequate, even if they are creative and sponsor considerable educational development among the students. The learning offered, even by Quadrant 2 curricula, is too much designed to reproduce academic identities. On this reasoning, creative and imaginative chemists and philosophers can only carry society so far. What is needed is a different kind of transformation, a transformation in which the student can move in an accomplished way in the wider society. It is out of such thinking that we have seen develop a curricular discourse of 'skills' including even 'generic skills'.

Here, in this discourse of skills, we are offered a curricular approach that promises to transform students but it is relatively risk-free. It is a paradox of this pedagogy that it claims to be able to bring students out of their academic domains into forms of human being more adequate for a changing world than a more purely academic curriculum could offer (no matter how creative) but it does so by attempting to specify clearly the skills that are to be developed among the students. In short, we are confronted in this idea of education with the nonsense belief that we can generate human being for uncertainty through a new kind of certainty in the curriculum.

Even generic skills offer no succour here for, in a world of uncertainty, in which the self is destabilized, an educational project built around skills cannot meet the bill. For what is in question is human being in a world of conceptual and ontological uncertainty; and that is not going to be addressed by talk of skills, generic or otherwise. A different order of educational response is called for.

Quadrant 4: Human Beings as Such

The final quadrant offers us the possibility and the challenge of a curriculum not only of educational transformation but also of high risk. This is a curriculum that is aimed at the transformation of human being; nothing less. At the same time, it intends to strive to this end through pedagogies that are themselves characterized by uncertainty. A pedagogy for uncertainty cannot be—as in Box 3—technological in nature, in which ends and outcomes are tightly specified. *This* pedagogy allows for human flourishing as such. A human flourishing here is precisely that of living effectively amid uncertainty. At the heart of such a curriculum will be an exposure to dilemmas and uncertainties. These may spring from complexities within a field of knowledge (as in Box 2) but, here, they will widen such that human being itself is implicated.

Dilemmas and uncertainties, in this curriculum approach, may include, for example, a confrontation with the limits of knowing in the field, and with the limitations of the field as such. Here, in this exposure to supercomplexity (to draw on one of our earlier terms), students will come to understand that academic disciplines can only carry us so far in addressing the open-textured challenges of supercomplexity. Where there are multiple descriptions of the world, further knowledge is going to be inadequate. What is called for are new modes of human being that just might be adequate to such a challenge.

Pedagogical disturbance

A curriculum for supercomplexity, of the kind prompted by Box 14.4 of our schema, will be aided and abetted by a pedagogy for supercomplexity. Thinking imaginatively about the components of a curriculum that is likely to sponsor a learning for uncertainty is a necessary condition but it cannot be a sufficient condition of bringing off the educational aspiration at work here. For that, the actual learning processes themselves will also need to be both high-risk and transformatory in character.

A pedagogy of this kind will be a pedagogy that engages students as persons, not merely as knowers. A pedagogy of the kind located in Box 14.2 will be one that entices students into new cognitive spaces. It will offer disciplinary delight and challenge (Reeves, 1988). It will invite the student to take up his or her own stances, and help form the courage to do so. The pedagogical journey will be one of encountering strangeness, of wrestling with it, and of forming one's own responses to it. There are disturbances here but it is a set of disturbances that are the outcome of trying to understand and then making one's interventions in an already pre-structured world. Much as it prompts significant forms of individual development, those forms of development are largely framed, at best, by the uncertainties generated by navigating a field of knowledge. This is a largely epistemological journey.

In contrast, in a pedagogy of the kind that is located in Box 14.4, the disciplinary field is still present but it recedes somewhat. More to the fore here are educational processes that disturb human being as such. A pedagogy for uncertainty gains its ultimate achievement when the self is engaged. As we have seen, academics in their teaching role are bringing off this educational aim on a daily basis. Such a pedagogy is to be understood not primarily through pedagogical strategies, but is much more to be caught through metaphorical descriptors. It is not unimportant to consider the balance between different forms of student experience; between the use of lectures, seminars, projects, and student-led tasks, whether individual or collective. But considerations of that kind are liable to drag us back to Box 14.2.

If we are to capture the kind of pedagogy that is in question here (in Box 4), then a quite different language is required. A language for risk, uncertainty and transformation of human being itself calls for imagination. It may be a poetic language, a language that speaks to human being. It might be a language of love, of becoming, of disturbance, or of inspiration. What is it for human beings to be encouraged, to be brought forth, out of themselves? Smiles, space, unease, frisson, humanity, empathy, care and engagement may be helpful as descriptors; but each pedagogical situation sets up its own educational challenges and the imagined possibilities will be sensitive to each setting (cf. hooks, 1994; Mills, 1994; Nussbaum, 2000).

Basil Bernstein (1996) offered the concept of 'framing', which may seem to be helpful here. Is the pedagogy being urged here not one that we might characterize as one of relatively open frames? In other words, a pedagogy for uncertainty requires relatively open relationships between teacher and taught. Clearly, that is the case. Indeed, if students are expected to come into an educational situation of some risk, and so make themselves vulnerable, we can expect nothing less from their teachers. In pedagogical risk, all are vulnerable. The pedagogical frames, therefore, are bound to be open, as each party in the pedagogical transaction discloses her/himself to the other.

But the openness of the pedagogical frame here is of a particular kind. After all, Box 14.2 itself requires an open pedagogical frame. In that curricular quadrant, the teacher teaches the students as much as he or she teaches the subject. There is a human reciprocity present, as the teacher empathizes with her students in bringing them to a position of epistemic delight. But it is an epistemic delight: it is a delight fostered as the student comes to live in a new cognitive universe and to enjoy the new capabilities that that process has opened up. In contrast, in Box 14.4, the risk and the mutual disclosure are more of a disclosure of human being as such. The openness of the pedagogical frames is not just epistemological but it is ontological in nature. The students come to know each other as persons; and to a degree, too, they come to know their teachers as persons. This is unbridled openness of the pedagogical frame.

But what, then, is being fostered in such a pedagogy for uncertainty? Where does this openness, this mutual disclosure, this personal risk and disturbance, lead? The outcomes, we have seen, characteristically lie neither in knowledge nor in skills: neither domain can carry the day in a world of uncertainty. What counts, it surely follows from our explorations here, is sheer being itself. But how, then, are we to understand *being-for-uncertainty* and how are we to understand such being in such a way that it can help orient pedagogies in higher education?

Being-for-uncertainty does not especially know much about the world nor have at its disposal a raft of skills to deploy in and on the world. Being-for-uncertainty stands in certain kinds of relationships to the world. It is *disposed* in certain kinds of way. It is characterized, therefore, by certain kinds of disposition. Among such dispositions are carefulness, thoughtfulness, humility, criticality, receptiveness, resilience, courage and stillness.

It is, perhaps strangely, dispositions such as these that will yield the 'adaptability', 'flexibility' and 'self-reliance' that the corporate sector so often declares it looks for among its graduate employees. So these dispositions will have economic and performative value. But that cannot be the educational justification for designing curricula and engaging in pedagogies that are likely to sponsor the formation of these dispositions. They are to be fostered because they offer the prospects of an education adequate to a world of uncertainty. They offer, in short, the fashioning of being that may thrive in such a world.

Conclusions

Learning for an unknown future cannot be accomplished by the acquisition of either knowledge or skills. There is always an epistemological gap between what is known and the exigencies of the moment as it invites responses, and this is particularly so in a changing world. Analogously, skills cannot be expected to carry one far in a changing environment: there can be no assurance that skills—even generic skills—appropriate to situations of the past or even the present will help one to engage with the future world in a meaningful way. Indeed, in a changing world, it may be that nonengagement is a proper stance, at least in some situations. A more positive term, to encapsulate right relationships between persons and the changing world in which they are placed, might be 'wisdom'.

These reflections take on added weight given the characteristics of the unknown future that awaits. The unknown-ness derives not just from the complexity of interlocking systems—and new technologies, for instance, can be seen in this way. The unknown-ness derives from the complexity of multiplying descriptions of the world such that we cannot even describe the challenges that face us with any assuredness. It is this latter form of complexity of rival descriptions of the world—this supercomplexity—that poses particular challenges for learning.

For what is in question in a situation of supercomplexity is neither knowledge nor skills but *being*. The pedagogical task is none other than the eliciting of a mode of being that can not just withstand incessant challenge to one's understandings of the world, such that any stance one takes up is liable to be challenged. It is the even more demanding task of encouraging forward a form of human being that is not paralysed into inaction but can act purposively and judiciously. It is a form of action in the face of incessant challenge that can still find reasons for such action. Such action springs from a form of being that is authentic in character.

Construing the pedagogical task as the formation of authentic being turns us towards neither knowledge nor skills as central categories but rather to certain kinds of human qualities. They are the qualities that both make authentic being possible and are also, in part, generated by a drive towards authenticity. They are qualities such as carefulness, thoughtfulness, humility, criticality, receptiveness, resilience, courage and stillness. The achievement of qualities such as these calls for a transformatory curriculum and pedagogy which are themselves understood to be and practised as endeavours of high risk; high risk not just for the participants but also for the academic staff in their educational roles.

Why, it might be asked, is this of significance in the context of higher education? Are not these educational challenges characteristic of many educational settings, especially those connected with projects of lifelong learning? So they are; but it may be observed that there is a particular connection between the kind of learning sketched out here and higher education. For the learning as sketched out here can surely, without hubris, be understood as a form of higher order learning. It looks, after all, to human being and becoming that offer the wherewithal for standing up to the world and engaging with it and in it purposefully. It is a learning for an unknown future that enables the self to come to understand and strengthen itself, much as it recognizes that there is always a gap between that self-awareness and the need to act in the world.

Part, therefore, of such a learning is acquiring the capacity to live with the existential angst that derives from an awareness of the gap between one's actions and one's limited grounds for those actions. Understood in this way, a pedagogy for an unknown future becomes a pedagogy with the unknown built into it as living principles of educational exchanges and accomplishments. Designing a curriculum and practising a pedagogy of this kind is not a set of practices that we readily understand. They are, in turn, matters about which we need to go on learning.

Chapter 15

Configuring learning spaces
Noticing the invisible

(from Anne Boddington and Jos Boys (eds) *Re-shaping Learning: A Critical Reader. The Future of Learning Spaces in Post-Compulsory Education*, 2011, Rotterdam: Sense Publishers)

Outline

The idea of learning space has many attractions but it holds traps for the unwary. The idea is at once educationally expansive, potentially emancipatory and even subversive. It opens up the hope of students becoming authors of their own learning in spaces that they claim as their own. But the idea of learning space, as it is being taken up, deserves to carry warning signs. There are invisibilities associated with it, invisibilities connected with a potential psychological overload on learners and with a possible down-valuing of knowledge, as the student's own learning journey is given prominence. This, at least, is the argument I shall try to make in this chapter. To do that, we shall need, en route, to essay a brief exploration of the conceptual landscape of learning spaces and to attempt a preliminary taxonomy. Finally, having developed a somewhat cautionary account of learning spaces, I shall turn – via the idea of an ecology of learning spaces – to intimate a positive way forward that addresses the challenges sketched out.

Valuing learning spaces

The idea of learning spaces is – on the surface, at least – emancipatory. It conjures themes of freedom, openness, personal realisation and creativity on the part of the learner. It also conjures a dissolution of the boundaries that have hitherto characterised formal learning – between different forms of knowledge, between forms of knowledge and forms of practice and between the teacher and the taught. Now the learner is free to roam by herself where so ever she wishes, in whichever direction she prefers and in whichever mode of learning she enjoys. In its intimations of the breaking of boundaries of higher education, the idea of learning spaces is subversive as, in its wake, the fixities and barriers that are characteristically so much part of the academy are set aside. This is a pedagogy that offers a new conception of education, in which the learner is much more the designer of her learning experiences.

The idea of learning spaces, then, flies in with large and even universal themes attaching to its wings. It is not shy of its ethical pretensions but proclaims them boldly and loudly. In associating itself with such tropes as freedom, openness, personal realisation and creativity, it stakes large claims for itself, claims that are not only pedagogical and educational but also ethical. The idea of learning spaces is a kind of educational radicalism, an outrider in its energies, its claims and its hopes. It attempts to storm the ethical high ground, to secure a vantage point from which other educational doctrines and dogmas may easily be vanquished.

It has considerable right on its side. Only so long as students have some degree of space to themselves can they flourish. Only insofar as they have space to themselves can they acquire and be authentically themselves in their learning and their own development. The idea of learning space is a radical concept that seeks to grant the individual student – and students collectively – space in which to become truly themselves, free from constraint. There is both negative and positive freedom here (Berlin, 1969/1979): on the one hand, the limitations – of discipline, of bounded curricula and of tight pedagogical frames – are reduced as the student is freed from constraints; on the other hand, the student is thereby empowered and indeed encouraged to take their courage in their hands and to venture forth by and for themselves. There is an existential calling lurking in the idea of learning space.

We should note too that the terms 'learning space' and 'learning spaces' are often here treated as if they were synonymous. This is a telling insight into the way in which language has ideological force. The learning space opens into learning spaces (plural). The one leads naturally to the other; and various *forms of learning space* may be identified. It is not merely that students can have access to different rooms, as it were, of the educational mansion through which they may roam, in and through its different spaces. Rather, the students may now have access to quite different kinds of mansion, configured quite differently and affording quite different kinds of experience.

The idea of learning space, thereby, offers an unending opening up of pedagogical space. Its spaces are presumably – at least in theory – infinite in their scope. The idea heralds, as we may term it, a pedagogy of air (Barnett, 2007). It is a space in which students take off and fly and breathe for and by themselves. They fly with courage and with confidence, and direct their own flight. They become themselves in this space. It is a space not just for greater understanding but a space in which students' own re-becoming as persons becomes possible. It is a space that offers to change students' lives.

Towards a taxonomy of learning spaces

It is surely already evident that learning spaces are of multiple kinds. Let us, then, hazard an attempt at forming a preliminary taxonomy of learning spaces (cf. Savin-Baden, 2008). I would want to classify learning spaces as forming three broad domains:

a. *Material space and physical space*: These two – material space and physical space – are intimately related but are crucially different. Or to put it another way, the terms point us to different aspects of the geography of learning space. In relation to the student's material space, we can inquire into the materiality of the student's learning experience, its technologies, and its material structures (are there lecture halls?) and the spaces that they open (or close off). In relation to the student's physical space, we can inquire into the location of the student's learning (to what extent is it on campus or off it? To what degree are the tutors and other students visibly present?). Design can enter both forms of space here but it is the client and architect who come into play in the design of material space whereas it is the educationalist as designer who acts in relation to physical space.

b. *Educational space*: This is a set of intentional spaces that are revealed in the playing out of the curriculum and pedagogy. Curriculum spaces and pedagogical spaces are intertwined but again should be distinguished. *Curriculum spaces* are the spaces intentionally opened to the student, in the ordering of specific knowledge and its practice elements. *Pedagogical spaces* are the spaces of the relationship – the pedagogical relationship – between the tutor and student, and among the students. Curricula and pedagogical spaces are *both* structured and unstructured; but curricula spaces tend more by structure and pedagogical spaces more by improvisation. This is because, in higher education, curricula are formed crucially by assemblies from disciplinary fields that are, to some extent, given, whereas pedagogies are more open to experiment and innovation. Within both curricula and pedagogical spaces are to be found other spatial zones, in particular those of knowledge and of practices; so we can talk of *epistemological spaces* and of *practical spaces*. Issues arise as to the kinds of journey a student is being invited to make and as to the freedom extended to explore forms of knowledge. To what extent are the boundaries between forms of knowledge kept tight and even policed? Are there no-go areas? Issues also arise as to the kinds of actions that a student is enabled to conduct: with what freedom and in which direction might a student go? In some disciplines, related to life-threatening situations, there may be good reason for quite tight boundaries containing practical ventures.

c. *The student's interior space*: This is a psychic space, but it is more than that. This is a kind of ontological space: it is the space of the student's being. It has a liquid character: her educational being flows in and out of her wider being as a person. It is a zone in which is to be found much of the meaning of that complex concept of *Bildung* (Lovlie, Mortenson & Nordenbo, 2003). Here, the student's own self-formation is implicated. To what extent does the student have a will to venture forth? How secure does she feel in doing so? Does she really wish to explore the spaces that are opened to her? What forms of explorations does she prefer? Concrete and practical or ideational and cognitive? Is she a nomadic learner or a stay-at-home learner? Is her world local or global – or both? How spacious is her interior space?

These three sets of spaces could be depicted as intersecting circles but that would be misleading. There is a dynamic between all three: each interacts with and influences the other two. But they are more like clouds, flowing into each other and setting turbulences. The unbrokenness and the fixity of Venn diagram circles is far from this situation. The zones of the spaces outlined above are much more fuzzy, inchoate and fluid.

There is another difference between Venn diagrams and clouds. Characteristically, the circles of Venn diagrams are fairly empty; clouds on the other hand are more or less opaque; they are cloudy! Correspondingly, learning spaces may be populated; they may even be congested. There is perhaps too readily an assumption that learning spaces are open, uncluttered and readily available to the student's freely chosen explorations. But the opposite may be the case. Not infrequently, especially in the hard sciences and in the newer institutions of higher education, the learning spaces of the curriculum have been and are unduly full. Students have been sometimes been left with little room to reflect and hardly even to breathe, educationally speaking. So the arrival of the idea of 'learning spaces' is a call to the academic world to remove unnecessary clutter. The new dispensation is an implicit plea for more openness in the students' learning spaces.

Languages of learning spaces

Trailing in the wake of the idea of learning spaces are the different languages through which it is articulated. There is a language that speaks to the pedagogical experience of students as they make their way amongst the learning spaces afforded to them and which they are increasingly invited to design and construct for themselves. There is a language, for example, of 'liminality', of the 'fluid' and 'liquid', of the 'transitional' and 'provisional', of the 'transgressing of borders' and of 'fragility'. There is 'risk' here, risk that learning may not advance effectively or even efficiently; risk that the student's will to learn may falter, as the personal load becomes unbearable. There is also a language of the student as 'traveller', as a 'voyager', as a 'nomad', a 'sojourner', hardly able to put down roots, as the student glides from one learning space (with its experiences) to another (with *its* experiences).

These two languages (of the absence of borders on the one hand and of the student's crossing of borders on the other hand) point to the ephemeralism of the student and her experiences as an ever-continuing traveller. The metaphors – at once of fragility and of personal travel – are metaphors of the contemporary age; or at least, of perceptions of it. For the current age, of 'post-modernity', of 'hyper-modernity', is seen precisely as a fluid age, somewhat rudderless, and lacking in the anchors of sure and uncontestable values and principles. As such, the individual is seen as bearing responsibility for making his or her way in the world, not just materially but also conceptually. A curriculum of learning spaces, accordingly, is a response to the challenges of a liquid world.

The educational philosophy – as we might term it – behind informal learning spaces is one that diminishes the place of knowledge and instead throws its weight behind *being* and *becoming*. Here, it is less important that the student knows or even that she is able to do particular things; what counts is that she is a certain kind of human being, able to take on unexpected challenges and move ahead even in murky waters. This is a philosophy not of filling up (with knowledge) nor even of filling out (with skills) but of opening out; opening out of the person, ready to take on the world; willing to go on a voyage of exploration by and for oneself. Accordingly, the curriculum is to be characterised much more by relative open spaces, spaces both on and off campus, spaces of the mind and of body. There is a freedom here, a freedom better termed here not so much 'academic freedom' but a 'learning and personal freedom'. It is a space in which the student's voice can be developed and will be developed; it will be valued and will be heard and even heeded. (Witness the continuing and expanding efforts to monitor and evaluate students' 'satisfaction' with their courses and their entire university experience.)

There are ideological currents at work here. The idea of learning space implies an in-between space. It is a space that is not fully accounted for. Unforeseen experiences may arise in such spaces. There is a tension, therefore, between the idea of learning space and that of learning outcomes. The one speaks of spaciousness, of air, of freedom, of self-authorship; the other speaks of predictability, of control, of lack of freedom. So the idea of learning space is a subversive concept, containing the prospect of challenging the hegemony of contemporary dominant curricular thinking (which in the UK, for example, is predicated on a rigid structure of specific learning outcomes, explicitly linked to defined evaluation criteria which are then used to formally assess each teaching unit).

There are also other strains embedded in the idea of learning space. A key question is this: To what extent are learning spaces designed and who designs them? In other words, the idea of learning spaces could also herald a new kind of pedagogic control. It could presage a kind of Foucaultesque experiment, in which curricula and pedagogies are designed precisely to bring about the kinds of 'subjectivities' felt to be required by a globalised learning economy (Foucault, 1991). For such spaces might be designed and even engineered so as to elicit specifically desired qualities and dispositions – of venturousness, resilience, fortitude, self-endeavour and so forth. Far from heralding a critique of contemporary curricula, learning spaces may just be a device for bringing about a new order of student domestication.

The idea of learning spaces, then, is a discursive space in which different and perhaps somewhat antipathetic agendas come together. It is emancipatory, at least in its self-presentation: and it yet may serve as a pedagogic vehicle for the needs of the market and the global learning economy, and thereby serve the dominant interests in society. Its inner perception of the student as a free spirit, fearlessly exploring the learning spaces being opened may also here be coexisting with an educational response to calls for greater efficiency. And yet the idea of learning spaces, properly pursued, may lead to 'inefficient' learning as students are granted pedagogical space in which to make and to learn from their own mistakes. There is, therefore, in the idea of learning spaces an ideological complex, as competing educational philosophies jostle together.

The potency of learning spaces

Higher education has long been associated with learning through subject disciplines. 'Disciplines' are aptly named: they require discipline for their study. They impose limits (of reasoning, argumentation, truth claims and ways of proceeding) and require understandings, whether of a horizontal character (across a broad range of concepts and schemas, as in the humanities) or of a vertical character (going into a limited range of concepts in an ordered way and to ever greater depth, as in the natural sciences) (Bernstein, 1999; Wheelahan, 2010). Disciplines require that the learner yield to their demands, if learning is to take place. The learner has to displace him or herself, to some extent. Learning spaces, to the contrary, encourage the learner forward. Disciplines provide a kind of learning *super-ego*: they call the learner to account, inviting an internalisation of the standards and forms of life particular of each discipline. Learning spaces, on the other hand, sponsor a learning *ego:* they invite the learner to become more fully him or herself, independently of external expectations.

Within the idea of learning spaces, therefore, lurks a psycho-dynamic dimension in which the individual appears to be freed from the perceived impositional tyranny of disciplines and is instead encouraged to become their own person. But learning spaces are inert in themselves. Under certain conditions, however, they can take on an educational power: they can become potent. Learning spaces can provide – as we may term it – *educational energy*. They can elicit and encourage a self-realisation among students; a new *becoming*. It is through the provision of learning spaces that a student can testify to the fact that her experience at university has changed her life. Nor is this potency a *fixed* quality of learning spaces, even where it is present: learning spaces can be assessed as to their degree of potency. The following theorem therefore presents itself:

> *availability (of learning spaces)*
> *+ a will to explore*   =   *potency*
> *+ pedagogical encouragement*   (1)

Potency here, therefore, is a function of real openness for the student to make their own explorations, combined with a will on the part of the student to take advantage of that openness. This also requires an encouragement to do so from the pedagogical environment. Under such a set of circumstances, the idea of learning spaces can be realised.

But what is this potency? Potency of what? It is, as implied, a potency for student *becoming*. In the centre is the flowering of the student's learning age. She comes to have confidence in herself and her own understandings. However, as implied too, there are epistemological implications. For, insofar as the student's becoming becomes the pedagogical fulcrum here, there is – or is liable to be – a consequent diminution in the extent to which the student yields to and is initiated into *the discipline of the discipline*. This may be an empty triumph for the ontological quest of the student's being and becoming. For, if it is at the cost of the student's effective appropriation of a discipline, the resulting ego may be educationally empty at best and downright dangerous – being full of assertive dogma and personal opinion – at worst.

Another way of expressing these reflections is to observe that the disciplines themselves help to form perspectives on the world. In that way, they illuminate the world: they reveal it in ways not ordinarily perceived. They are themselves vistas of strangeness. They offer, in the words of Deleuze and Guattari, a set of 'striated' spaces as against the 'smooth' spaces of 'learning spaces' (Deleuze & Guattari, 2007). Disciplines are slices into the world; learning spaces are educational vehicles for traversing the world. A course of study, in and by the disciplines, is a programme that runs its course; it is channelled. Perspectives may be limited, therefore, but may run true and steady. Learning spaces offer excitement, a rare freedom and personal exploration; but the very open ended nature of the learning experience may be problematic. Not merely may the learning spaces be empty as the student is encouraged to make her own pedagogical journey; but the resulting experience may be largely empty as well. Without the insights of disciplinary perspectives, little understanding of any rigour may be gained. This is not so much a liquid learning as a glassy learning, in which the student skims across the learning surfaces and, in the process, accumulates very little.

Noticing the invisible

I have been hinting that there are hidden aspects in the idea of learning spaces. That thesis can now be brought more fully into the open. The idea of learning spaces is of its time. It offers – or seems to offer – the sponsoring of a learning 'subjectivity' in which the student embarks on a never-ending journey of self-learning. The learning, too, is a free-floating enterprise, that skates confidently over the existing representations of the world. Both these aspects of learning spaces have a pedagogical appropriateness in and for the 21st century; or so it may seem. The never-ending journey of self-learning that the idea of learning spaces seems to sponsor is a learning style fitting for a liquid world (Bauman, 2000), a world that seems to call forth a nomadism, a learning without roots, a learning that evinces disdain for disciplinary-bound learning. The world presents, so we are continually told, with changing, interdisciplinary and hybrid problems. It is, too, a world of fluid institutions, employment patterns, geographic movements and learning media. No one set of representations can sustain the kind of educational self-help that such a world requires; or so the argument seems to run.

There are a number of exclusions and hidden preferences in this ideology. Firstly, there is the exclusion of attachment. The contemporary world appears to call for a kind of learning promiscuousness in which the individual moves effortlessly from one topic to another, from one concept to another, and from one set of data to another. 'Multimodality' perhaps captures the hallmark of the discourse here and its appropriate learning processes (Kress & Van Leeuwen, 2001). Secondly, there is a preference for learning in the world and a down valuing of learning apart from the world. The reasoning runs this way. Effortless movement across situations – from which individuals learn – calls for a readiness to adopt different schemas. An education in a single discipline is thereby no longer useful. Such an education not merely restricts vision and access to learning tools; it severs the individual from the world, when what is desired is the capability and confidence of negotiating the world in all its messiness. Thirdly, the learning spaces that are encouraged are spaces in which the student is active and preferably literally so; active in visible performances. Spaces for mere contemplation are largely off-limits here. Finally, there is an embedded set of assumptions to the effect that all 'employability' requires this framing of knowledge and skills and that students en masse are in turn open to such malleability.

So, within the working out of the rhetoric of learning spaces, issues arise as to the rules of inclusion and exclusion. Not all learning spaces are equal;

some are more equal than others. Some planes of learning – the disciplinary, the visionary, the theoretical, the contemplative – may be largely hidden or occluded; or banished completely. In the curricula construction of these learning spaces, students are carefully enjoined to go on certain kinds of learning journey rather than others. There is thus a major dimension of invisibility attaching to the educational project of learning spaces.

We may distinguish two kinds of the invisible. Firstly, there is the kind of learning spaces that is excluded by reason of educational intention. Opening up learning spaces of action, of 'training', of 'professional education' or even of 'service', whether on or off campus, whether in formal or structured settings or in informal and unstructured settings, can diminish spaces which enable a deep engagement within disciplines. It is not merely disciplines which fade from sight; so too do their perspectives and their power to transform perceptions. Such spaces are closed off *intentionally*. This is a form of *ideological invisibility*: the liberal idea of higher education is implicitly repudiated and banished. Secondly, learning spaces of former kinds may remain but become unnoticed. In an age of increasing e-learning, and group-based projects, books may remain on the shelves of the library but become invisible – less a learning resource and more a symbolic emblem of a former idea of the academy. Students are oriented to the task, the collective and the here-and-now. Private, in-depth and reflective study – of which dedicated reading is an obvious example – is not outlawed as such but instead passes out of sight. We may term this a 'myopic invisibility'.

For Heidegger, 'being' strives for to become transparent to itself. It becomes 'cleared in itself' in such a way 'that it is itself the clearing' (Heidegger, 1962/1998, p. 171). A key question for learning spaces, therefore, is the extent to which they allow students a *clearing* to come into themselves, to be disclosed to themselves. Far from encouraging such 'disclosedness' (ibid.), learning spaces may shut off – intentionally or unintentionally – such clearings as would allow a student genuinely to come into themselves, to develop authentic understandings of the world for and by themselves. Far from opening up real and challenging vistas, learning spaces may consign students to the immediate, the familiar and the safe as they move rapidly from one learning space to yet another. The idea of learning spaces loses its meaning if it means yielding one set of closures for another. The very breadth of view, the interconnectedness and largeness of outlook, the vision and even the wisdom (Maxwell, 2009) that the idea of learning spaces holds out may be vitiated if it is implemented as an ideological vehicle for external interests.

An ecology of learning spaces

We can, therefore, speak of *an ecology of learning spaces*. An ecology of learning spaces points to interconnectedness between learning spaces and thence to modalities of that interconnectedness. Learning spaces primarily of knowing, learning spaces primarily of doing and learning spaces primarily of sheer being: what are their relationships? To what degree and in what ways does the student have freedom to roam across those spaces? What are the values informing the shaping of these various learning spaces? To speak of an ecology of learning spaces, therefore, is not only to advert to patterns and shapes in and between learning spaces, but also it is to underscore their ethical dimensions. What ends are these learning spaces intended to sustain? Which sustainabilities are favoured here? Do these learning spaces look outwards or at least open windows outwards, towards the learning economy perhaps or to ideas of civic society? Or do they look inwards, to the student's own sustainability and development across her lifespan?

There is literally incredible complexity here. A student's programme of undergraduate studies typically runs its course over three or four years. Each is a set of learning spaces, with their own ecologies. There is a dynamic here, the modules and units tension with each other, firing off each other, drawing from each other. They open spaces for the students, who take differential advantage or their opportunities. Some venture forward excitedly; others hold back. After all, students need courage to move into learning spaces of their own volition. This courage is a kind of gift on the part of the student to him or herself. But, because of the risks, it is a gift he or she can often barely come to bestow. It is an expression of goodwill, to make good of the open spaces, but the outcome is unclear.

This ecology is a complex of ecologies. It is a knowledge ecology, a learning ecology (itself a complex of learning modalities), an ecology of being and becoming and an ecology of praxis all at once, and all working in an extraordinary dynamic with each other. There is, too, as there has to be, all manner of inter-connectednesses across these domains. These inter-connectednesses are themselves constantly shifting, as curricula, pedagogies, students, learning opportunities on and off campus, changing members of course teams, disciplinary developments and alterations in resources all play their part in helping to shape the ecological landscape. The student makes her way in and across these learning spaces, perhaps hesitantly, perhaps with some confidence; but there is unpredictability here; there has to be. No matter how far some of the spaces are rule-bound – are 'striated' – still there is some glassiness here. The student slides across the 'smooth spaces', just hoping that the ice will not crack.

These are adventures, ventures of discovery. The potential discoveries are as much discoveries of self – of being in the world – as they are about knowledge and of practice. In these learning processes, there is room inevitably for misadventure, not only for wrong turnings but for learning encounters where the discoveries of self are even, at first, injurious (Meyer & Land, 2006). There has to be always a possibility of genuine learning spaces, but ecologies may founder; may not be sustained.

The idea of ecology, to use a term of Bernard Williams (2008), is a 'thick concept'. It is fact and value at once. So, too, are learning spaces considered as learning ecologies: we can inquire into them as sets of actual curricula and pedagogical spaces and we can inquire into the hopes and commitments circling in them and around them. Learning spaces are always pools of *learning–possible*. They are potentials for learning in all manner of directions, learning that has ultimately to be at least partly under the control of the student. They constitute a retort to the dominant ideologies encircling these learning spaces.

As ecologies, learning spaces are full of hopes for improvement, for the student's own personal improvement, for her being in the world, and for her knowing and for her practices in the world. They hold out the wish for some kind of existential liberation from the pulls and pushes that attend those spaces, even from the existing educational communities of knowers and would-be knowers (the other students) participating in those spaces. Learning spaces, even in their ecological moments, are sites of some anarchy (Barnett, 2010) as students take their chances and realise their own possibilities, amid the inter-connetivities that characterise the many ecologies at work.

To couple the ideas of learning spaces and learning ecologies is to inject both an intention and a value-component into what otherwise might be – *a priori* – a neutral concept, open to any manner of curricula aims. Now, seen as the formation and sustaining of learning ecologies, learning spaces are imbued with high and virtuous hopes and ideals. The idea of learning spaces, which (as noted) is itself inert, is now given a forward and progressive momentum. As the formation of a learning ecology, it is no longer blind to ideological presences (of the kind observed earlier). On the contrary, this ecology now keeps open a watchful eye for ideological presences and directly engages them in combat. This is not fanciful. Students these days are often very aware of ideological presences, of the state or corporations, of discourse and of power structures that affect their learning and their student experience. As inhabitants of learning spaces, afforded their own autonomy to take some charge of their own learning, they become active and may even adopt a critical and radical stance as they forge their own learning situation, reflective of their own – doubtless developing – values. An ecology of learning spaces is dynamically in favour of improvement of and for a better world, even if just what is to count as a better world is kept under critical review.

Conclusion

The idea of learning spaces holds traps for the unwary. It comes full of promises and hopes, of liberation, emancipation and authenticity for the learner, now freed to take charge of her learning experiences and to win through to new stages of her own self-becoming. But its contemporary and forceful arrival as an idea isn't happenstance. It has taken off as an idea because multiple and indeed even antagonistic groupings find it a useful vehicle for furthering their various interests. As well as it being a vehicle for emancipatory hopes, it is also a vehicle for technical and instrumental interests, in a context of mass post-compulsory education, rising student:staff ratios and an attunement to a global learning economy that calls for individuals to have powers of self-renewal throughout their lifespan. The single term 'learning spaces', therefore, denotes a contested ideological terrain.

There are also education pitfalls arising from learning spaces considered as an emancipatory project. If the student's learning spaces are initially empty, to be filled only by the student's creative endeavours, what becomes of knowledge, knowing and deep understanding? There is a risk here of epistemological superficiality as the educational enterprise focuses on the student's self-becoming.

In this complex of considerations, two further questions arise: what is to count as maturity on the part of the student? And, is it possible to derive a conception of learning spaces that, at once, addresses the three concerns of educational maturity, of knowing and understanding, and of potential ideological entrapment? I have suggested that consideration of learning spaces as a *set* of ecologies may offer a way forward. This conception of learning spaces may turn out to be epistemologically, ontologically and practically efficacious. Learning spaces considered as a set of ecologies both opens up spaces and at the same time places severe epistemological burdens on the student as learner. The knowledge wanderings of students are still subject to the forms of life of academic disciplines, even as they find their own path through and form their own images of the world. Such a journey is precisely one means of achieving maturity as it opens up the prospect of the student coming into herself or himself in a totally new way; of 'finding' themselves, and of securing the personal resources through which to gain a genuine authenticity. And such a voyage of discovery, too, opens the prospect of a student engaging with the world and coming to form a care for the world. The sustainability of the world, the student and even knowledges, can all be in evidence here.

Of course, the framing of curricula and the adoption of pedagogies that are going to do justice to all of these hopes is full of challenge. Fortunately, there are indications that such educational achievements are possible and, indeed, are already present. Not infrequently, students can be heard to say at graduation ceremonies, in introducing a tutor to the proud parents, not that 'I've gained a lot of knowledge on this course' or that 'I've acquired many skills on this course' but that 'this course has changed my life'. Is that not a shorthand and telling testimony to the presence of ecological learning spaces?

Coda
Threads of an academic life

The corpus of work, built over thirty years, from which the papers in this volume have been drawn, could not have been sustained without it being invested with considerable personal meaning; and both intellectual and professional meaning at that. The themes present in the titles of the chapters here have both threads running through them, threads that connect with personal apperceptions and recollections of mine over the past years.

For instance, the concept of 'supercomplexity' (chapters one and eleven) is not only an analytic term but reflects the felt complexity of an academic life as in, for instance, the chairing of a meeting of eighty course leaders or some sixty-plus professors in one's own institution, or of some forty-plus experienced colleagues drawn from across all the colleges and faculties of the federal University of London, such meetings being spaces of multitudinous and nuanced, and even conflicting, views and beliefs: were not those endeavours efforts in some way of 'situating the learning university' (chapter two)? The idea of 'learning for an unknown future' (chapter fourteen) embodies a sense that while the future is unknown (for example, in drawing up an institutional strategy), we may yet assemble some resources that may enable us to venture forth more securely. The idea of 'noticing the invisible' (chapter fifteen) implies that there lie to hand, in the interstices of academic life, unrealised possibilities: their hiddenness is partly a matter of us not fully being open to the opportunities for recognition and human flourishing that lie to hand, perhaps towards the student who is strangely silent from one lesson to another or the committee member who is hesitating to make an intervention. 'The strange case of entrepreneurialism' (chapter eight) points to the felt ambivalent potency of university transformations, as one's institution becomes ever more financially self-sufficient. And the idea of 'recapturing the universal in the university' (chapter three) tacitly asks whether all the happenings of one's academic life are so many disparate events with little or no connecting tissue or rather can be seen to be a playing out of some large and even universal themes.

Again, 'the coming of the ecological university' (chapter five) calls to mind the textual challenges of crafting a report for a national body that both respected the interests of that national body and was also duly sensitive to an academic community across the UK (which was, at that moment, critical of the national audit practices under review). The ecological university, after all, is precisely a university that tries to live out carefully and fully its interconnectedness(es) with the world, despite the difficulties that such multiple interconnections bring. And the question 'Does higher education have aims?' (chapter seven) reminds us of the profound difficulties of teaching, that dedicated teachers sometimes fall short of fulfilling their hopes towards their students' flourishing. (I recall setting up a module so as to encourage participation and a sense of equality, the chairs – including mine – arranged in a circle. Across a term, one student appeared at each session but remained silent throughout. Should I have intervened, even quietly at the close of a session?) Such self-questioning and self-recollecting could run for some time; perhaps even unendingly.

On the edge

There is a further thread to my academic life that might perhaps be worthy of mention and this is the matter of being something of an outsider. It will be difficult for many to have a sense as to the intellectual aloneness that I felt at the start of my efforts in my postgraduate research work in the 1970s and 1980s, leading to my first book – *The Idea of Higher Education* in 1990. At that time, there was really nothing in the way of a philosophy of higher education (save – as I observed in the Introduction – for a rather thin book by John Brubacher, published in 1977 in the USA entitled *On the Philosophy of Higher Education*). As a consequence, the bibliography for my doctorate thesis (in 1984) was something of a fiction, in that even though it ran to many pages, it consisted of a creative amalgamation of resources for what was a new kind of intellectual venture. I was acutely conscious then that I was breaking new ground in wanting to attempt to understand higher education with a philosophical perspective. It wasn't just that what I wanted to say was necessarily original but that I was having to map out a territory anew in order to make *any* kind of argument. There could be no serious engagement with the literature for there was no such literature.

 This intellectual liminality, this sense of being on the edge of the current academic field, had a number of reinforcements over the succeeding thirty years. I began my doctoral studies while working as an administrator in a London polytechnic and, while my (evening) studies were supported by the polytechnic, I nevertheless felt unable to share my thinking with work colleagues, who perhaps viewed such academic work with some suspicion. My academic base lay in the philosophy department at the Institute of Education in London and it was heavily oriented both to school education and to a conceptual philosophy deriving from R S Peters. That approach had considerable influence and weight but my own work, being situated in the Frankfurt School of Critical Theory (especially the oeuvre of Jurgen Habermas) and being focused on higher education, was intellectually somewhat homeless.

I continued with my studies (working in the evenings) while being an administrator at a national body, the Council for National Academic Awards. Again, while I was given support for my studies, my scholarly work – which by then was examining higher education as ideology – placed me in an orthogonal relationship with my professional situation, both as insider and as critic. This insider/outsider location came again in becoming a senior academic manager at the Institute of Education: there I was in the strange situation of being part of a system and acting out a management role that, in the evening, I would be critiquing in the writing of my books. I had also become active in the Society for Research into Higher Education and ploughed a rather lonely furrow in my interests in philosophical issues. For the most part, 'research' was understood as lying in empirical studies. Within the journals, too, purely conceptual and philosophical research – for a long time – had no obvious location. So, for many years, I felt that my work was outside the mainstream, even though in many ways, my work received recognition and indeed much valued support in all of the organisations with which I was involved.

That much of this landscape has changed fundamentally over the years – work on higher education has expanded, there are outlets for and even an encouragement of conceptual work and the philosophical ground has changed, being much more receptive of continental philosophy – has made life easier, intellectually. But still some edginess remains, to which a recent map of higher education research bears testimony. There (Macfarlane, 2012), I am positioned – at 'Barnett point' – as the lone inhabitant of a 'philosophy reef', some way off from the main islands in the total 'higher education research archipelago'; so it seems as if my sense as to my intellectual location as being outside of the main currents of the field is not unique to myself.

Other than in providing some passing anecdotal interest, why offer these reflections here? These continuing sensations of intellectual and professional apartness have, I believe, affected my writing in this sense. This abiding liminality has meant that I have had, in my writing, to forge a readership. At least, in the early days, there was no ready readership for my work for it was breaking new ground. The task of writing, therefore, was in part a matter of reaching out to potential readers and of even, over time, developing a readership. Consequently, much effort lay in striving for clarity. Nothing could be presumed on the part of potential readers (not least because I was attempting to reach out to multiple audiences, including practitioners, managers and planners, who were unlikely to be familiar with the ground I was covering). I have always felt that it should be possible to write clearly about technical matters and that if the reader found my writing hard-going, the fault lay with me. There being no certainty as to there being readerships for my work provided an added spur to this self-imposed demand for clarity.

There is, though, another point here. Adorno, Derrida, Gramsci and others have advanced their work while in a state of some exile from the university system and that extra-mural location has provided a space from which their work could take on heightened elements both of critique and of reconstruction. My own liminality has helped in both these ways; not only according one space in which to go against the grain but also space in which to eke out a position for oneself. Inhabiting different worlds simultaneously – academic life, administration, empirical work, management, state ideologies, theory, critique, abstraction, philosophy, practice, teaching, scholarship, committee work, organisational life and consultancy, and at local, national and global levels – has furnished resources that have fuelled my writings. Out of the edginess of professional and academic life has emerged some kind of writing voice.

Unending quest

Unended quest was the title of Karl Popper's intellectual autobiography (Popper, 1978). My own sub-title here, it will have been noticed, is slightly different, that of an 'unend*ing* quest'. By this slight variation, I want – in these remaining closing words – to move attention from my work as *my* work and see it as a form of inquiry as such. My work is but a personal attempt to develop a form of inquiry that might also be seen in the work of others. And 'work' here is both practical and thoughtful in character. It is a matter of delight when I learn that a university – or a group within a university – somewhere in the world is picking up some part of my corpus and is putting it to work, seeing how far and in what ways it might cash out in the interstices of a specific university context.

This work has been an unending quest too in that the form of inquiry in which I have been engaged can always sensibly be conducted, so long as there are institutions with the title of 'university' and educational processes that are understood to be forms of a 'higher education'. How might that be so? And what would constitute the elements of such an inquiry?

Universities, so it is often observed, have had a long innings, stretching back at least to mediaeval times (with some institutions being able to trace their own history to that period). That longevity, and the present flourishing of such long-standing institutions, is indicative of a capacity for change, and internal self-willed change at that (as well as responses to more external promptings). Universities are characterised, to use a term from Roy Bhaskar's philosophy, by a quality of emergence (Bhaskar, 2008). They have internal properties such that they are always changing, and always morphing into new forms. Emergence, after all, is the attribute of an entity to become something other than it is at any point in time. The enumeration of its elements at any point in time can neither be reduced to the elements of its constitution at a previous point in time and nor could have been entirely predicted. This is the case with the university; with any university. And nor, therefore, is it possible to give a complete specification as to the elements of a university at some *future* point in time.

Emergence, accordingly, is not a deterministic process, but nor is it an entirely random process. Some like to speak of, and continue to keep alive, the idea of a dialectic. It is not an unhappy term, for it conveys something of the dynamic and antagonisms inherent in the nature of an entity; in the nature of a university indeed. But it can sometimes be brought into play to paper over difficulties in understanding the workings of complex processes, as the university continues to evolve.

Emergence is both conceptual and practical. There are always openings for the university to be other than it is as an institution in the world. Putting it more formally, we might say that the university has an ontologically open nature. Its very being in the world is such that it has openings available to it in its most intimate practices. Teaching can be enacted more to bring out the potentialities that lie within individual students so that each one may be better able to live purposefully in a complex world; research may be practised with more of an eye on promoting wellbeing in the wider world; members of academic communities could sometimes exhibit even more of a graciousness towards each other. But the university is also *conceptually* open. We can think of it, comprehend it, in numerous ways. We can picture it through deploying all manner of images and metaphors. We can even imagine it differently.

Of course, there are limitations that bear both on its practical situation and on its conceptual – or ideational – situation. Characteristically, the university is hedged in politically, and financially and in its relationships with other social institutions (and, with world rankings, globally so); and thinking about it is hedged in by current ways of seeing and imagining the university. And both of these dimensions come together in ideologies of the university, those conglomerations of practices and thought that so work together as to produce a sense of their naturalness. ('For sure, all universities are embarked on a process of entrepreneurialism . . .') But even ideologies have their moments of openness: unguarded, they let in critiques. The entrepreneurial university can be and is critiqued; the idea that teaching has to be written up – before the event – in so many 'learning outcomes' comes in for critical comment (or more likely is honoured in the breach more than in the observance); the assessment of the quality of research partly in virtue of its impact on the wider society (in the UK at least) is subject to intensive critical debate; and managerial practices (through which academic staff come to constitute a minority of the staff of a university) are also a topic for wry commentary from *within* the university.

Potent presences

The contemporary university, accordingly, is marked not just by tensions and even negativities but also, paradoxically, antagonisms and struggles. (Will the humanities survive? Is there time for care, for sensitive advice to students? What might it mean for the university to acquire an ecological spirit in an instrumental age? Is the digital age one of closure or openness?) Where is the paradox here? For the bracketed questions tell of an institution, the university, riven with dissent and even conflict. Famously, Kant observed a 'conflict of the faculties' (1992) but now the conflict is wider, over the very ideological foundation – as we may put it – of the university and its relationship with the wider world. But how, again it will be insisted, is this paradoxical? It is paradoxical because the very presence of such ideological conflict on campus – usually rather hidden or quiet but lying there, dormant, volcano-like – is evidence of a positive presence. This ideological antagonism is an indication of the university being fully a university, allowing and sustaining dissent on campus.

But then and there opens the possibility of potentialities that lie latent, ready to be sparked off with imaginative ideas. The university can continue to become itself not in spite of the contending forces with itself but because of them. The university will always fall short of its possibilities and its potential. There is always a beyond. And it is part of the intellectual task to help to sketch out this possible beyond, a sketching out that ultimately has to find its way into, and struggle with, the messiness of practical and organisational life that constitutes the forms of the university. However much they may be filled by imaginative concepts, the spaces of the intellect have quite quickly to be brought into an imaginative searching for spaces in the university as an institution; in the daily round, the common – and not so common – task.

A social philosophy of the university of this kind – which I have been trying to develop and sustain over these last decades – has been at once critical, imaginative, practical, global and personal in character. It is also, and inescapably, an unending quest. It may play a part, if only a very modest part, in the continuing reshaping of a worldly significant social institution that is the university. This is not so much to help the university to become other than it is but to be more of what it is *now* and could reasonably emerge into, in a contested age.

The university is more than, or should be more than, its constituent parts. The university has agency of its own: it may have powers acting on it but it is also an agent itself with its own powers. And so the matter arises as to how those powers are going to be put into effect. What might it mean to put them authentically into effect? Can the university realise even more its possibilities in the world? And in being more itself, the university may even contribute to the larger task of the formation of a wider wellbeing in the world.

Appendix
Key publications

Major works

2013	-	*Imagining the University.* (Routledge) (190pp)
2011	-	*Being a University.* (Routledge) (190pp)
	-	*Korean edition published, with a Foreword from RAB.*
2007	-	*A Will to Learn: Being a Student in an Age of Uncertainty* (McGraw-Hill/Open University Press) (200pp)
2005	-	(with Kelly Coate) *Engaging the Curriculum in Higher Education.* McGraw-Hill: Maidenhead (188pp)
	-	*Portuguese edition also published* (2005)
2003	-	*Beyond All Reason: Living with Ideology in the University* (Open University Press) (220pp)
	-	*Turkish edition in press*
2000	-	*Realizing the University in an age of supercomplexity* (Open University Press)
	-	Awarded 'Highly Recommended' prize, Society for Educational Studies.
	-	*Spanish edition published* (2003)
	-	*Portuguese edition published* (2005)
1997	-	*Higher Education: A Critical Business* (Open University Press) (200pp)
1994	-	*The Limits of Competence* (Open University Press) (200pp) (October) (reprinted)
	-	Awarded second prize, for books on education, Standing Conference on Studies in Education (SCSE), 1995
	-	*Spanish edition* (2000).
1992	-	*Improving Higher Education: Total Quality Care* (Open University Press) (240pp) (reprinted)
1990	-	*The Idea of Higher Education* (Open University Press) (244pp) (reprinted)
	-	Awarded first prize, SCSE, for books on education, 1991.
	-	*Chinese edition* (Peking University Press, 2012).

Editor or joint editor or team-authored

2014 - (jt Editor with Paul Gibbs) *Thinking about Higher Education*. Springer.
2012 - (jt Editor with Joy Higgs et al.) *Practice-Based Education: Perspectives and Strategies*. Sense Publishers.
2011 - (Editor) *The Future University: Ideas and Possibilities*. Routledge.
 - (2013) paperback version published.
 - *Winner of 2013 prize, Comparative International Education Society (Higher Education SIG)*
2009 - (John Strain, Ronald Barnett and Peter Jarvis, co-editors) *Universities, Ethics and Professions: Debate and Scrutiny*. Routledge.
2008 - (Nicholas Maxwell and Ronald Barnett (Eds)) *Wisdom in the University*. Routledge.
 - *paperback edition published 2009.*
 - (co-edited with Roberto Di Napoli) *Changing Identities in Higher Education: Voicing Perspectives*. Routledge.
 - *paperback edition published 2009.*
2005 - (Editor) *Reshaping the University: New Relationships between Research, Teaching and Scholarship*. McGraw-Hill: Maidenhead.
 - *Spanish edition in press.*
 - *Arabic edition in press.*
1997 - *The End of Knowledge in Higher Education* (edited jointly with Anne Griffin) (Cassell)
1994 - *Academic Community: Discourse or Discord?* (Editor) (Jessica Kingsley Publications) (202pp)
1993 - with Bertil Rolf and Eskil Ekstedt, Kvalitet ock kunskasprocess i hogre utbilding ("Quality and knowledge processes in higher education") (published in Sweden)
1992 - *Learning to Effect* (Editor) (Open University Press) (230pp)
 - *Reissued in paperback.*
1991 - *Part-time Students and their Experience of Higher Education*, Bourner T with Hamed M, Reynolds A and Barnett R (Open University Press)

Major reports have included

2014 - *Conditions of Flexibility: Securing a More Responsive Higher Education System*, report for HEA – an overarching report for its 'Flexible Pedagogies' programme of projects.

1997 - *Report on National Consultation* (Report for National Committee of Inquiry, chaired by Sir Ron Dearing). Volume published with Report of National Committee. (London)
1994 - *Assessment of the Quality of Higher Education: A Review and an Evaluation*, report on the quality assessment approach of the Higher Education Funding Councils for England and for Wales (HEFCE)

A full list of Ronald Barnett's publications and his full CV are available via www.ioe.ac.uk/about/documents/LCE_Ron_Barnett_CV.pdf

Bibliography

Abercrombie, N. (1980) *Class, Structure and Knowledge* (Oxford: Blackwell).
Adelman, C. (Ed.) (1984) *The Politics and Ethics of Evaluation* (Beckenham: Croom Helm).
Adelman, C. and Powney, J. (1986) *Institutional Self-validation and Course Validation*, Society for Research into Higher Education annual conference (Guildford: SRHE).
Ainley, P. (1994) *Degrees of Difference: Higher Education in the 1990s* (London: Lawrence and Wishart).
Albrow, M. (1996) *The Global Age* (Cambridge: Polity Press).
Althusser, L. (1969) *For Marx* (Harmondsworth: Penguin).
Althusser, L. (1971) *Lenin and Philosophy and Other Essays* (New York: Monthly Review Press).
Althusser, L. (1972) Ideology and ideological state apparatuses, in: [his] *Lenin and Philosophy and other Essays*, pp. 123–173 (London: New Life Books).
Apple, M. (1979) *Ideology and Curriculum* (Henley: Routledge & Kegan Paul).
Association of Graduate Recruiters (1995) *Skills for Graduates in the Twenty-first Century* (Cambridge: Association of Graduate Recruiters).
Badiou, A. and Zizek, S. (2009) *Philosophy in the Present* (Cambridge: Polity).
Bakhurst, D. (2011) *The Formation of Reason* (Oxford: Blackwell).
Ball, C. (1985) *Fitness for Purpose* (Guildford: SRHE & NFER-Nelson).
Ball, C. (1992), The Learning Society, *RSA Journal* CXL, 5429, 380–390.
Barnes, B. (1974) *Scientific Knowledge and Sociological Theory* (Henley: Routledge & Kegan Paul).
Barnes, B. (1977) *Interests and the Growth of Knowledge* (Henley: Routledge & Kegan Paul).
Barnes, B. and Edge, D. (1982) *Science in Context: Readings in the Sociology of Science* (Milton Keynes: Open University Press).
Barnett, R. (1981) 'Integration in Curriculum Design in Higher Education', *Journal of Further and Higher Education*, 5 (3), 33–45.
Barnett, R. (1985) 'Higher Education: Legitimation Crisis', *Studies in Higher Education*, 10 (3), 241–255.
Barnett, R. (1987) 'The Maintenance of Standards in the Public Sector of UK Higher Education', *Higher Education*, 16 (3).

Barnett, R. (1990) *The Idea of Higher Education* (Milton Keynes: Open University Press).
Barnett, R. (1992) *Improving Higher Education: Total Quality Care* (Buckingham: Open University Press).
Barnett, R. (1992) 'What Effects? What Outcomes?' in R. Barnett (ed.) *Learning to Effect* (Buckingham: Open University Press).
Barnett, R. (1994) *The Limits of Competence: Knowledge, Higher Education and Society* (Buckingham: Open University Press).
Barnett, R. (1997) *Realizing the University* (London: Institute of Education).
Barnett, R. (2000) *Realizing the University in an Age of Supercomplexity* (Buckingham: Open University Press).
Barnett, R. (2003) *Beyond All Reason: Living with Ideology in the University* (Buckingham: Open University Press).
Barnett, R. (2007) *A Will to Learn: Being a Student in an Age of Uncertainty* (Maidenhead: McGraw-Hill/Open University Press).
Barnett, R. (2011) *Being a University* (Abingdon: Routledge).
Barnett, R. and Coate, K. (2004). *Engaging the Curriculum in Higher Education* (Maidenhead: McGraw-Hill/Open University Press).
Barnett, R. and Phipps, A. (2005) 'Academic Travel', *Review of Education and Pedagogy*, 27 (1) 1–14.
Bauman, Z. (1998) *Liquid Modernity* (London: Sage).
Bauman, Z. (2000) *Liquid Modernity* (Cambridge: Polity).
Becher, T. (1981) 'Towards a Definition of Disciplinary Cultures', *Studies in Higher Education*, 6, 109–122.
Becher, T. (1987) 'Disciplinary Discourse'. *Studies in Higher Education*, 12, 261–274.
Becher, T. and Trowler, P. (2001) *Academic Tribes and Territories* (Buckingham: Open University Press).
Beck, U. (1992) *Risk Society: Towards a New Modernity* (London: Sage).
Beck, U. (1998) 'Politics of Risk Society', in Franklin, *op. cit.*
Bell, D. (1973) *The Coming of Post-Industrial Society* (Harmondsworth: Penguin).
Berdahl, R. (1980) The planning and coordination of higher education, *The Select Committee's Recommendations & Future Policy*, Fifth Festival Hall Conference on Higher Education (North East London Polytechnic/University of Warwick).
Berger, P. L. and Luckman, T. (1971) *The Social Construction of Reality* (Harmondsworth: Penguin).
Berlin, I. (1969/1979) *Four Essays on Liberty* (Oxford: Oxford University Press).
Bernstein, B. (1996) *Pedagogy, Symbolic Control and Identity* (London: Taylor & Francis).
Bernstein, B. (1999) 'Vertical and Horizontal Discourse: An Essay'. *British Journal of Sociology of Education*, 20 (2), 157–173.
Bernstein, R. J. (1983) *Beyond Objectivism and Relativism* (Oxford: Blackwell).
Bernstein, R. J. (1991) *The New Constellation: The Ethical-Political Horizons of Modernity* (Cambridge: Polity Press).
Berrill, K. *et al.* (1983) *Excellence in Diversity* (Guildford: SRHE).
Bevan, J. (1984) *The Inter-relationships and Impact of Performance Criteria for Higher Education*, talk to Standing Conference of Principals and Directors, Waldorf Hotel (London, National Advisory Body) (mimeo).

Bhaskar, R. (2002) *From Science to Emancipation: Journeys towards Meta-reality – A Philosophy for the Present* (New Delhi: Sage).
Bhaskar, R. (2008) *Dialectic: The Pulse of Freedom* (London and New York: Routledge).
Bhaskar, R. (2008/1975) *A Realist Theory of Science* (London: Verso).
Birch, W. (1988) *The Challenge to Higher Education: Reconciling Responsibilities to Scholarship and Society* (Milton Keynes: Open University Press).
Birnbaum, N. (1970) *The Crisis of Industrial Society*, pp. 131–158 (New York: Oxford University Press).
Bjarnason, S. and Coldstream, P. (2003) *The Idea of Engagement: Universities in Society* (London: Association of Commonwealth Universities).
Bligh, D. (1971) *What's the Use of Lectures?* (London: University Teaching Methods Unit).
Bloom, A. (1987) *The Closing of the American Mind: How Higher Education has Failed Democracy and Impoverished the Souls of Today's Students* (London: Penguin).
Bloor, D. (1976) *Knowledge and Social Imagery* (Henley: Routledge & Kegan Paul).
Boud, D. (1985) *Studies in Self-assessment: Implications for Teachers in Higher Education*, Tertiary Education Research Centre, Occasional Publication 26 (University of New South Wales).
Bourdieu, P. (1971) Intellectual field and creative project, in: M. F. D. Young (ed.) *Knowledge and Control* (Basingstoke: Macmillan).
Bourdieu, P. (1973) Cultural reproduction and social reproduction, in: R. Brown, (ed.) *Knowledge, Education and Cultural Change* (London: Tavistock).
Bourdieu, P. (2000) *Pascalian Meditations* (Cambridge: Polity).
Bourdieu, P. and Passeron, J.-C. (1979) *The Inheritors: French Students and their Relation to Culture* (London: University of Chicago Press).
Boys, C., Brennan, S., Henkel, M., Kirkland, N., Kogan, M. and Youll, P. (1988) *Higher Education and the Preparation for Work* (London: Jessica Kingsley).
Brady, M. and Pritchard, D. (eds) (2003) *Moral and Epistemic Virtues* (Malden, MA and Oxford: Blackwell).
Brecher, B., Fleischmann, O. and Halliday. J. (eds) (1996) *The University in a Liberal State* (Aldershot: Avebury).
Brennan, J. (1985) 'Preparing Students for Employment', *Studies in Higher Education*, 10, 151–162.
Brockbank, A. and McGill, I. (2007) *Facilitating Reflective Homing in Higher Education* (Maidenhead: McGraw-Hill).
Brown, R. (1999) Diversity in higher education: has it been and gone? Professional Lecture, Goldsmiths College, University of London.
Brubacher, J. S. (1977) *On the Philosophy of Higher Education*, p. 1 (London: Jossey-Bass).
Burgess, T. (1981) Bias is of the essence, in: D. Warren-Piper (ed.) *Is Higher Education Fair?* (Guildford: SRHE).
Butler, J., Laclau, E. and Zizek, S. (2000) *Contingency, Hegemony, Universality: Contemporary Dialogues on the Left* (London: Verso).
Cameron, J. M. (1978) *On the Idea of a University* (Toronto: University of Toronto Press).
Carr, W. and Kemmis, S. (1986) *Becoming Critical: Education, Knowledge and Action Research* (Lewes: Falmer).

Castells, M. (1996) *The Rise of the Network Society* (Oxford: Blackwell).
Chomsky, N. (1968) *Language and Mind* (Cambridge, MA: Massachusetts Institute of Technology).
Christopherson, Sir D. (1973) *The University at Work* (London: SCM Press).
Clark, B. R. (1983) *The Higher Education System: Academic Organisations in Cross-national Perspective* (London: University of California Press).
Cmnd 2154 (1963) *Higher Education*. Report of a Committee Appointed by the Prime Minister under the Chairmanship of Lord Robbins (London: HMSO).
Cockburn, A. and Blackburn, R. (eds) (1969) *Student Power* (Harmondsworth: Penguin).
Coffield, F. and Williamson, B. (1997) *Repositioning Higher Education* (Buckingham: Open University Press).
Colebrook, C. (2002/2005) *Gilles Deleuze* (Abingdon and New York: Routledge).
Collier, K. G. (1982) 'Ideological Influences in Higher Education', *Studies in Higher Education*, 7, 13–19.
Connerton, P. (1980) *The Tragedy of Enlightenment: An Essay on the Frankfurt School* (London: Cambridge University Press).
Cooper, D. (2002) *The Measure of Things: Humanism, Humility, and Mystery* (Oxford: Clarendon Press).
Cutright, M. (ed.) (2001) *Chaos Theory and Higher Education: Leadership, Planning, and Policy* (New York: Peter Lang).
CVCP (1986) *Performance Indicators in Universities: A First Statement by a Joint CVCP/UGC Working Party* (London: CVCP).
CVCP (1987) *Academic Standards in Universities* (London: CVCP).
CVCP (1987) *Performance Indicators in Universities: A Second Statement by the Joint CVCP/UGC Working Party* (London: CVCP).
Delanty, G. (2001) *Challenging Knowledge: The University in the Knowledge Society* (Buckingham: Open University Press).
Deleuze, G. (2001) *Difference and Repetition* (London: Continuum).
Deleuze, G. (2012/1965) *Pure Immanence: Essays on a Life* (New York: Zone).
Deleuze, G. and Guattari, F. (2007/2004/1987/1980) *A Thousand Plateaus: Capitalism and Schizophrenia* (London and New York: Continuum).
Derrida, J. (1992) Mochlos; or, the conflict of the faculties. In R. Rand (ed.) *Logomachia: the conflict of the faculties* (London: University of Nebraska Press).
Derrida, J. (2004). Mochlos, or the conflict of the faculties. In his *Eyes of the university. Right to philosophy 2* (pp. 83–112). (Stanford: Stanford University Press).
DES (1985) *The Development of Higher Education into the 1990s*, Cmnd 9524 (London: HMSO).
DES (1987a) *Higher Education: Meeting the Challenge*, Cmnd 114 (London: HMSO).
DES (1987b) *Changes in Structure and National Planning for Higher Education: Contracts between the Funding Bodies and Higher Education Institutions*, Consultative Paper (London: DES).
Dienstag, J. F. (2006) *Pessimism* (Princeton, NJ: Princeton University Press).
Duke, C. (1992) *The Learning University: Towards a New Paradigm* (Buckingham: Open University Press).
Ecclestone, K. and Hayes, D. (eds) (2009). *The Dangerous Rise of Therapeutic Education.* (London: Routledge).

Edwards, E. G. (1982) *Higher Education for Everyone* (Nottingham: Spokesman).
Ehrlich, T. (ed.). (2000) *Civic Responsibility and Higher Education* (Phoenix, AZ: American Council on Education/The Oryx Press).
Ekman, R. and Quandt, R. E. (1999) *Technology and Scholarly Communication* (Berkeley, CA: University of California Press).
Eraut, M. (1994) *Developing Professional Knowledge and Competence* (London: Falmer Press).
Erdinç, Z. (2002) 'Australia Online: Borderless University', *Turkish Online Journal of Distance Education*, 3 (4).
Evans, N. (1981) *The Knowledge Revolution* (London: Grant McIntyre).
Evans, N. (1985) *Post-Education Society: Recognising Adults as Learners* (Beckenham: Croom Helm).
Feyerabend, P. (1975) *Against Method* (London: Verso).
Fleming, D. (1991) *The Concept of Meta-competence. Competence and Assessment*, No. 20 (Sheffield: Employment Department).
Foucault, M. (1991/1975) *Discipline and Punish: The Birth of the Prison* (London: Penguin).
Franklin, J. (ed.) (1998) *The Politics of Risk Society* (London: Polity/IPPR).
Fuller, T. (ed.) (1989) *The Voice of Liberal Learning: Michael Oakeshott on Education* (London: Yale University Press).
Galbraith, J. K. (1969) *The New Industrial State* (Harmondsworth: Penguin).
Gellert, C. (1985) 'State Interventionism and Institutional Autonomy: University Development and State Interference in England and West Germany', *Oxford Review of Education*, 11, 283–293.
Gellert, C. (undated) A comparative study of the changing functions of English and German universities, unpublished PhD thesis (University of Cambridge).
Gellner, E. (1969) *Thought and Change* (London: Weidenfeld & Nicolson).
Gellner, E. (1970) Concepts and society, in: D. Emmett and A. MacIntyre (eds) *Sociological Theory and Philosophical Analysis*, pp. 115–149.
Gellner, E. (1974) *Legitimation of Belief* (Cambridge: Cambridge University Press).
Gellner, E. (1988) *Plough, Sword and Book: The Structure of Human History* (London: Paladin).
Gellner, E. (1998) *Language and Solitude: Wittgenstein, Malinowski and the Habsburg Dilemma* (Cambridge: University Cambridge Press).
Gibbons, M., Limoges, G., Nowotny, H., Schwartzman, S., Scott, P. and Trow, M. (1994) *The New Production of Knowledge: The Dynamics of Science and Research in Contemporary Societies* (London: Sage).
Gibson, R. (1986) *Critical Theory and Education* (Sevenoaks: Hodder & Stoughton).
Giddens, A. (1995) *Beyond Left and Right* (Cambridge: Polity Press).
Giddens, A. (1995) *Modernity and Self-identity: Self and Society in the Late Modern Age* (Cambridge: Polity Press).
Giddens, T. (1994) *Beyond Left and Right* (Cambridge: Polity Press).
Gokulsing, K. and DaCosta, C. (eds) (1997) *Usable Knowledges as the Goal of University Education* (Lampeter: Edwin Mellen Press).
Goodlad, S. (1976) *Conflict and Consensus in Higher Education* (London: Hodder and Stoughton).
Goodlad, S. (ed.) (1984) *Education for the Professions: Quis Custodiet?* (Guildford: SRHE/NFER–Nelson).

Gouldner, A. (1976) *The Dialectic of Ideology and Technology*, pp. 28–58 (Basingstoke: Macmillan).
Gouldner, A. (1979) *The Future of Intellectuals and the Rise of the New Class* (Basingstoke: Macmillan).
Graham, G. (2002) *Universities: The Recovery of an Idea* (Thorverton: Academic Imprint).
Gratton, P. and Panteleimon Manoussakis, J. (eds) (2007) *Traversing the Imaginary: Richard Kearney and the Postmodern Challenge* (Evanston, IL: Northwestern University Press).
Guattari, F. (2005 [1989]) *The Three Ecologies* (London: Continuum).
Habermas, J. (1970) Knowledge and Interest, in: D. Emmett and A. MacIntyre (eds) *Sociological Theory and Philosophical Analysis* (Basingstoke: Macmillan).
Habermas, J. (1972) *Towards a Rational Society* (esp. chs 1, 4, 6) (London: Heinemann).
Habermas, J. (1976) *Legitimation Crisis*, pp. 46–48 (London: Heinemann Educational Books).
Habermas, J. (1978/1968) *Knowledge and Human Interests* (London: Heinemann).
Habermas, J. (1979) *Communication and the Evolution of Society* (London: Heinemann).
Habermas, J. (1979) What is universal pragmatics? In his: *Communication and the Evolution of Society* (London: Heinemann).
Habermas, J. (1990) *The Philosophical Discourse of Modernity*: (Cambridge: Polity).
Habermas, J. (1991) *The Theory of Communicative Action*, Vol. 1 (Cambridge: Polity).
Habermas, J. (1991) *The Theory of Communicative Competence*, Vol. 1 (Cambridge: Polity).
Hallden, S. (1987) *Intellectual Maturity as an Educational Idea*, Studies of Higher Education and Research Newsletter (Sweden, National Board of Universities and Colleges).
Halpin, D. (2003) *Hope and Education: The Role of the Utopian Imagination* (London: Routledge).
Halsey, A. H. (1992) *Decline of Donnish Dominion* (Oxford: Clarendon Press).
Hamilton, P. (1974) *Knowledge and Social Structure* (Henley: Routledge & Kegan Paul).
Harris, K. (1979) *Education and Knowledge* (Henley: Routledge & Kegan Paul).
Harvey, L. (1996) *Transforming Higher Education* (Buckingham: Open University Press).
Hassam, R. (2003) *The Chronoscopicic Society: Globalization, Time and Knowledge in the Network Society* (New York: Peter Lang).
Heidegger, M. (1998/1962) *Being and Time* (Oxford: Blackwell).
Heidegger, M. (2001/1971) *Poetry, Language, Thought.* (New York: Harper).
Held, D. (1983) *Introduction to Critical Theory* (London: Hutchinson).
HMSO (1966) *A Plan for Polytechnics and Other Colleges*, Cmnd 3006 (London: HMSO).
HMSO (1984) *A Strategy into the 1990s: The University Grants Committee Advice* (London: HMSO).
Hollis, M. and Lukes, S. (eds) (1982) *Rationality and Relativism* (Oxford: Blackwell).

hooks, b. (1994) *Teaching to Transgress: Education as the Practice of Freedom* (New York: Routledge).
Horton, R. (1970) 'African Thought and Western Science', in: B. Wilson (ed.), op. cit., pp. 131–171.
Horton, R. (1982) 'Tradition and Modernity Revisited', in: M. Hollis and S. Lukes (eds), op. cit., pp. 201–260.
Jacoby, R. (2005) *Picture Imperfect: Utopian Thought for an Anti-utopian Age* (New York: Columbia University Press).
Jaques, D. (1984) *Learning in Groups* (Beckenham: Croom Helm).
Jarratt, Sir A. (1985) *Report of the Steering Committee for Efficiency Studies in Universities* (London: CVCP).
Jarvis, P. (1992) *Paradoxes of Learning: On Becoming an Individual in Society* (San Francisco: Jossey-Bass).
Jarvis, P. (2001) *Universities and Corporate Universities: The Higher Education Industry in Global Society* (London: Kogan Page).
Jaspers, K. (1946, 2nd imp. 1965) *The Idea of the University* (London: Peter Owen).
Jenkins, C. (1977) *Rationality, Education and the Social Organisation of Knowledge* (Henley: Routledge & Kegan Paul).
Joseph, Sir K. (1984) Speech to the House of Commons, 26 October, *Parliamentary Debates*, 65 (210) 470.
Kant, I. (1992/1979/1798) *The Conflict of the Faculties*. (Lincoln, NE and London: University of Nebraska Press).
Kearney, R. (2007) Foreword. In: P. Gratton and J. Panteleimon Manoussakis (eds), *Traversing the Imaginary: Richard Kearney and the Postmodern Challenge* (Evanston, IL: Northwestern University Press).
Kells, H. R. (1992) *Self-Regulation in Higher Education* (London: Jessica Kingsley).
Kerr, C. (1972) *The Uses of the University* (Cambridge, MA, and Oxford: Harvard University Press).
Kress, G. and Van Leeuwen, T. (2001) *Multimodal Discourse: The Modes and Media of Contemporary Communication* (London: Arnold).
Kuhn, T. (1970) *The Structure of Scientific Revolutions* (London: University of Chicago Press).
Laclau, E. (2000) 'Identity and Hegemony: The Role of Universality in the Constitution of Political Logics', in: J. Butler, J. Laclau and E. Zizek (eds) op cit.
Lakatos, I. and Musgrave, A. (1977) (eds) *Criticism and the Growth of Knowledge* (London: Cambridge University Press).
Larrain, J. (1979) *The Concept of Ideology* (London: Hutchinson).
Lawson, K. H. (1982) *Analysis and Ideology: Conceptual Essays on the Education of Adults* (Nottingham: University of Nottingham).
Leavis, F. R. (1943) *Education and the University* (reprinted 1979, London: Cambridge University Press).
Leavis, F. R. (1969) *English Literature in our Time and the University* (London: Chatto & Windus).
Lessem, R. (1991) *Total Quality Learning: Building a Learning Organisation* (Oxford: Blackwell).
Lewis, D. (1986) *On the Plurality of Worlds* (Oxford: Blackwell).

Liedman, S.-E. (1993) In search of Isis: general education in Germany and Sweden, in S. Rothblatt and B. Wittrock (eds), *The European and American University since 1800: Historical and Sociological Essays* (Cambridge: Cambridge University Press).

Light, G. and Cox, R. (2001) *Learning and Teaching in Higher Education: The Reflective Practitioner* (London: Paul Chapman).

Lovlie, L., Mortensen, K. P. and Nordenbo, S. E. (2003) *Educating Humanity: Bildung in Postmodernity* (Oxford: Blackwell).

Lukasiewicz, J. (1994) *The Ignorance Explosion: Understanding Industrial Civilization* (Ottawa: Carleton University Press).

Lyons, F. S. L. (1983) 'The Idea of a University: Newman to Robbins', in: N. Phillipson (ed.) *University Society and the Future* (Edinburgh: The University).

Lyotard, J. F. (1984) *The Postmodern Condition: A Report on Knowledge* (Manchester: Manchester University Press).

Macfarlane, B. (2012) 'The Higher Education Archipelago', *Higher Education Research & Development*, 31 (1) 129–131.

MacIntyre, A. (1982) *After Virtue* (London: Duckworth).

Malatesta, E. ([1891] 2001) *Anarchy* (London: Freedom).

Marginson, S. and Considine, M. (2000) *The Enterprise University: Power, Governance and Reinvention in Australia* (Cambridge: Cambridge University Press).

Marton, F. (ed.) (1984) *The Experience of Learning* (Edinburgh: Scottish Academic Press).

Marton, F., Hounsell, D. and Entwistle, N. (eds) (1984) *The Experience of Learning* (Edinburgh: Scottish Academic Press).

Maxwell, N. (2008) 'From Knowledge to Wisdom: The Need for an Academic Revolution', in: R. Barnett and N. Maxwell (eds) *Wisdom in the University* (pp. 1–33) (Abingdon: Routledge).

McCarthy, E. D. (1996) *Knowledge as Culture* (London: Routledge).

McIlrath, L. and Labhrainn, I. M. (eds). (2007). *Higher Education and Civic Engagement: International Perspectives* (Aldershot: Ashgate).

Mepham, J. (1979) *The Theory of Ideology in Capital*, in: J. Mepham and D. H. Ruben (eds), p. 163 (op. cit.).

Mepham, J. and Ruben, D. H. (eds) (1979) *Issues in Marxist Philosophy, Volume Three, Epistemology, Science, Ideology* (Sussex: Harvester).

Meyer, J. H. F. and Land, R. (2005) 'Threshold Concepts and Troublesome Knowledge: Epistemological Considerations and a Conceptual Framework', *Higher Education*, 49, 373–388.

Meyer, J. H. F. and Land, R. (eds) (2006) Threshold concepts and troublesome knowledge: Issues of liminality. *Overcoming Barriers to Student Understanding: Threshold Concepts and Troublesome Knowledge* (Abingdon: Routledge).

Miliband, R. (1970) *The State in Capitalist Society*, Ch. VIII (London: Weidenfeld & Nicolson).

Mill, J. S. (1969/1987) 'Inaugural Address at St. Andrews', in: W. Levi (ed.) *The Six Great Humanist Essays of John Stuart* (New York: Washington Square Press).

Mills, J. (ed.) (1994) *A Pedagogy of Becoming* (New York: Rodopi).

Minogue, K. R. (1973) *The Concept of a University* (London: Weidenfeld & Nicolson).
Moberley, Sir W. (1949) *The Crisis in the University* (London: SCM Press).
Montefiore, A. (ed.) (1975) *Neutrality and Impartiality: The University and Political Commitment* (London: Cambridge University Press).
Moodie, G. C. (1986) 'Fit for What?', in: G. C. Moodie (ed.), *Standards and Criteria in Higher Education* (Guildford: SRHE/NFER-Nelson).
Moodie, G. and Eustace, R. (1973) *Power and Authority in British Universities* (London: George Allen and Unwin).
Moore, T. W. (1974) *Educational Theory: An Introduction* pp. 7–9 (Henley: Routledge & Kegan Paul).
Murphy, M. and Fleming, T. (eds) (2012) *Habermas, Critical Theory and Education* (Abingdon and New York: Routledge).
NAB (1987) *Management for a Purpose: The Report of the Good Management Practice Group* (London: National Advisory Body).
NACETT (1994) *Review of the National Targets for Education and Training: Proposals for Consultation* (London: NACETT).
Nash, A. (1945) *The University and the Modern World: An Essay in the Social Philosophy of University Education* (London: SCM Press).
National Advisory Body for Local Authority Higher Education (1984) *A Strategy for Higher Education in the Later 1980s and Beyond* (London: NAB).
National Advisory Body for Local Authority Higher Education (1984) *Report of the Continuing Education Group* (London: NAB).
National Committee of Inquiry into Higher Education (1997) *Higher Education for a Learning Society* (London: HMSO).
Newman, J. H. (1852 reprinted 1976) in: I. T. Ker (ed.) *The Idea of a University* (London: Oxford University Press).
Niblett, W. R. (1974) *Universities between Two Worlds* (London: University of London Press).
Niblett, W. R. (1979) review of Brubacher, (op. cit.) *Higher Education*, 8, pp. 349–350.
Niblett, W. R. (Ed.) (1975) *The Sciences, the Humanities and the Technological Threat* (London: University of London Press).
Nisbet, R. (1971) *The Degradation of the Academic Dogma: The University in America, 1945–1970* (London: Heinemann Educational).
Nixon, J. (2004) 'Learning the Language of Deliberative Democracy', in: M. Walker and J. Nixon (eds) *Reclaiming Universities from a Runaway World* (Maidenhead: McGraw-Hill/SRHE).
Nixon, J. (2008). *Towards the Virtuous University: The Moral Bases of Academic Practice* (New York: London).
Nixon, J. (2011, forthcoming) *Higher Education and the Public Good* (London: Continuum).
Nowotny, H., Scott, P. and Gibbons, M. (2001) *The New Science* (Cambridge: Polity).
Nowotny, H., Scott, P. and Gibbons, M. (2001). *Re-thinking Science: Knowledge and the Public in an Age of Uncertainty* (Cambridge: Polity).
Nussbaum, M. (2000) *Cultivating Humanity: A Classical Defense of Reform in Liberal Education* (Cambridge, MA: Harvard University Press).

Ortega y Gasset, J. (1946) *Mission of the University* (London: Routledge & Kegan Paul).
Pateman, T. (1972) *Counter Course: A Handbook for Course Criticism* (Harmondsworth: Penguin).
Pattison, M. (1969) *Memoirs* (Fontwell, Sussex: Centaur Press).
Perry, W. G. (1970) *Forms of Intellectual and Ethical Development* (New York: Holt, Rinehart & Winston).
Peters, M. (2009) 'Education, Creativity and the Economy of Passions', in: M. A. Peters, S. Marginson and P. Murphy (eds) *Creativity and the Global Knowledge Economy* (New York: Peter Lang).
Peters, M. (2011, forthcoming) 'Universities and the Intellectual Commons: Revisiting the Concept of Openness in the 21st Century', in: R. Barnett (ed.) *The Idea of the University in the Twenty-first Century* (New York: Routledge).
Peters, M. and Olssen, M. (2005) 'Useful Knowledge: Redefining Research and Teaching in the Learning Economy', in: R. Barnett (ed.) *Reshaping the University: New Relationships between Research, Scholarship and Teaching* (Maidenhead: McGraw-Hill/Open University Press).
Peters, M. A., Marginson, S. and Murphy, P. (2009) *Creativity and the Global Knowledge Economy* (New York: Peter Lang).
Peters, R. A. (1970) *Ethics and Education* (London: Routledge & Kegan Paul).
Peters, R. S. (1959) 'Must an Educator Have an Aim?', In his: *Authority, Responsibility and Education* (London: Allen & Unwin).
Peters, R. S. (1966) *Ethics and Education* (London: Allen & Unwin).
Peters, R. S. (1967) 'What is an Educational Process?', in: R. S. Peters (ed.) *The Concept of Education* (London: Routledge & Kegan Paul).
Peters, R. S. (1972) 'The Role and Responsibilities of the University in Teacher Education', reprinted in his (1977) *Education and the Education of Teachers* (London: Routledge & Kegan Paul).
Peters, R. (1973) 'Aims of Education – A Conceptual Inquiry', in R. Peters (ed.) *The Philosophy of Education* (London: Oxford University Press).
Peters, R. (1977) 'Ambiguities in Liberal Education and the Problem of its Content', in: R. S. Peters (ed.) *Education and the Education of Teachers*, Ch. 3 (London: Routledge & Kegan Paul).
Phipps, A. (2005) 'Making Academics: Work in Progress', in: R. Barnett (ed.) *Reshaping the University: New Relationships between Research, Scholarship and Teaching* (Maidenhead: McGraw-Hill/Open University Press).
Piaget, J. (1971) *Structuralism* (London: Routledge & Kegan Paul).
Plamenatz, J. (1970) *Ideology*, ch. 5 (Basingstoke: Macmillan).
Plumb, J. H. (1964) *The Crisis in the Humanities* (Harmondsworth: Penguin).
Popper, K. (1970) 'Normal Science and its Dangers', in: I. Lakatos and A. Musgrave (ed.) *Criticism and the Growth of Knowledge*, 51–8 (Cambridge: Cambridge University Press).
Popper, K. (1975) *Objective Knowledge: An Evolutionary Approach* (Oxford: Oxford University Press).
Popper, K. (1976) *Unended Quest: An Intellectual Autobiography* (Glasgow: Fontana/Collins).
Powell, J. P. (1974) 'Theories of University Education in Victorian England', *The Australian University*, 12, 197–212.

Ramsden, P. (1984) *The Context of Learning*, in: Marton (ed.), op. cit.
Ramsden, P. (1988) *Improving Learning: New Perspectives* (London: Kogan Page).
Ranson, S. (1994) *The Learning Society* (London: Cassell).
Readings, B. (1996) *The University in Ruins* (Cambridge: MA: Harvard University Press).
Reeves, M. (1988) *The Crisis in Higher Education* (Milton Keynes: Open University Press).
Robbins, Lord (1963) *Higher Education: Report of the Committee*, Cmnd 2154 (London: HMSO).
Robbins, Lord L. (1966) *The University in the Modern World*, address given in 1964, reprinted in his book of the same title, Ch. 1 (London: Macmillan).
Robertson, D. (1994), *Choosing to Change: Extending Access, Choice and Mobility in Higher Education* (London: HEQC).
Robins, K. and Webster, F. (eds) (2002) *The Virtual University? Knowledge, Markets and Management* (Oxford: Oxford University Press).
Rorty, R. (1980) *Philosophy and the Mirror of Nature*, chs VII, VIII (Oxford: Blackwell).
Rose, H. and Rose, S. (eds) (1976) *The Political Economy of Science: Ideology of/in the Natural Sciences* (Basingstoke: Macmillan).
Rothblatt, S. (1993) 'The Limbs of Osiris: Liberal Education in the English-speaking World', in: S. Rothblatt and B. Wittrock (eds) *The European and American University since 1800: Historical and Sociological Essays* (Cambridge: Cambridge University Press).
Rowland, S. (2006) *The Enquiring University: Compliance and Contestation in Higher Education* (Maidenhead: McGraw-Hill/Open University Press).
Ryan, A. (1974) 'An Essentially Contested Concept'. *The Times Higher Education Supplement*.
Sartre, J.-P. ([1940] 2004) *The Imaginary* (London: Routledge).
Sarup, M. (1978) *Marxism and Education* (Henley: Routledge & Kegan Paul).
Savin-Baden, M. (2008) *Learning Spaces: Creating Opportunities for Knowledge Creation in Academic Life* (Maidenhead: McGraw-Hill/Open University Press).
Schon, D. (1983) *The Reflective Practitioner: How Professionals Think in Action* (New York: Basic Books).
Schopenhauer, A. (1997) *The World as Will and Idea* (London: Dent).
Scott, P. (1984) *The Crisis of the University* (Beckenham: Croom Helm).
Scott, P. (1995) *The Meanings of Mass Higher Education* (Buckingham: Open University Press).
Shaw, M. (1977) *Marxism and Social Science: The Roots of Social Knowledge* (London: Pluto).
Shils, E. (1983) *The Academic Ethic* (London: University of Chicago Press).
Silver, H. (1981) *Expectations of Higher Education: Some Historical Pointers*, p. 65, Paper No. 1 (Expectations of Higher Education Project, Brunel University).
Sizer, J. (1982) 'Assessing Institutional Performance and Progress', in: L. Wagner (ed.), *Agenda for Institutional Change in Higher Education*, Ch. 2 (Guildford: SRHE).
Slaughter, S. and Leslie, L. L. (1997) *Academic Capitalism: Politics, Policies and the Entrepreneurial University* (Baltimore: Johns Hopkins University Press).

Sloman, A. (1964) *A University in the Making* (London: BBC).
Snelders, P. (1981) 'An Essentially Contesting Philosopher: A Reply to John Wilson', *Journal of Philosophy of Education*, 15, 17–22.
Snow, C. P. (1978/1959) *The Two Cultures* and *A Second Look* (Cambridge: Cambridge University Press).
Squires, G. (1990) *The Undergraduate Curriculum* (Milton Keynes: Open University Press).
Standaert, N. (2009) 'Towards a Networked University', in: R. Barnett, *et al.* (eds), *Rethinking the University after Bologna: New Concepts and Practices beyond Tradition and the Market* (pp. 11–15) (Antwerp: UCSIA).
Standish, P. (2003) 'Higher Education and the University', in: N. Blake, R. Smith and P. Standish (eds), *The Blackwell Guide to the Philosophy of Education* (Oxford: Blackwell).
Standish, P. (2007) 'Towards an Economy of Higher Education', *Critical Quarterly*, 47 (1–2), 53–71.
Stehr, N. (1994) *Knowledge Societies* (London: Sage).
Stehr, N. (2001) *The Fragility of Modern Societies: Knowledge and Risk in the Information Age* (London: Sage).
Steiner, G. (2003) *Lessons of the Masters* (Cambridge, MA: Harvard University Press).
Strathern, M. (2004) *Commons and Borderlands: Working Papers on Interdisciplinarity, Accountability and the Flow of Knowledge* (Wantage: Sean Kingston).
Taylor, C. (1969) 'Neutrality in Political Science', in: P. Laslett and W. G. Runciman (eds) *Philosophy, Politics and Society*, 3rd series (Oxford: Blackwell).
Taylor, C. (2007) *Modern Social Imaginaries* (Durham, NC: Duke University Press).
Taylor, C. (2007). 'On Social Imaginaries', in: P. Gratton and J. Panteleimon Manoussakis (eds), *Traversing the Imaginary: Richard Kearney and the Postmodern Challenge* (pp. 29–47) (Evanston, IL: Northwestern University Press).
Taylor, R., Barr, J. and Steele, T. (2002) *For a Radical Higher Education: After Postmodernism* (Buckingham: Open University Press).
Test, K. (1992) *Civil Society* (London: Routledge).
Thompson, J. (1984) *Studies in the Theory of Ideology* (Cambridge: Polity Press).
Thompson, K. (1984) 'Education for Capability: A Critique', *British Journal of Educational Studies*, 32, 203–212.
Toulmin, S. (2001) *Return to Reason* (Cambridge, MA: Harvard University Press).
Toyne, P. (1985) 'Mission and Strategy: A Case Study of North East London Polytechnic', *International Journal of Institutional Management in Higher Education*, 9.
Trow, M. (1994) *Managerialism and the Academic Profession: Quality and Control*. Higher Education Report No. 2 (London: Open University Quality Support Centre).
Trow, M. (2007) 'Reflections on the Transitions from Elite to Mass to Universal Access: Forms and Phases of Higher Education in Modern Societies since WWII' in: J. Forest and P. Altbach (eds) *International Handbook of Higher Education* (Dordrecht: Springer).
University Grants Committee (1984) *Report of the Continuing Education Working Party* (London: UGC).

University Grants Committee (1985) Circular letter 22/85, para 21, quoted in para 6.7, Cmnd 81, 1987, *Review of the University Grants Committee (Croham Report)* (London: HMSO).

Walford, R. (1987) *Restructuring Universities: Politics and Power in the Management of Change* (Beckenham: Croom Helm).

Wegener, C. (1978) *Liberal Education and the Modern University* (Chicago: University of Chicago Press).

Weidemeyer, C. (1981) *Learning at the Back Door: Reflections on Non-traditional Learning in the Life-span* (University of Wisconsin Press).

Wheelahan, L. (2010) *Why Knowledge Matters in Curriculum: A Social Realist Argument* (Abingdon: Routledge).

Whitburn, J., Mealing, M. and Cox, C. (1976) *People in Polytechnics: A Survey of Polytechnic Staff and Students 1972–3* (Guildford: Society for Research into Higher Education).

White, J. (1982) *The Aims of Education Restated* (London: Routledge & Kegan Paul).

Whitehead, A. N. (1932) 'Universities and their Function', in his *The Aims of Education* (London: Williams & Norgate).

Williams, B. (2002) *Truth and Truthfulness* (Princeton, NJ: Princeton University Press).

Williams, B. (2008/2006/1985) *Ethics and the Limits of Philosophy* (London: Routledge).

Wilson, B. (1970) *Rationality* (Oxford: Blackwell).

Wilson, J. (1981) 'Concepts, Contestability and the Philosophy of Education', *Journal of Philosophy of Education*, 15, 3–16.

Winch, P. (1958, sixth imp. 1970) *The Idea of a Social Science and its Relation to Philosophy*, pp. 27–28 (Henley: Routledge & Kegan Paul).

Wittgenstein, L. (1958, third edn 1978) *Philosophical Investigations* (Oxford: Blackwell).

Woods, J. (1973) Commentary on R. S. Peters' 'The Justification of Education', in: R. Peters (ed.) op. cit., p. 30.

Young, M.F.D. and Whitty, G. (eds) (1977) *Society, State and Schooling* (London: Falmer Press).

Young, R. (1992) 'The Idea of a Chrestomathic University', in: R. Rand (ed.) Logomachia: The Conflict of the Faculties (Lincoln and London: University of Nebraska).

Zizek, S. (1993) *Tarrying with the Negative: Kant, Hegel, and the Critique of Ideology* (Durham, NC: Duke University Press).

Zizek, S. (2009) *The Parallax View* (Cambridge, MA: MIT).

Name index

Adelman, C 172
Adorno, T 250
Ainley, P 39
Albrow, M 180
Althusser, L 29, 100, 109

Badiou, A 198
Ball, C 37–38, 156
Barnett, R 2, 32–33 38, 58, 70, 72, 84, 120, 125, 136, 146, 153, 186, 194, 200, 212, 220, 225, 245, 249
Bauman, Z 55, 69, 82, 146, 242
Bearn, G 148
Becher, T 105, 119, 144, 158, 165
Beck, U 4, 53, 130, 180, 217, 220
Bell, D 105
Berdahl, R 157
Berlin, I 236
Bernstein, B 179, 187, 189, 231, 240
Bernstein, R J 33, 76, 109
Bevan, J 172
Bhaskar, R 16, 66, 251
Birch, W 37
Bjarnason, S 148
Bligh, D 126
Bloom, A 50
Bloor, D 109
Boud, D 168
Bourdieu, P 109, 128
Boys, C 178
Brady, M 14, 201
Brecher, B 26
Brennan, J 159
Brockbank, A 200
Brown, R 187
Brubacher, J 17, 94, 248
Burgess, B 157
Butler, J 18

Cameron, J 9, 165
Carr, W 39
Castells, M 32
Chomsky, N 121
Christopherson, D 109
Clark, B 178–79
Coate, K 225
Cockburn, A 101
Coffield, F 180
Coldstream, P 148
Colebrook, C 8, 75
Collier, G 100
Connerton, P 161
Considine, M 129
Cooper, D 86
Cox, C 2
Cox, R 200
Cutright, M 54

DaCosta, C 28, 181
Dearing, R 33
Delanty, G 25, 27, 33
Deleuze, G viii, 8, 16, 66, 75, 241
Derrida, J 67, 75, 87, 144, 149, 196, 250
Dienstag, J 70
Duke, C 39

Ecclestone, K 69, 85
Edwards, E 95
Ekman, R 222
Eraut, M 52, 224
Ehrlich, T 68
Eustace, R 78

Feyerabend, P 18, 109
Fleming, T 15, 204
Foucault, M 196, 240

Name index

Franklin, J 130

Galbraith, J 148
Gellert, C 163
Gellner, E 1, 18, 77, 93, 98–99, 105, 108–109, 196, 220
Gibbons, M 33, 38, 51–52, 54, 80, 136, 184, 223
Gibson, R 161, 163
Giddens, T 32, 180, 184, 197
Gokulsing, G 28, 181
Goodlad, S 34, 109, 193
Graham, G 147
Gramsci, A 250
Guattari, F viii, 8, 16, 73, 241

Habermas, J 8, 15, 18, 38, 45–47, 78, 93–94, 105, 108–109, 115, 121, 145–146, 161, 165, 167, 196, 206, 218, 249
Hallden, S 122
Halpin, D 81
Halsey, A H 26
Harvey, D 186
Hayes, D 69. 85
Hegel, G 17, 50
Heidegger, M 3, 16, 70, 74–75, 82, 84, 227, 243
Held, D 161
Hoffman, S 94
hooks, b 231
Huxley, T 114

Jacoby, R 66
Jacques, D 122
Jarvis, P 32, 38, 56, 147, 218
Jaspers, K 102, 109, 115, 144
Joseph, K 156

Kant, E 10, 210, 252
Kearney, R 64–6
Kells, H R 29
Kemmis, S 39
Kerr, C 101, 119, 145, 159, 166
Kress, G 52, 242
Kuhn, T 109

Labhrainn, I 68
Laclau, E 13, 18
Land, R 199, 244
Leavis, F R 1, 99–100, 109, 115–116, 211

Leslie, L 54, 79, 128
Lessem, R 37
Lewis, D 52
Liedman, S E 210
Light, G 200
Lovlie, L 192, 238
Lukasiewicz, J 194, 222
Lyons, F 114
Lyotard, J F 27–8, 38, 52, 144, 180, 184, 196

Macfarlane, B 249
MacIntyre, A 51, 55, 65
Malatesta, E 67
Marginson, S 78, 129
Marton, F 166, 214, 218
Maxwell, N 70, 243
McCarthy, E D 28
McGill, I 200
McIlrath, L 68
Mealing, M 2
Meyer, J 199, 244
Miliband, R 101, 109
Mill, J 113–14
Mills, J 231
Minogue, K 109, 117–118, 145
Moberly, W 109, 112, 144
Montifiore, A 109
Moodie, G 78, 168
Moore, T 106
Mortenson, K 192, 238
Murphy, M 15, 78

Newman, J H 3, 18–19, 76, 99–100, 102, 114, 145, 192–193, 215
Niblett, R 96, 105, 109, 118
Nietzsche, F 196, 227
Nisbet, R 77, 79
Nixon, J 70
Nordenbo, S E 192, 238
Notwotny, H 54, 223
Nussbaum, M 231

Oakeshott, 214
Olssen, M 51
Ortega y Gasset, 109, 112

Parker, J 70
Pateman, T 101
Pattison, M 121
Perry, W G 212
Peters, M 51, 78, 87, 96

Name index

Peters, R 116–19, 121, 158, 169, 205, 214, 248
Phipps, A 59, 136
Plato 193
Plumb, J 105
Popper, Sir K 18, 85, 105, 108–09, 195, 211, 250
Powell, J 114
Powney, J 172
Pritchard, D 14, 201

Quandt, R 222

Ramsden, P 166, 200
Ranson, S 39
Readings, B 144–146
Reeves, M 230
Robbins, L 1, 11, 101, 115–116
Robins, K 69
Rorty, R 109
Rothblatt, S 210
Rowland, S 86
Russell, B 201
Ryan, A 97

Sartre, J P 64–66
Savin-Baden, M 237
Schon, D 52
Schopenhauer, A 82
Scott, P 26, 54, 115
Shils, E 143
Silver, H 109
Sizer, J 162
Slaughter, S 54, 79, 128
Sloman, A 2
Snelders, P 97
Snow, C P 1

Socrates, 195
Squires, G 178
Standaert, N 69
Standish, P 88, 148
Stehr, N 153, 181, 220
Steiner, G 59
Strathern, M 136

Taylor, C 11, 63–66, 80–81, 86
Taylor, R 147
Test, K 38
Thompson, J 167
Toyne, P 168
Trow, M 11, 29, 50
Trowler, P 145

Van Leeuwen, T 52, 242
von Humboldt, 19

Walford, R 120
Webster, F 69
Wheelahan, L 240
Whitburn, J 2
White, J 116–117, 119
Whitehead, A 112
Whitty, G 109
Williams, B 69, 88, 144, 245
Wilson, J 97
Winch, P 98
Wittgenstein, L 98
Woods, J 97

Yeats, W B 201
Young, M 109
Young, R 70

Zizek, S 16, 18, 198

Subject index

NB: *The main references are emboldened.*

'academic capitalism' 54, 79, 128, 136
academic community 120, 143, 164, 166, 170, 173, 251
academic freedom 93, 106, 143
   See also freedom of speech
academic identity 79, 137–138, 178–179
academic life 20, 44, 46, 165, 169
academic professionalism 44
academics 8, 181
access 142, 164, 170
action 188–189, 227
adaptability 181
agency, university 252
aims
   See higher education
air
   See pedagogy of air
alterity 88
anarchy 245
andragogy 209
anxiety 9, 222
antagonisms 17, 18, 21, 252
anthropology 133, 143, 220
archaeology 120
architecture 185
audiences 249
audits 3
authentic university, the 85
authenticity 5, 12, 46, 86–88, 201, 227, 233, 236, 243, 245–246
autonomy 11, 13, 26, 28–29, 106, 169–170

becoming 5, 9, 82, 89, 203, 215, 239, 241, 244

being 5, 9, 36, 44, 75, 77, 79, 130, 137, 153, 188, 198, 203, 227, 233, 239, 244, 251
being for uncertainty 232
Bildung 27, 191, 210, 238
borderless university, the 69
boundaries 31
bureaucratic university, the 69, 84
bureaucracy 9
business-facing university, the 68

capability 88
capital 128–129, 131, 133–134, 204
   See also cultural capital; social capital
care 6, 9, 13, 84, 246, 252
carefulness 9, 19
challengeability 33, 58, 61, 153
change 129–130, 220, 232, 250
chaos 44, 54, 153, 220, 222
chemistry 133, 185, 225, 229
citizenship 12, 19–20
civic university, the 67–68
civil engineering 120
classification 179
committee meetings 3
Committee of Vice-Chancellors and Principals (CVCP) 125, 162–163
commitment 121
communication 15, 152, 166
communicative competence 32
community 19–20, 26
   See also academic community
competence 5, 14, 120
competences 120, 122
competition 80, 142

complexity 5, 19, 31, 53–54, 60, 180, 220, 227
computing 120, 133
concepts 4–5, 28, 31
　subversive concepts 239
　'thick concepts' 69, 88, 245
　See also universal concepts
conceptual landscape 812
concern 5, 84
'Conflict of the Faculties' 252
constructivism 12
contestability 33, 58, 61, 153
continuing education 101
contradictions 30
control 78, 84, 179
convergence 127, **131–135**, 138
corporate university, the 62, 69
Council for National Academic Awards (CNAA) 2, 111, 158, 249
courage 152, 230
creativity 235–236
criteria of adequacy 62, **71–73**
critic 8
critical action 6
critical being 6
critical discourse 46
critical inquiry 170
'critical interdisciplinarity' 13
criticality 9, 15, 19, 49, 108, 120, 126, 173
　self-criticality 197–199
critical mind 124
critical realism 4, 16, 66
critical reason 46, 49, 108, 151
critical standards 47
critical theory 16, 248
critical thinking 6, 155
critique 9, 46, 88, 152, 199
cultural capital 79, 128, 204
cultural studies 151
culture 27, 50, 56, 100, 134, 144, 204
　disciplinary cultures 119
'Culture of Critical Discourse' 167, 170
curricula 91, 227, 234
　hidden 183
curriculum 5, 29, 44, 84, 114, 125–26, 166, **177–190**, 239

Dearing inquiry
　See NCIHE
delegitimization 26
delight 9

democracy 26, 29, 152
Department of Education and Science (DES) 166
dialectic 251
dialogue 4, 15, 17, 196
　See also internal dialogue
digital world 10, 252
disciplines 10, 55, 77, 119, 133, 179, 189, 203, 240–243
　See also STEM disciplines
discourse 167
disinterestedness 18
displacement 213–215
dispositions 14, 191, 200–201, 219–220, 232
disputations 49
dissensus 144
distance learning 11
domestication 240
double undermining 12, 107, 154
　See also epistemological undermining; sociological undermining
doubt 201–202
dystopian university, the 70
dystopias 70–1

ecological registers 73
ecological spirit 252
ecological university, the 7, 62, 67, 72–3, 76, 89–90, 247–248
ecology 5, 9, 12, 19–20, 72, 88, 235, **243–246**
economic capital 80
economy 29, 99, 181
educational development 228
educational energy 240
efficiency 240
emancipation 6, 19–20, 28, 30, 93, 103, 106–107, 120, 155, 190, 240, 245–246
emancipatory empiricism 8
emergence 250–251
empirical work 7
empirical world 8
　See also legitimacy, empirical; transcendental empiricism
employability 9, 242
empty signifier 13
enchantment 12
engagement 55, 148–149
　civic 88
engineering 137–138, 177, 185

Subject index

enlightenment 152, 155, 222
enquiring university, the 86
enquiry 57
  See also enquiring university; inquiry
enterprise 129
entrepreneurial university, the 7, 10, 15, 62, 67–68, **79–80**, 81, 90, **127–139**
entrepreneurialism **128–135**, 247
  See also entrepreneurial university
epistemic virtues 14
epistemological gap 232
epistemological space 237
epistemological undermining 12
epistemologies 30, 36, 45, 51
epistemology 15, 46, 76, 103, 184, 198–199
equal opportunities 151
  See also access
equity 12, 19
ethics 36, 46
Europe 9
European university, the 69
excellence 144
experiential learning 105, 209

fairness 12
faith 192, **198–199**
feasible utopias 7–8, 15, 62, **65–67**, 74–75, 81
fitness-for-purpose 156–157, 160, 164, 171
flexibility 181, 204
flourishing 84, 230
fluidity 9, 220, 238
flying 236
  See also trajectory
fragility 31, 53, 153, 180, 220, 222–224
fragmentation 220
frameworks 31, 179, 195, 213
  metadisciplinary 213
framing 179, 231
freedom 11–12, 26, 28, 64–6, 70, 235–236, **239**
freedom of speech 9, 18

generative mechanisms 16
generosity 152
global alliances 142
global economy 40, 42

globalization 6, 26, 32, 48, 51, 56, 142, 180
'grand narratives' 29–30, 33

happiness 20
Her Majesty's Inspectorate (HMI) 172
higher education 5–6, 8–9, 15, 17, 20, 106–107, 191, 196–197, 250
  aims of **111–126**
  concept of 13–15, 19, **94–99**, 101, **103–106**, 111, 120–121, 125, 141, 161, 197, 248
  emancipatory concept of 120–121, 123, 167
  conditions of 96, 157
  Institutions of (IHEs) 94, 141, **157–172**
  mass 26, 45, 50, 55, 127, 142, 177, 179, 182, 184–188, 246
  philosophy of **140–143**, 146, 148, 150–151, 248
  processes of 122, 171
  purposes of 157, **158–159**, **167–170**
  theory of 149
higher learning 13, 151, 171, 199, 201
history 177, 226
hope 5, 21, 47, 192, 198–199
humanities 9, 13, 77, 151, 163, 185, 252
human rights 20, 151–152
hybridity 184
hyper-modernity 239

ide*a*logy 15
'ideal speech situation' 15, 46, 57, 146
identity
  See academic identity
ideological complex 240, 252
ideological presences 63, 99, 245–246
ideological structures 72, 239
ideologies 3, 8–9, 15, 19, 5, 66, 100, 108, 220, 251
ideology, 16, 36, 40, 67, 99, 106–107, 144, 209–210, 242, 249
  concept of 5
ignorance 44, 222
imaginaries 80
imaginary 11, 63–65, 81
imagination 4–5, 9, 15, 17, 21, 47, 63–65, 67, 69–70, 74, 152, 231, 252

imaginative structure 68
impact 9, 79
improvement 245
identity
    See academic identity
inquiry 26, 86
instability 54, 195, 224–225
Institute of Education, London 2, 249
institutions of higher education
    See higher education
instrumentalism 43
integration 2
internal dialogue 3
internet 18, 86
invisibility 243
ivory tower 104

Jarratt report 163
justice 12, 30

knowing 76–77, 188–189
knowledge 5–6, 10–12, 14–15, 25–26,
    28, 30, 44–46, 53, 57, 76–77, 106,
    118–19, 142, 147, 152–153,
    164–165, 178, 183, 194, 219, 224,
    235, 244
    disciplinary 204
    propositional 28
    See also modes 1 and 2; objective
    knowledge; universal knowledge
'knowledge constitutive interest' 78
knowledge economy 78, 134
knowledge entrepreneurs 137
knowledge exploitability 13
knowledge production 26
knowledge society 25, 52, 78, 142, 181
knowledge travel 128, **136–138**
knowledges 52, 80, 186, 189

labour markets 37
Latin 9, 49
Latin America 9
leaders, institutional 7
leadership 7
learning 5–6, 20, 35, 38–39, 42–45, 57,
    126, 153, 165–166, **191–202**, 206,
    209, 211, **214**, **219**, 223, 235, **242**,
    245
    adult 209
    concept of 98, 191, 205
    ecology of 245
    e-learning 13

empirical 193–194
group-based 209
higher 30, 233
independent 185
lifelong 46
open 170
planes of 243
self-learning 40
societal 42, 46
see also distance learning;
    experiential learning; learning
    university
learning anomie 193
learning communities 39–40, 217
learning economy 63
learning ego 240
learning epochs 191–194
learning experience 241
learning organisations 37
learning outcomes 29, 202, 239–240,
    251
learning society 35–36, 39–47, 88, 181
learning spaces 235–236, **237–244**
learning strategies 182
learning super-ego 240
learning university, the **35–47**, 247
legitimacy, empirical 7
legitimation crisis 15, 93–94, 107–108,
    112
    See also delegitimization
legitimation of higher education
    108–109
Leverhulme Inquiry 95, 101
liberal education 99–100, 113, 117,
    154–155, 161, 173
liberation 245
liberty 6, 9, 12, 17, 19–20
life-world 37, 40–44, 218
liminality 238, 248–250
'lines of flight' 16, 19
liquid, the 9, 238, 242
'liquid modernity' 55, 220
liquid university, the 67, 69, 82

magic 185
management 7, 53, 163, 182, 251
managerialism 9, 29
    See also new public management
managers 32, 163, 211
marketization 9, 29, 140, 178
markets 127, 132, 141, 178, 182–183
    quasi-markets 51, 132, 178

mass higher education
　　See higher education
maturity 246
mediaeval universities 9
mediaeval university, the 49
metacriticism 109
metanarratives 27
metaphysical university, the 62, 67–68, 76, 81, 90
metaphysics 193–194
　　See also metaphysical university
midwifery 177
mind 46, 50, 65, 205
mission statements 3, 158
mobius strip 17
modern university, the 30
modes 1 and 2 51–52, 80, 136, 223
mode 3 224
modular programmes 2
MOOCs 11
multimodality 10, 52, 242
'multiplicities' 8, 16
multiversity 145
mystery 76

NACETT 3
narratives 65–66
National Advisory Board (NAB) 95, 156, 172
National Committee of Inquiry (NCIHE) 33, 187
negations 64–65, 252
neoliberalism 5, 51, 128, 136
network society 32
networked university, the 69, 8
neutrality 12
new public management 5
Nobel prizes 170
nomadic learners 238–239, 241
non-completion 161
North East London Polytechnic 125
nursing 177, 185, 226

objective knowledge 85, 93, 103, 106–107
　　See also knowledge
objectivity 12, 15
ontological space 237
ontological turn 16, 59, 84
ontological voyaging 137
ontology 59, 66, 76, 198–99, 201, 220, 225

opennness 49, 87, 236, 238
open spaces 239
Open University 122
open university, the 67, 69
optimism 190
outcomes
　　See learning outcomes

parochialism 89
particularity 135
particulars 19
　　cf universals
part-time study 215
patience 9
peace 19
pedagogical control 240
pedagogy 191, 227, **230–232**, 234, 237
'pedagogy of air' 236
'pedagogy of recognition' 59
peer review 168
performance indicators 17, 161, 163, 168–169, 171–172
performativity 5, 26, 52, 79, 129, 149, 180, **184–186**, 189–190, 203
personal development 29
persons 232
pessimism 8, 70, 190
pharmaceutical industry 9, 57, 185
philosophy 5, 7, 143, 150, 229
　　See also higher education, philosophy of; social philosophy; potholing, philosophy as.
physics 185
pluralism 106
poets 3
polytechnics 2
possibilities 5, 16, 47, 252
postmodern university, the 67, 145
postmodernism 12, 25, 27, 44–45, 48–49, 51, 58, 149, 204
postmodernity 26–28, 30, 239
post-structuralism 49
potholing, philosophy as 7–9
power 78, 179
powers 252
practice 4
practices 6
presences 252
problem nets 185
problems 6

professional education 105, 114, 171, 178
professor, idea of 150
public good 12, 133
public intellectuals 86
public sphere 59

qualities 14, 191, 200–201, 219, 233
quality 6, 133, 142
quality assurance 29
Quality Assurance Agency 187
quality of life 12

rationality 41, 106, 164, 196
reading 4
reason 5, 9, 11, 17, 20, 45, 106, 144
   dialogic 32, 186
   instrumental 156, 160, 162–164, 186
   technical 26, 30, 32
   See also critical reason; space of reason
reciprocity 231
reflexivity 153
regulation
   self-regulation 29
Reith Lectures 1
relativism 16, 28, 50–51, 66, 104, 107, 147
research 20, 26, 32, 57–58, 77, 119, 143, 153, 179, 182, 249, 251
research university, the 62, 68, 77–79, 90
researchers 32
respect 12, 19
responsibilities 20, 28–29, 37, 43, 67
responsibility 87–88, 149, 190
'Rhizome' 16
risk 33, 44, 53, 79, **128–130**, 133, 180, 184, 206, 217, 225, **228–230**, 233, 238
   pedagogical 231
Robbins report 1

'satisfaction' 217, 239
scholars 9
scholarship 13
sciences 10, 51, 123
   See also STEM disciplines
self 29, 189
scientific university, the 77
self-criticality 197
self-reliance 181, 187
skills 6, 13, 29, 37, **40**, 120, 181–183, 185, 226–229
   disciplinary 204
   transferable 193, 204
social capital 79, 128
social philosophy 6–7, 75, 144, 252
social sciences 10
social work 185
Society for Research into Higher Education 95, 217, 249
sociological undermining 12
sociology 103
space 5, 26, 82, 89, 150
space of reason 12
spaces **237**, 241, 244, 252
   See also learning spaces
spirit 12, 50, 73
'Squid', university as 16
state, the 76, 157
state apparatus 107
STEM disciplines 10
strangeness 53, 58, **60–61**, 230
student, concept of 5, 14, 40, 203, 210, 216–217
student experience 170, 203, **207–210**
students 7, 26, 33, 41, 84, 126, 208, 232, 252
student, the 121, 123–124, 205–207, 247
students-as-customers 9
supercomplex university, the 69
'Supercomplexity' 6, 14, 30–32, 53–55, 59–60, 146, 154, 180–181, 186–90, 193–94, 220–222, 224–25, 227, 230, 233, 247
sustainability 72, 89, 246

talloires network 87
teaching 6, 32–33, 57, 59, 119, 143, 153, 163, 165–166, 179, 182, 211, 248, 251
   scholarship of 55
teaching strategies 182
technology 51, 161
theatrical university, the 70
theorem 241
therapeutic university, the 67, 69, 84
time 5, 9, 26, 82, 130
trajectory 215–216
transcendental empiricism 8, 66
transcendental realm 76, 89

278 Subject index

transferable skills
  See skills
transformation 12, 28, 230
transport studies 185
travelling 136, 238
  See also knowledge travel; nomadic learner
troublesomeness 199
trust 26
truth 9, 11–12, 26, 28, 46, 48, 50, 56–57, 76, 103, 118, 147, 153
truthfulness 19, 121

uncertainty 6, 13, 33, 61, 153, 222, 224, **227–232**
  'Authoritative uncertainty' 197
understanding 5, 12–13, 17–18, 20, 26, 28, 38, 123–124, 147, 185, 205–206, 217, 227
universality 10, 49–51, 54–57, **60**, 86–87, 135, 142, 150, 186, 236
universality of access 11
university of strangeness, the 59
universality of universities 11, 49, 60
universal knowledge 10, 115, 164
universal reason 10
universal, the **48–61**, 146, 247
universals 6, 10, 12, 17–20, 28, 58, 63, 89, 155, 184, 190
universitas 9, 164
universities 9–10, 20, 45, 53, 74, 250
  corporate 56, 141
  virtual 141
  See also higher education – institutions of; Mediaeval universities
universities as organizations 54–55, 57, 59
university agency
  See agency
university as critical space 56
university as institution 94
University Grants Committee (UGC) 95, 162, 172
university in crisis 154
'university in ruins' 66, 154

University of Aberdeen 76
University of Essex 1
University of Galway 88
University of Lancaster 125
University of London 247
University of Oxford 121
  See also Open University
university, the 1, 5, 7–10, 19–20, 25, 48–49, 75, 251–252
  being a 74
  concept of 13, 15, 47, 56, 63, 65–67, 70, 73, 141, 151, 222
  title of 250
  value background of 26–28, 30
university mission 54
university purposes 54, 152l
unknown, the 219, 223–234
unpredictability 33, 61, 130, 153, 222–223
USA 141–142, 248
utopian university, the 70–71
utopias 47, 66, 71, 73, 75
  See also dystopias; feasible utopias

value background 26, 81
value freedom 36
value-ladenness 45
values 27, 82, 87, 99, 118–119
venture 192
virtue 12
virtual university, the 69
virtuous university, the 70
vision 71
voice 250

wellbeing 12, 19–20, 84, 89–90
western university, the 26–30, 46, 56, 222
will 201
will to learn 201
wisdom 12, 76, 214, 233, 243
wonder 12, 76
words 3
work 29, 152
worthwhileness 95
writing 3–4, 247–248, 249
  writing as autobiography 2